Critical and effective histories

This book places Foucault's methodologies against central currents in social theory and philosophy in order to provide a guide to doing historical sociology in particular and social science more generally. It has several purposes. First, it seeks to make Foucault's contribution comprehensible to a wide range of professional and non-professional readers. Second, it rescues the originality and usefulness of Foucault's work, and his critical project from both the welter of ill-informed criticism and the obfuscation of sympathetic commentators. Third, it embodies a conviction that Foucault's approaches could inform the metamorphosis of sociology into an effective, open-ended, multi-focused, present-relevant discipline, capable of problematising the grand frameworks and assumptions of earlier social theory. Finally, it demonstrates that Foucault's methods provide the necessary condition for any state-of-the-art social research today. The book thus addresses the many formulations of Foucault's methodological position and seeks to establish its relation to such figures as Nietzsche, Kant, Weber, Elias, Habermas, Giddens and the *Annales* and Frankfurt Schools. Furthermore, it explores the interconnected substantive themes of Foucault's work: truth, knowledge and rationality; power, domination and government; and the self and ethical practice. The book is less a commentary on Foucault than a use of Foucault's methods to chart an original position on the condition of social science today. It is directed not only at readers interested in Foucault's legacy but to any social scientist or student working at the cutting edge of contemporary research and to the non-professional audience concerned with the central ethical, political, and theoretical problems of our time.

Mitchell Dean lectures in Sociology at Macquarie University, Sydney. He has contributed to journals such as *Economy and Society* and *Theory and Society* and is the author of *The Constitution of Poverty: Toward a Genealogy of Liberal Governance* (Routledge 1991).

Critical and effective histories

Foucault's methods and historical sociology

Mitchell Dean

London and New York

First published 1994
by Routledge
11 New Fetter Lane, London EC4P 4EE

Simultaneously published in the USA and Canada
by Routledge
29 West 35th Street, New York, NY 10001

Typeset in Garamond by
Ponting–Green Publishing Services, Chesham, Bucks
Printed and bound in Great Britain by
Mackays of Chatham PLC, Chatham, Kent

British Library Cataloguing in Publication Data
A catalogue record for this book is available from the British
Library.

Library of Congress Cataloging in Publication Data
Critical and effective histories: Foucault's methods and
historical sociology / Mitchell Dean.
   p.   cm.
  Includes bibliographical references and index.
  1. Historical sociology.
  2. Foucault, Michel.
I. Title.
HQ104.D43 1994
302'.0722–dc20   93–28834
                             CIP

ISBN 0–415–06494–5 (hbk)
ISBN 0–415–06495–3 (pbk)

For Deborah

I shall take from things the illusion they produce to preserve themselves
from us and leave them the part they concede to us.

René Char

The only rule and method I have kept is contained in a text by Char, where
the most urgent and restrained definition of truth may also be read: 'I shall
take from things the illusion they produce to preserve themselves from us
and leave them the part they concede to us.'

Michel Foucault

Contents

Acknowledgements

One of the origins of the present work was Chris Rojek's suggestion in 1990 that I might write a book on Foucault's historical sociology. I warmly thank him for the suggestion and for his support during the time I have been working on this book. However, as many thinkers have noted, outcomes cannot be assimilated to origins. In the present case, that topic soon proved impossible for no other reason than the fact that Foucault was not a sociologist and, if he contributed to historical sociology, it was from some distance. I hope that the finished product proves capable of maintaining a sense of the integrity of both Foucault's work and that of historical sociology. I also hope that, by venturing into related fields of social and political philosophy and theory, the present work stands as more than a commentary on either of these domains, and is received as an attempt to advance the state of our knowledge-practices in the contemporary social sciences.

I must also thank Barry Hindess, Peter Miller and Barry Smart for the patience displayed in reading a draft of this book and their promptness in making comments on it. If I have failed to address all of their suggestions, it is perhaps less to do with our disagreements and more with the constraints of time and energy. A book is a beginning and not an end, and it is in this spirit I present it, knowing that it is criticism above all which makes it so. It is also a laboratory, a record of thought experiments, and as such should faithfully record those experiments without concealing them under the later rationalisations of the author. Finally, I add my thanks to Zygmunt Bauman for his extraordinarily encouraging and perceptive report on this book. He understood both the task of the book and the role of the publisher's report in a way only a thinker of his stature could.

Introduction

This book addresses the uses of history in sociology from a position informed by the methods of Michel Foucault and his project for a 'history of the present'. The prominent names here, Max Weber, Norbert Elias, Anthony Giddens, Jurgen Habermas, Horkheimer and Adorno, and Fernand Braudel, as well as Foucault himself, suggest the terrain investigated is somewhat larger than a sub-discipline of sociology or a hybrid of sociology and history. I hope the reader will grant me the liberty of calling this terrain 'historical sociology'. As she or he will find, however, it is marked out here not only by sociology and history, but also by social philosophy and political thought, by cultural and intellectual history as much as the history of 'economies, societies and civilisations' (to quote the title of the journal, *Annales*) and by pursuits and projects that seem to ignore all of these divisions and pursue an unexpected path not mapped out in advance within disciplinary territories.

The latter is true of the elusive work of Foucault himself. Reading a recent biography (Eribon 1991) one gains the impression of a thinker, so concerned with the regularities of thought and so integrated within the institutional hierarchy of the French academy, who somehow escaped the maze of disciplines and specialisms and the compulsive siting of intellectual endeavour within a science, school, or tradition. This does not mean Foucault was without intellectual affiliation or that his thought evaded social and discursive constraints to trace an original arc. It does mean he refused not only the mantle of science but even the conceptual terminology of a scholarly discipline. He preferred instead to address a broad learned public in a language that, while replete with brilliant conceptual innovation, was most decidedly not of the specialist.

To describe the *style* of Foucault's writings and other public communications, I am tempted to cite Norbert Elias' observations (1978: 36–7) on the integration of the intelligentsia into aristocratic circles in seventeenth and eighteenth century France. This, suggests Elias, left a distinctive non-specialist mark on intellectual activity that endured the Revolution and was adopted by universal enlightenment intellectuals. Here, writing follows from the courtly 'law of right speaking' that 'the technical term and everything that betrays the specialist is a stylistic blemish' (Nietzsche, quoted by Elias 1978: 36). It might be suggested a certain principle of right speaking persists in a modified form in both Foucault's writing and his speech. On the one hand, he is well known for having announced the transition from the 'universal intellectual', speaking from a position of universal values, to the 'specific intellectual' (in Foucault 1980h), combating 'power–knowledge' relations at the point of contact. On the other, he does so in a language and a manner that is never specialist. This thinker, whose historical horizon was so often the 'classical age' of the seventeenth and eighteenth centuries and, later, classical antiquity, wrote, one might venture to say, not as a 'classical theorist' – a term familiar to all students of sociology – but as a classical stylist.

When reading Foucault, it is important to keep in mind that the conceptual innovation, even at its most prolix as in *The Archaeology of Knowledge* (1972), is not seeking to initiate or develop a science or discipline, but to explore how it is possible to think in a certain way and how far a specific language can be used. This is why so little of what Foucault was to write could be described as an application of concepts or methodological principles and why, having offered accounts of method at certain points, he appears to jettison them or take them up in an entirely different fashion. Methodological codification, in this regard, is best regarded as a summary that revisits and clarifies analysis *after* the event rather than a rationalistic plan put into practice by analysis. The present work is not an attempt to codify those methods but to find out how far one can get by reflecting on them in the context of particular problems of sociology and history. Indeed, to speak of following 'Foucault's methods' is as paradoxical as speaking of ascending stairs or cascading waterfalls in the graphic work of M. C. Escher.

The impact of Foucault, then, upon sociology and history has not been felt directly as a specialist within the social sciences, but from a number of rather oblique angles. Above all, there are his scholarly writings in which he undertook a series of successive displacements in the history of ideas, thought, and science – in, to put it more simply, the history of truth. These displacements were first toward an analysis of the regularities of the formation of discourse, then toward the embeddedness of that discourse in institutional practices and power relations, and finally toward the relation of such practices to ones concerning the self and forms of ethical conduct. In this personal and biographical journey, Foucault has become a kind of touchstone for many of those working in the humanities and the social sciences seeking to address questions to three broad domains: first, one of reason, truth, and knowledge; secondly, one of power, domination, and government; and finally, one of ethics, self, and freedom. Foucault (e.g. 1982, 1985) came to understand his own contribution in this way and it is certainly helpful to think of a 'Foucauldian triangle' of truth, power, self (Flynn 1988).

However, his impact cannot be accounted for by his writings alone. Of course, one should not neglect his status as a political militant, whose practice might offer new ways of inventing and participating in political action. More important, perhaps, was his status as a speaking subject, as a lecturer both at the *College de France* and at American universities, and, above all, a conversationalist, whose lucidity and creativity can be felt through virtually every one of his interviews and which would reach a kind of art-form at the end of his life. There is here an affirmation of the conventions of dialogue, not so much in a Socratic form, but with something of the highly developed sense of 'stylistic conventions, the forms of social intercourse . . . esteem for courtesy, the importance of good speech and conversation, articulateness of language', that Elias (1978: 36) understood as part of the lasting legacy of the French court. In an era when German critical theory has sought normative grounding in the conditions of an ideal of communication, Foucault's interviews themselves exemplify the open possibilities of speech as a practice that constructs an impossible intersubjectivity.

ON THEORY AND HISTORY

From what I have already said, it is clear the present work will be identified as a variety of what, in English-speaking countries, is called social theory. Perhaps something should be said in advance about the strange little word 'theory'. It might be useful to offer a sketch of three forms of intellectual practice to distinguish what I am undertaking here.[1] The first is a *progressivist theory*. It proposes a model of social progress through the teleology of reason, technology, production, and so on. This is the model that might be called 'high modernism', and is exemplified by the narratives of the Enlightenment, by the nineteenth century positivism of Comte, and by elements of Marx's theory of history and certain interpretations of Weber's conception of rationalisation. It is a form of theory that seeks to adopt the prestige of the natural sciences, and often gives its statements the form of general causal explanations which have a law-like character.

The second type is a *critical theory*. It proposes a dialectic in which the present forms of reason and society are both negated and retained in a higher form. Critical theory offers a critique of modernist narratives in terms of the one-sided, pathological, advance of technocratic or instrumental reason they celebrate, in order to offer an alternative, higher version of rationality. Instead of narratives of progress, we have narratives of reconciliation of the subject with itself, with nature, with the form of its own reason. Such narratives promise emancipation and secular salvation. This form of theory, instanced by 'Western Marxism' generally, and by Habermas' theory of communicative rationality and Horkheimer and Adorno's dialetic of enlightenment, can be characterised as a form of 'critical modernism'. It typically adopts the 'neo-Kantian' distinction between the natural an social sciences written into sociology by Weber's methodological statements. This eschews the model of the natural sciences in favour of the methods and perspectives specific to the sphere of culture and society.

The third type of intellectual practice is a *problematising* one. It establishes an analysis of the trajectory of the historical forms of truth and knowledge without origin or end. This form of practice has the effect of the disturbance of narratives of both progress and reconciliation, finding questions where others had located answers. It seeks to remain open to the dispersion of historical transformation, the rapid mutation of events, the multiplicity of temporalities, the differential forms of the timing and spacing of activities, and the possibilty of invasion and even reversal of historical pathways. It seeks to problematise those versions of history which regard it as the resting place of the identity of an ahistorical subject, and the scene of a final reconciliation of humanity with nature, reason or itself. Such a discourse remains critical as it is unwilling to accept the taken-for-granted components of our reality and the 'official' accounts of how they came to be the way they are. Yet in so far as it refuses to submit the critical impulse to both high and critical modernist narratives, it becomes what Foucault (1977b), following Nietzsche, called an 'effective history', and sets itself against what might be called the colonisation of historical knowledge by these synthetic philosophies of history. It is a central thesis of the present work that historical study can become effective because it is able to exercise a perpetual vigilance and scepticism toward the claims of various philosophies to prescribe the meaning of history.

The present work then, is an engagement with a theoretical domain rather than an argument for a type of theory. It remains theoretical since it seeks a displacement of what has counted as history within sociology and social theory. However, it interrogates progressivist narratives of social progress or critical ones of human emancipation from the perspective of what it calls *critical and effective history*. This displacement of both types of modernist discourse and the global philosophies of history in which they are embedded leads to a necessarily historical intellectual practice. As I shall show, this form of critical history then is quite a different practice from what is called critical theory. For the moment, I would stress its status as a problematising activity. Indeed, if the widely used term 'postmodernism' is defined as the restive problematisation of the given, I would be happy to regard this type of history as an exercise of postmodernity.

CONTENTS AND ORGANISATION

This book, then, is an exploration of the implications of leading themes of what Foucault called a 'history of the present', and I have called critical and effective histories, for historical–sociological studies. It has pretensions neither to exhaustive treatment of any particular body of texts nor to be a completed and definitive theoretical argument. It does not attempt a commentary on the totality of Foucault's *œuvre*, the entire body of historical sociology, or the histories of the present. What it does is identify and develop arguments around a number of concepts, themes and theories that are germane to the delineation of what these Foucauldian histories of the present have to offer historical–sociological studies. Broadly, four thematic areas might be identified in the following pages: an overarching one of historical perspective and methods; one around problems of rationality, discourse, and the production of truth; another around practices of government, power, and domination; and a final one around subjectivity, the self, and ethical practice. As such, the present work seeks to make a statement of key issues of a critical and effective historical study of rationality, subjectivity, and power.

This book remains, nevertheless, one about historical practice and the uses of history, of how to do this 'critical and effective' history. If the injunctions it issues are often expressed in the negative, it is because of an underlying conviction that this form of historical practice only becomes available when we rid ourselves of the vestiges of the philosophies of history and their transcendental and synthetic ambitions.

The first chapter works toward a delineation of this work of a critical and effective history by examining the most recent 'historical turn' in sociology and the reflection on the uses of history offered by Foucault. The second and third chapters focus on the practice and use of history by developing the problem of the relationship between history and the present. Chapter 2 examines the relationship between Foucault's 'genealogy' and 'archaeology' against theses on the relationship between sociology, history, and the present, put forward by Norbert Elias and Fernand Braudel. It is followed by a brief excursus on the relations between Foucault and the *Annales* School in France. Chapter 3 goes some way toward qualifying the notion of a history of the present by examining both Kant's 'historical writings' and Foucault's commentaries of Kant and enlightenment. It discusses the problems presented by the Enlightenment philosophies and teleologies of history and Foucault's juxtaposition of an 'ontology of the present' to an 'analytic of truth'.

The fourth and fifth chapters represent an extended meditation on the theme of rationality through the writings of Max Weber. The fourth chapter compares Weber's suppositions concerning rationality and the methodology of the cultural sciences with the position of Foucault's critical histories of rationality and their status as 'counter-sciences' in relation to the human sciences. The fifth chapter demonstrates how such a critical history of rationalities differs from the development of the notion of rationalisation in Weber and Weberian historical sociology. The project for an historical sociology of civilisations, implicit in Weber's sociology of religion, and in his notion of the development of the West, is shown to be problematic. However, the Weberian theme of the implications of rationalised practices for the 'conduct of life' remains to be fully explored.

The sixth and seventh chapters continue this concern with the historical comprehension of problems of rationality and enlightenment in the work of the Frankfurt School of critical theory. Now, however, they are inflected with themes of power and domination, of the subject and subjectivity, and of modernity and its potential. These chapters address respectively the 'dialectic of enlightenment' proposed by Horkheimer and Adorno and the implications of the 'discourse of modernity' detected by Jurgen Habermas. I distinguish Foucault's critical history of rationalities, his notion of power–knowledge, and approach to subjectivity, from the philosophy of history that interprets the trajectory of the West in terms of the indefinite extension of instrumental rationality. I also seek to demonstrate the shortcomings of Habermas' reading and extended 'critique' of Foucault as a total theorist of transcendental power. Each of these chapters contains a postscript. The first examines the notion of 'critique' and its usefulness for our purposes; the second the question of the ethics of the intellectual as exemplified by the work of Foucault.

The final chapters address Foucault's various historical enterprises in terms of the major themes of his work in the years 1970–84. This is the closest to commentary on substantive analysis the present work comes. Rather than a linear treatment of his work, I identify the key areas in which he was working in these years. Chapter 8 addresses the themes of his famous microphysics of power and the problem of political individualisation in its relation to similar themes of the historical sociology of the state. An excursus addresses the issues of the relation between time, space, and power, through an examination of Anthony Giddens' comments on Foucault's notion of disciplinary power. Chapters 9 and 10 follow the transformation of the theme of power under the new rubric of governmentality and the related transformation of his history of sexuality into a history of ethics or of the 'techniques of the self'. The relation between techniques of government and techniques of the self is compared with and distinguished from the work of Norbert Elias on state formation and the civilising process.

In a conclusion, I argue that Foucault's legacy to historical–sociological studies is contained in both his methodological treatments which constitute a critical and effective history and his historical analyses of forms of rationality, ethics, and government, and their interrelations.

Chapter 1

Sociology, Foucault, and the uses of history

The relations between sociology and history are indeed problematic. Since its post-Enlightenment beginnings, the development of what is today regarded as sociological thought has been intertwined with historical analyses and schemas for interpreting, understanding, and explaining, history. The focus of this relationship has been the attempt by sociologists and social theorists to comprehend what Karl Polanyi (1944) called 'the great transformation', the broad historical movement that led to the characteristic social relations of what is today named 'modernity'.

The features of this modernity are in principle inexhaustible. In different theories, the core of the great transformation is identified as one or a combination of any of the following: industrial technology, capitalism or generalised commodity production, bureaucratic modes of administration, urbanism, the liberal-democratic state, affective individualism, the public/private dichotomy, and so on. These accounts then give rise to the host of process terms which circumscribe different features of this great trans-formation: modernisation, industrialisation, rationalisation, urbanisation, secularisation, bureaucratisation, etc. It is apparent that sociology has had a degree of success in generating terms that describe and define the contours of modernity. This is perhaps why one influential view proposes that sociology 'focuses particularly upon the "advanced" or modern societies' (Giddens 1984: viii).

In many ways, then, the fundamental claim of sociology is to have captured the historical movement embodied in the great transformation in its essential processes and elements, and in doing so, to have erased both the troublesome particularities revealed by historical analyses and the necessity to revisit the other side of this transformation. It is also to claim the effective unity of all trajectories of transformation and so free sociology from worrisome concerns about the nature of historical time. Sociology thus can present itself as a generalising or 'nomothetic' discipline, one which formulates theories to be applied across a range of phenomena, while it attributes to history the 'idiographic' description of the unique and the singular (Goldthorpe 1991). Sociology, and in this it is like Marxism, can therefore claim to be a science of history that has, paradoxically, dispensed with the necessity of concrete historical analysis. Having captured the historical movement in which the present is caught, it can avoid the difficulties of the singular and the unique, and of differential rhythms and times, and get on with the business of the synchronic analyses of social totalities and their future directions. Historical analysis, in so far as it is regarded as dealing with the understanding of contingent events, different cycles and temporalities, and diverse and ir-reducible diachronic processes, stands at the margins of this science of historical movement.

Posed in this way the relationship of sociology to history has remained an unresolved one. In many respects sociological theory has been made by ignoring or at least bracketing-out the difficulties and complexities that effective historical analysis must pose for explanatory generalisation. This was certainly true of mid-twentieth century sociological theory, whether in the ahistorical typologies of 'pattern variables' of structural functionalism, or the plethora of sociologies of everyday life. Postwar Western Marxism exhibited a distaste for the problems of historical analysis, preferring either a humanist philosophy of history or a fundamentally ahistorical science of historical materialism. Even the critical theory of the Frankfurt School, despite its closeness to the tragedies of the mid-twentieth century, added little that was new to the historical sense of sociology and social theory. For the three decades prior to the 1980s, historical study was at best a preliminary to the comprehension of contemporary social reality or something that could be reduced to a set of rarely examined, self-explanatory, categories, whether of modernisation and theories of development, the advance of instrumental rationality and its irrational effects, or the transition to industrial capitalism.

Since that time it has become increasingly rare to find a form of sociology able to dispense with history and historical analysis as a core component. If earlier students had been prevented from examining the implications of careful historical analysis for taken-for-granted theoretical schemas, the next generation would have found reworkings of history to be indispensable to a whole range of areas. This was especially true in the sociologies of medicine and psychiatry, of sexuality, of deviance and social control, of the modern world system, and of the political sociology of the modern state.[1] There has been the widespread recognition of a hybrid activity called 'historical socio-logy', at least within sociology.

The empirical richness of this activity has not been matched, however, by the attempts to provide a theoretical rationale. Indeed such attempts to provide a justification have tended to be merely syncretic. They have taken conventional grounds for distinguishing between the disciplines – i.e. the oppositions, general/particular, synchronic/diachronic, nomothetic/idio-graphic, present/past, theoretical/empirical, etc. – and turned these into tendencies internal to the new hybrid. This is especially the case where the problem of the relations between sociology and history are posed in terms of agency and structure. In an influential paper, Philip Abrams wrote of what he called the 'problematic of structuring' in which sociology and history are together involved in the same enterprise:

> Both seek to understand the puzzle of human agency and both seek to do so in terms of the process of social structuring. Both are impelled to conceive of those processes both chronologically and logically, as both empirical sequence and abstract form ... Sociology must be concerned with eventuation because that is how structuring happens. History must be theoretical because that is how structuring is apprehended. History has no privileged access to the empirical evidence relevant to the common explanatory project. And sociology has no privileged theoretical access.
>
> (Abrams 1980: 5)

The puzzle of human agency in question pervades a certain type of sociological theory: how do actions of human subjects constitute a social world that in turn constitutes the conditions of possibility of the actions of those subjects? For Abrams' theory of structuring, as for Giddens' better-known theory of structuration, the separation of sociology and history has no rational justification. For these thinkers, history and sociology become methodologically indistinguishable because the dualism between agency and structure cannot be sustained. There are, however, major problems with this view. Before reviewing them, it is worth noticing that if history and sociology are methodologically indistinguishable, then it makes little sense to restrict sociology to the domain of modernity.

Such attempts at combining and overcoming the problems of this dualism of agency and structure are inherently unstable. Above all, their conception of social agency is reductive. Social agency becomes identified with the human subject and its capacities and attributes. Other forms of social agency, including various forms of collective or corporate agency, are either written out of these accounts, or themselves conceived as composed of and reducible to human agents. Secondly, a further untenable conflation is made between human agents and the actions of individuals or persons. Since Mauss' seminal essays (1979), sociologists have known that categories of the person, self, and individual are dependent upon particular cultural and historical practices and techniques. These categories cannot therefore be used as universal data of human existence and experience as they are in attempts to found a general sociological theory upon them. Attempts to grasp the properties of social relations and social systems from such categories of agency cannot be sustained. When such categories are combined in basic sociological concepts themselves, such as in the famous 'duality of structure', they form an unstable amalgam sliding between a structure whose effectivity knows no limits and a form of agency that knows no determination.

Attempts of this type cannot therefore provide the basis for a meeting of sociology with history. Just as their central concepts replicate the dualism they seek to overcome within themselves, so any project for an historical sociology grounded on such concepts replicates the principal grounds for distinguishing between the disciplines within a new inter-disciplinary project itself. Historical sociology now becomes the study of both the structure-forming practices of human actors, and the enabling/constraining effects of those structures upon their actions. The dichotomies, event/process, past/present, diachrony/ synchrony, agent/structure, idiographic/nomothetic, and so on, no longer form the basis of a distinction between two disciplines, but are reproduced as *tendencies* within the new interdisciplinary field. Such manœuvres may provide the basis for reorganising academic life but they do little to overcome what seem to be conceptual inadequacies endemic to these disciplines. These dichotomies simply may be the conditions of possibility of the human and social sciences generally (Smart 1982).

I want to argue with Abrams in favour of historical–socioligical studies, but without relying on his arguments that sociological explanation is necessarily historical and that historical sociology 'is of the essence of the discipline' (Abrams 1982: 2). I suggest there are reasons for undertaking historical sociologies other than conceiving history in an ontological sense as the 'nexus of action and structure' (ibid. 14). If something like an historical sociology is now to be found at the intellectual core of sociology, it may be for reasons that are less theoretical than *strategic*. Indeed, its strategic location may be marked out by the rejection of older uses of history in sociology that functioned to oppose forms of historical analysis rather than embrace them, to deny the contingency and singularity of events and processes, and to repress what Braudel (1980: 49) has called the 'violence' of historical time. This is certainly the case when one considers the broad teleological processes, evolutionary schemas, and generalising typologies which sought to explain historical development in the last half century of sociology. While laying claim to englobing explanatory schemas for historical process, both structural func- tionalism and Marxism could effect what Norbert Elias (1987b) dubbed 'the retreat of sociologists into the present'.

If more recently there has been something of a slowing of that retreat, it is undoubtedly less to do with a recognition of the historical ontology of social forms than with the loosening of the purchase of global theoretical schemas. A new form of intellectual practice, then, rather than a theoretical transcendence of the action/structure dichotomy, is at the root of the recent return to historical studies in sociology. Instead of a union of two disciplines, historical sociology has become a project *internal* to the transformation of sociology itself. Sociology's most recent historical turn is neither new nor a rediscovery of a classic vocation. Rather, it is a strategic reformation of the complex relations between sociology and history that are the conditions of existence of sociology as a discipline. What has occurred is a realignment or, rather, a multiplicity of interconnected realignments, only indistinctly glimpsed in the debates over modernity and postmodernity, of the place of historical analysis and historical time in sociology, and the relations between past, present, and future.

Why has this occurred, and what can we learn from it? The historical dimension of sociology may have moved from a position of supporting its central theoretical schemas to one of qualifying, opposing, or even seeking to undermine them. Theda Skocpol (1982: 12–17) perceptively notes that many of the practitioners of historical sociology situate themselves within the frame of reference of Marxism or structural functionalism while seeking to offer critical analyses of the presuppositions of functionalism, economism, and evolutionism. If a critical historical sociology is largely an enterprise within sociology, this is perhaps because it is this discipline which has been most profoundly subject to the legacy of what Skocpol calls 'transhistorical generalisations and teleological schemas' (1982: 2), of grand social theories and the metanarratives of modernisation, development and increasing affluence, or of the crisis-ridden tendencies of the capitalist mode of production.

It might be said that the historical return in sociology is a part of the resolution of what Gouldner (1971) diagnosed as the coming crisis of Western sociology. It is not necessary to participate in this prophetic mode of intellectual activity to note that sociology has manifest the features of such a crisis, if by that is meant a conjuncture which prefigures either metamorphosis or catastrophe. In any case, sociology has become a form of study without a unifying theoretical edifice, or even consensual norms of validity and meaning, a polycentric, chaotic, even if critical undertaking (cf. Smart 1990). In keeping with this, historical sociology, or what might be better described as critical historical studies, perhaps forms less a unified discipline, or even a new interdisciplinary field, than a *trans*disciplinary, critical, contestatory, erudite, intellectual activity. Indeed, this activity could be said to encompass an *anti*-sociology in so far as it represents so many multiple lines of flight from grand social theory, and from the object 'society' as a global entity, critically examining theoretical claims against those of historical learning and specific social and political analysis. The rise of historical–sociological studies might be said to constitute a series of multiple ruptures, a 'de-formalisation' of the discipline from within that prepares a transformation of sociology into an engaged but learned practice. Such a practice would privilege analytical sophistication over theoretical system, conceptual productivity over fidelity to established models, and plural and diverse intellectual adventures rather than the search for foundations. The reversal of the retreat of sociologists into the present would not lead to an end of sociology but to its metamorphosis into a new kind of critical historical–sociological practice with a diversity of theoretical trajectories. Indeed, the renewed interest in hitherto neglected or marginalised historical–sociological thinkers, such as Karl Polanyi and Norbert Elias, the far more serious reflection on the historical writings of Max Weber, the concern to draw upon other versions of history, such as that of the *Annales* School and, indeed, the historical writings of Michel Foucault and others in the history of knowledge and science, may all attest to the imminence of such a metamorphosis.

However, beyond the transformation of sociology lies a far more serious issue. In displacing, from within and without, the claims of grand social theory, this historical turn seems to imply a particular form of the 'politics of truth', a contestation of the way in which statements are validated within a particular practice of knowledge. Conventional social theory took a hyper-rationalist path. Whether Durkheimian, functionalist, or Marxist, it established a hierarchy of discursive objects in which those with the greatest levels of generality and abstraction held the strongest explanatory force. The characteristics of social systems, divisions of social labour, or modes of production, or the nature of modernity, capitalism, and industrialisation, had to be invoked in order to understand anything held to be within their purview. One does not have to oppose hyper-rationalism to a hyper-empiricism to notice that little room existed for a form of analysis which sought to maximise the intelligibility of regional domains such as those of sexuality, madness, delinquency, poverty, and so on, and particular forms of practice and rationality, those of governing, curing, punishing, confining, etc. Certainly, existing schemas could provide some intelligibility. Yet the encounter of the historical contents revealed by meticulous analysis with grand social-theoretical schematas was one that was peculiarly sensitive to the claims of theoretical and hierarchising knowledges.

It is certainly true that not all historical sociologies involve the contestation of the regime of grand theory and its claims to scientificity. Yet the existence of such projects suggests that the narratives and typologies deployed by such theories are in some ways problematic. At a minimum, the emergence of historical sociologies attests to the need of global theories for a new empirical validation to establish themselves as active research programmes. It may be, however, that the existence of these renewed critical historical studies may also suggest that these theories have become *epistemological obstacles* (to invoke loosely Gaston Bachelard's famous term[2]) to effective knowledge and analysis of historical trajectories. If historical sociologies are an effect of the resolution, or attempted resolution, of the crisis of sociology struggling with the legacy of grand social theory, then there is little reason to seek a renewed theoretical container for them. To do so would not only undermine the potential for greater intelligibility they possess, but would also be inimical to the kind of politics of truth they represent.

This is of course a conjectural version of the changing historical sense of sociology and to what it might lead. I want now to introduce some leading themes of the one major recent thinker who has perhaps devoted most effort to considering questions of historical sense and what constitutes what we might call a 'critical and effective history', Michel Foucault. Far from making Foucault into a sociologist in disguise, I want here to reflect on *his* historical sense and what it might offer the new historical sense in sociology. In the following chapters, we follow that historical sense through its various aspects, attempting to specify the relationship between genealogy and archaeology, his principal methodological approaches, his understanding of a critical history of rationality, and his notion of a 'history of the present'. The rest of this chapter is devoted to an introduction to some of the key terms necessary to understanding Foucault's specific contribution.

FOUCAULT'S TIMELY MEDITATIONS

Michel Foucault has been called the 'greatest modern philosophical historian' (Murray 1990: viii), the 'historian in a pure state' (Veyne, qutoed by Habermas 1987a: 275), the inventor of a 'properly philosophical form of interrogation which is itself new and which revives History' (Deleuze 1988: 49). It would be inexcusable to remake him a social theorist or to regard him as a sociologist in disguise. To do so is to risk exposing these flowerings between philosophy and history to the arid climate of theoretical systems and the brutal search for ultimate foundations. To do so is to deny the specificity subtly caught in the title of the chair he held at the *College de France*, *Histoire des systèmes de pensée* (History of Systems of Thought), and to turn away from the real achievements of his critical excursions into the history of reason. For our purposes, Foucault is approached as he was, as somewhere 'in between' and 'across' established boundaries of knowledge. As such we might mobilise his achievements for an enterprise that is also between and across established disciplines and modes of thought.

This philosophical historian's (or historical philosopher's) studies, first termed 'archaeologies' and later 'genealogies', as well as his writings on the use and practice of history, particularly *The Archaeology of Knowledge* (1972) and the essay on Nietzsche (1977b), offer a point of reflection on our changing historical sense. They suggest a form of critical historical study that leaves behind the methods and objectives of conventional, empiricist historiography without recourse to sterile theoretical schemas. They raise again the problem of the uses and pertinence of historical study, and of the practice of history that is linked but not subservient to present theoretical, political, and ethical issues.

It is a quite senseless task to be faithful to a form of thought which itself seems designed to put the most loyal follower off track. This is a thought that, despite an internal consistency, never felt the need to be faithful to itself. It does not lend itself to a systematic theoretical elaboration. Rather, 'theory' is here embedded within substantive analyses. Its statement and restatement takes less the form of a progress toward increasing clarity than a vertiginous and prolix recreation, a continual renewal of itself, one which refuses to stand still, to be the same. As a consequence, I feel compelled to take an instrumental attitude toward Foucault's work and to admit that what follows is a use of his work for particular objectives concerning the historical–sociological study sketched above. It is my general hypothesis that Foucault's contribution to this historical sociology can be best understood as a delineation of a form of history which is both *critical* and *effective* and which displaces the invasion of historical analysis by what I shall call the *philosophy of history*. These are terms which must be approached with care. They are the nub of the following discussion.

Despite a concern with discourses as rule-governed systems for the production of thought, Foucault never sought to apply a particular system or to allow his own heuristics to congeal into a fixed, formal method. Every statement of method, ostensibly committed to the same overall framework, reveals subtle, and sometimes gross, shifts and reconfigurations. Indeed, Foucault engaged in the task of methodological formalisation in the *Archaeology* only after he had completed his 'empirical' studies, and almost immediately set off on a new path in which this approach was subsumed under another, quite different one, that of genealogy. Moreover, he left us no extended methodological statement of this genealogy. There are a series of essays, lectures, introductions, interviews, and other fragments, in which genealogical historiography is discussed but none of these settle on a fixed language and style of presentation. The one text that discusses genealogy in considerable detail is in fact a commentary on Nietzschean genealogy. No matter how much affinity there is between Foucault and Nietzsche the assumption of an identity between commentary and methodological approach is a perilous one that has derailed several of his admirers as well as his detractors.[3]

The relation between Foucault's reflections on the uses and pertinence of historical studies and his own histories cannot be understood in terms of the application of a method or theory. This again should give us cause for caution. It is just as likely that these 'methodological' statements are occasions for reshaping and re-positioning the historical work already done as they are ways of posing new directions and aims for research. Such statements are united by a fundamental rejection of the naïve empiricist account of historiography as a reconstruction of the past, and an approach to the use of historical sources to discover the reality of which these sources are traces. More generally, they are united by their rejection of the pedantry of method, the notion that historical practice is reducible to the application of a methodology to a particular field. Positively, these approaches to method are united by the insight that history is above all a practice, a practice undertaken in a particular present and for particular reasons linked to that present. For no matter how much historical writing is about dimensions or aspects of the past, and refers to events, irruptions, discourses, and social practices that can be given a particular time-space, it is in fact an activity that is irrevocably linked to its current uses.

One way of getting at this idea of history as a practice within a definite present is to note that certain kinds of history arise from the rather simple necessity of having to deal with the records of one sort or another produced within and across the boundaries of national societies. This is a problem raised in the introduction to *The Archaeology of Knowledge*. Here, history does not merely use documents as the fortunate by-product of the past that serves as its memory. Rather, history is an active marshalling of historical resources in so far as it 'is one way in which a society recognises and develops a mass of documentation with which it is inextricably linked' (1972: 7). Even if history is reduced to this kind of curatorial role, it is still of its own time and place, and the needs it serves are equally of this time and place.

This is not simply a repetition of the idea that all histories are written from a particular viewpoint or perspective, because it is also concerned to come to terms with history as a practice, as a particular set of actions brought to bear on a particular material. This material is not 'raw' but already the result of other practices of conservation and organisation. It follows that it is not a question of advocating the adoption of a perspectival history against a positivist one but of reflecting upon the possible uses of historical studies. Any critical, transdisciplinary historical study then must not only avoid empiricist *naïveté* but also actively thematise the problem of the uses to which history is put and the necessity to which it answers. The resolution Foucault gives in his archaeology is not entirely satisfactory, and in the course of engaging with Nietzsche he came to a notion of genealogy as a 'history of the present' in which archaeology becomes a means of analysis rather than its end.

For the *Archaeology* (Foucault 1972: 6–8), the new kinds of historical study undertaken by both the *Annales* School and the French School of the history of sciences following from Bachelard and Georges Canguilhem arise precisely from the problematisation of documents. In both forms of history, the crucial question is not the relation between discontinuity and continuity but a new approach to the document. This new approach forsakes the reconstitution of the world of which the document seeks. Its primary function is *not* to interpret the document; instead, it 'organises the document, divides it up, distributes it, orders, arranges it in levels, establishes series, distinguishes between what is relevant and what is not, discovers elements, defines unities, describes relations' (ibid. 6–7). Here Foucault claims to be undertaking, from within the history of knowledge, the same displacement of conventional modes of historiography pioneered by the 'serial history' of the *Annales* school.

If Foucault's diagnosis of the new kind of history refuses the *naïveté* of the document as a trace through which the past can be reconstructed, it is not to fall for the seductive spiral of interpretation characteristic of hermeneutics. As early as his contribution to the Royaumont Colloquium of 1964 (1986c), Foucault had explicitly distanced himself from the nineteenth century discovery of the infinite task of interpretation in which nothing is primary since the sign itself is already an interpretation of other signs. Here he maintains that hermeneutics and what he calls 'semiology' are the two fiercest enemies (ibid. 5). If semiology is taken to mean any structural study of discourse or language, then it is clear where Foucault's sympathies lie. Indeed, this statement recalls the severe polemic against 'commentary' in the preface to *The Birth of the Clinic* (1973: xvi–xvii) as depending on a double plethora of meaning because it assumes a silent signified that must be given speech and a signifier subject to inexhaustible decipherment. This 'dooms us to an endless task nothing can limit'. Foucault is clearly not a hermeneuticist. Archaeology is not yet another mode of interpretation rendering into discourse the unsaid. It concentrates all its focus onto what is said, as Foucault repeats throughout the *Archaeology*, in a project which seeks 'a pure description of discursive events' (1972: 27). It is this affirmation of the reality of discourse as something to be analysed, described, and organised that prevents archaeology from retracing the interpretative spiral of hermeneutics. In this sense, archaeology undertakes a move parallel to that of Emile Durkheim. If the latter's dictum to 'treat social facts as things' is a demand to recognise the specificity of social reality, then one could perhaps say that Foucault exhorted us to treat discursive facts as an irreducible reality. However, it is more appropriate to say that Foucault's dictum was not to treat discursive facts as things but as, rather, *fields*, as systems of the dispersed relations that are are the conditions of discourses (cf. Major-Poetzl 1983: 3–5).

The name he gives to this form of study is 'archaeology'. This may be an unfortunate name in two respects of which Foucault showed himself to be aware in an interview (1989a: 46). Archaeology sought neither to reconstitute the *arche* or primary origin or deep foundation of forms of knowledge nor excavate or exhume the buried remnants of the past. Indeed, archaeology denies the search both for origins and for hidden depths of discourse in an attempt to define the level of the intrinsic description of the *archive*, which Foucault defines (1972: 130) as the 'general system of the formation and transformation of statements'. Perhaps this concern for the facticity of statements, their relations with each other, the rules under which they are formed and transformed, is best captured in the metaphors Foucault uses at the beginning of the *Archaeology* (1972: 7). Here, he argues, it is no longer the task of history to memorise monuments of the past and thus to transform them into 'documents' of a reality and a consciousness of which they are but the traces. Rather, history has become, he suggests, that which transforms documents into monuments, into a mass of elements to be described and organised. If archaeology had once aspired to become a form of history, he suggests that now history aspires to the condition of archaeology, concerned as it is with the intrinsic description of the monument. In an earlier essay, we find this suggestion posed as the treatment of 'discourse not as a theme of reviving *commentary*, but as a *monument* to be described in its intrinsic configuration' (1991a: 60).[4]

The *Archaeology* is a rigorous and exhilarating rethinking of the themes of conventional historiography and its relation to documents. However, it retains a certain positivism, admitted by Foucault (1981a: 73) and detected by Deleuze (1988: 12), that is unhelpful from the point of view of a concern for the uses of history in the present. In rejecting the naïve positivism that imagines history concerns itself with showing how it really was, Foucault replaces it with a sophisticated and rarefied form that insists on the irreducibility of the discursive order and the contents that appear within it. Thus, contrary to certain prevailing views, Foucault, at least in his archaeological methods, was neither a relativist nor a nihilist arguing that all is interpretation and denying the existence of facts or primary data. Indeed, for archaeology discourse has a specific density, solidity, and facticity, and constitutes a level of reality that is irreducible to the subjective attributes of those who participate in it. Instead of seeking to use documents to reconstruct the historical reality that lies behind and beyond them, Foucault asserts that the problem is to bring the positive reality of discourse into focus and attempt the description of its systems of formation.

The achievement of the *Archaeology* is great and is now way diminished by later phases of Foucault's thought. I would want to resist all the hasty claims that Foucault found himself enclosed in a structuralist account of discourse as fundamentally self-referential, and thus felt the need for a more adequate theorisation of what had remained the non-discursive background of discourse (e.g. Dreyfus and Rabinow 1983). Against such views, it is necessary to assert the unassailable discovery contained in *The Archaeology of Knowledge* and related texts of the positive and irreducible existence of discourse. Such a discovery remains fundamental throughout his work and, more importantly, is fundamental to any rethinking of the place of the study of discourse and rationality within historical sociology. Far from resorting to a notion of discourse as an ideal unity like a *Weltanschauung* or ideology, archaeology marks the advent of a materialist approach to the analysis of knowledge and belief if by that is meant an approach that respects the being of discourse, its materiality, its location in time and place, and seeks to account for it in terms of its conditions of existence.

The fundamental deficiency of archaeology is not therefore its account of the relation between discursive and non-discursive practices. Rather, it is the way it conceives the rootedness of historical study in present problems and necessities. *The Archaeology* gives no explicit account of how the historical description of the positivity of discourse is to be mobilised in terms of current purposes and issues.

This, more than anything, may be what led Foucault to reflect on the purposes and uses of history in the essay, 'Nietzsche, Genealogy, History', a little more than two years later. As suggested above, there is some difficulty in using this text as an account of Foucault's own position as it is quite clearly a form of intellectual labour performed on Nietzsche's writings and not, primarily, a statement of Foucault's method. Here, the terms which stand out are ones drawn from Nietzsche. Nevertheless, they are ones which help us gain a sense of what type of critical historical approach may be apt for a sociology in the process of refurbishing its own 'historical sense'. Indeed, Foucault finds scattered through Nietzsche's books a notion of an 'effective history', a *wirkliche Historie*, and an analysis of 'historical sense' (Foucault 1977b: 152). The historical sense commended by Nietzsche, according to Foucault, is something that parallels our diagnosis of sociology's historical turn: it questions those histories that are subordinate to suprahistorical perspectives, that reduce the diversity of time to a self-enclosed totality, that find in history a place for subjective recognition and reconciliation, and that imply the end of time in a completed development.

The historical sense is one which evades the myriad tentacles of what we shall call a synthetic *philosophy of history*, the imposition of transcendent perspectives on history that tell of the progress of reason, the rise and decline of civilisation, or the loss and alienation and final reconciliation and emancipation of humanity's true being. Beyond the reaches of this philosophy of history lies a Foucauldian–Nietzschean domain of effective history that contains more than a clue as to the possible directions of a critical historical sociology. This effective history 'places within a process of development everything considered immortal in man . . . deals with events in their most unique characteristics . . . and leave[s] things undisturbed in their own dimension and intensity' (Foucault 1977b: 153–6). In short, an effective history historicises that which is thought to be transhistorical, grasps rather than effaces the singularity of events and processes, and defines levels of analysis that are proper to its objects. An effective history both refuses to use history to assure us of our own identity and the necessity of the present, and also problematises the imposition of suprahistorical or global theory.

In so far as archaeology had engaged in a polemic against the subsumption of historical study to a philosophy of history that posits an ideal continuity of history around the story of its subject, it fulfilled this role as an effective history. However, while its 'positivism' may well be a technique capable of finding the level proper to its objects, it remained incapable of articulating its own purposes and relation to the present. The account of archaeology could reflect upon its own *theoretical* effects (e.g. the displacement of the history of ideas, the denial of the creative subject, the interruption of continuous histories etc.) without providing an account of its *strategic* purposes. Genealogy is far better placed to do so.

In establishing the shape of this effective history, Foucault invokes the second of the *Untimely Meditations* (Nietzsche 1983: 57–123) as a way of grasping the trajectory of Nietzsche's thought on history. Here, Nietzsche had discerned three fundamental uses of history: the monumental, devoted to the veneration of great events and deeds (ibid. 69–72); the antiquarian, dedicated to the preservation of the past as the continuity of identity in tradition (ibid. 72–75); and the critical, directed to the judgement and condemnation of parts of the past in the name of present truths (ibid. 74–75).

It is to these three figures, suggests Foucault, that the historical sense of Nietzsche's genealogy is opposed:

> The historical sense gives rise to three uses that oppose and correspond to the three Platonic modalities of history. The first is parodic, directed against reality, and opposes the theme of history as reminiscence or recognition; the second is dissociative, directed against identity, and opposes history given as continuity or representative of a tradition; the third is sacrificial, directed against truth, and opposes history as knowledge. They imply a use of history that severs its connection to memory, its metaphysical and anthropological model, and constructs a counter-memory – a transformation of history into a totally different form of time.
>
> (Foucault 1977b: 160)

Foucault thus found in these parodic, dissociative, and sacrificial uses of history three doubles of the monumental, antiquarian and critical modalities. Genealogy thus follows conventional uses of history with sufficient awareness of their foibles and pitfalls. It is able to laugh at the buffoonery of greatness and the great, to reveal the heterogeneity masked by presumed continuity of identity, and to turn its critical capacity from the past to the subject of knowledge.

It is this latter move that has disturbed Foucault's humanist critics. At the end of the essay, Foucault argues that Nietzsche reconsidered the critical use which was 'no longer a question of judging the past in the name of truth . . . but of risking the destruction the subject of knowledge in the endless deployment of the will to knowledge' (ibid. 164). This and surrounding passages have doubtless given rise to the charge that Foucault followed Nietzsche in refusing reason (Ingram 1986: 314) or that here 'Foucault yield[s] to the familiar melody of a *professing* irrationalism' (Habermas 1987a: 278). This is an untenable charge for several reasons. First, while Foucault is certainly attracted to Nietzsche's genealogy as a source of inspiration and of 'historical sense', it is a mistake to read this as a methodological statement. It is only within the exploration of the language and perspective afforded by Nietzsche's analysis of the rancorous will to knowledge that Foucault states that 'all knowledge rests upon injustice (that there is no right, not even in the act of knowing, to truth or a foundation for truth)' (1977b: 163). For Foucault, it is not a matter of accepting Nietzsche's provocation as an ersatz truth but of turning his insight into a critical problem. The restive force of criticism, turned to the subject of knowledge, will deny knowledge any secure foundation in that subject. I would suggest that Foucault's turn to Nietzsche is not for a model of a methodology to follow but for a kind of incitement that would force the conceptualisation of the relation of historiography to its present outside the rarefied positivism of archaeology. Nietzsche represents a pole that is capable of wresting historical thought from its complacency and from its typical moves, of inducing the effects necessary to examine our own purposes in historical study. This is not to deny Foucault's self-professed Nietzscheanism but to try to make clear the kind of use to which Nietzsche is put in Foucault's deliberations.

Indeed, there is some evidence to suggest that Foucault did not regard the critical use of history as problematic as did Nietzsche. More than a decade later, Foucault discusses (1983b: 201) his own approach to reason as a 'critical inquiry into the history of rationality', a 'rational critique of rationality', and insists on the possibility of a 'rational history of all the ramifications and all the bifurcations [of reason – M.D.], a contingent history of reason'. If archaeology displaces the delirium of interpretation with an analysis of the positivity of discourse, then genealogy displaces both the search for ultimate foundations and its opposite, nihilism, with a form of patient criticism and prob- lematisation located in the present. Foucault's critical history forsakes the critique of the past in terms of the truth of the present but not the critical use of the history of reason to diagnose the practical issues, necessities, and limits, of the present. Let us call history 'effective' to the extent that it upsets the colonisation of historical knowledge by the schemas of a transcendental and synthetic philosophy of history, and 'critical' in proportion to its capacity to engage in the tireless interrogation of what is held to be given, necessary, natural, or neutral.

In seeking to establish such a practice of history, I would argue, Foucault had already begun to chart the very same presuppositions that historical sociologies, in roughly the same period, would find in the social theories they had inherited: tendencies toward totalising abstraction, teleology, supra- historical generalisation, universalist conceptions of human existence, and confirmation of identity. If Foucault's encounter with Nietzsche suggests some broad perspectives which could be used to constitute an effective and critical history, his historical studies themselves realise a relevance and creative conceptual focus which historical sociologies might seek. At the beginning of *Discipline and Punish*, his famous, popular, study of punitive practice, he poses the question of why write such a history: 'Simply because I am interested in the past? No, if one means by that writing a history of the past in terms of the present. Yes, if one means writing the history of the present.' (Foucault 1977a: 31). The pertinence of this 'history of the present' to historical sociologies is the capacity of such history to be situated in an illumination of present reality without invoking the themes of memory, tradition, and foundations, and making history the haven in which the constitutive subject finds reconciliation. The general context for a con- sideration of genealogy and archaeology is, then, a third term which they both serve, that of a history of the present.

CONCLUSION

I have resisted a definition of 'historical sociology' due to a desire to keep the term as open and non-prescriptive as possible. Such a definition, if possible, must be broad enough to encompass projects that range across intellectual methods, styles, schools, traditions, and disciplines. Indeed, rather than reduce it to a comparative method or new hybrid discipline, I would prefer to regard historical sociology as any reflexive attempt to develop and elaborate social-theoretical concepts within a field of positive historical analysis.

In contrast, the 'history of the present' may be loosely characterised by its use of historical resources to reflect upon the contingency, singularity, interconnections, and potentialities of the diverse trajectories of those elements which compose present social arrangements and experience. Such a history renews a quest for methodologies adequate to the problems of division, dispersion, and difference within history, and seeks to prevent anachronistic understandings of the past that make the present a necessary outcome of a necessarily continuous past. Such a history is geared toward the critical use of history to make intelligible the possibilities in the present and so can yield to neither universalist concepts of rationality and subjectivity nor metanarratives of progress, reason, or emancipation. It is this latter move that makes his critical history an effective tool for historical sociologies.

I have argued so far as if there was a clear-cut division between two discrete intellectual movements. This, of course, is not the case. The history of the present has been one contributor to the changing historical sense in sociology, at first no doubt minor, but one which has become increasingly active. While some of the historical sociologies cited above, particularly those working in the fields of sexuality, deviance, medicine, and so on, incorporated themes and analyses derived from Foucault's histories to varying degrees, there has emerged, as though along a parallel track, a number of studies which took seriously his programme for a 'history of the present'.[5] These include studies of notions of madness and mental health and illness, and disciplines of psychiatry and psychology in France, the United States, and Britain, of the family and of social policy, of various forms of government, of education, and of poverty. These studies represent the first fruits of a new style of engaged historical practice in the space marked out between and in contradistinction to two competing 'regimes of truth': on the one hand, a social theory and sociology that seeks to sacrifice historical intelligibility in favour of models, types, and method; on the other, a conventional historiography that seeks to abandon concepts in the quest for exhaustive reconstruction of the past, for telling it like it was. The solution for historical sociology has often been a comparativist empiricism fuelled by theoretical, often classical, references, and so open to the charges of neglect of the historiographical use of sources (Goldthorpe 1991). The histories of the present, by contrast, have shown a much greater willingness to focus on the problems presented by historical resources, of the purpose of historical ventures, of their pertinence, and of the presuppositions inherited from the synthetic philosophies of histories with which the social and moral sciences have been entangled from their birth in the eighteenth century Scottish Enlightenment.[6]

In the next chapter we shall seek to comprehend the relation of genealogy to archaeology within this framework of the history of the present.

Chapter 2

Presentist perspectives

Implicit in what I have argued in the first chapter are two key propositions. First, history as an intellectual practice has no special, self-evident, merit or justification. There are no a priori grounds, in other words, on which one could justify 'doing' history, or the use of resources or materials that might be called historical. In fact, there is good reason to be suspicious of the various rationales for history and the uses to which it is put. Secondly, there is nothing about the nature of social or historical reality that can compel sociology – if we are to continue to take the perspective of that discipline – to take history seriously. It remains an open question as to whether adequate theoretical grounds for a 'marriage' of history and sociology can be adduced at all. However, it is clear that these grounds cannot be found in a putative ontology of a socio-historical reality as a process of structuring or structuration.

Despite these propositions, I argue for critical historical studies in general and historical–sociological studies in particular.[1] I conceive the latter, however, not in terms of an account of the relation between social agency and social structure, nor as a new synthetic science, inter-disciplinary field, or comparative method. Rather these studies constitute an endeavour which is perspectival and strategic, rooted in present-day concerns even as they reject the present as a necessary end-point of historical trajectories. The notion of 'presentism' has been central to one critic's evaluation of Foucault's contribution to the 'philosophical discourse of modernity' (Habermas 1987a). Whatever that term may be taken to mean, it is certainly right to suggest that the present is at the heart of the critical historical studies of Foucault. This is so in a double sense. On the one hand, these studies attain a focus from contemporary struggles, confrontations, and what Foucault began to call 'problematisations'. On the other, they are concerned with the present configuration and organisation of knowledge. These studies remain theoretical – in the sense of operating within the contested field of ideas and concepts – without ever creating a totalising theory. It is in this latter sense that they are strategic. Rather than seeking an absolute foundation, they give explicit acknowledgement of the fact of their own immersion within an existing, mobile field of knowledge. Their objective is not to produce the truth but to grasp the conditions which hold at any one moment for 'saying the true'.

The notion of 'the present' itself is not of course beyond problematisation, and the next chapter takes up that issue in relation to Foucault's engagement with Kant's philosophy of history. However, I want here to bring into focus those aspects of Foucault's approach that constitute a guide to a critical and strategic form of historical–sociological study. This is done by examining two alternative conceptions of the position of the present in historical and sociological study, those of Fernand Braudel, a key figure of the *Annales* school of historians in France, and Norbert Elias, the belatedly acknowledged (not least in England where he worked for more than thirty years) historical sociologist and theorist of civilisation, particularly in his essay, 'The retreat of sociologists into the present' (1987b). The two thinkers represent quite different attitudes toward the present from those of Foucault, that, none the less, remain instructive in themselves. Moreover, although their positions are not fundamentally inconsistent with Foucault's, they do allow us to clarify his contribution. The elaboration and clarification of Foucault's notion of a 'history of the present' forms the bulk of this chapter, particularly in regard to the relation between the approaches he termed 'genealogy' and 'archaeology'. It concludes with some remarks comparing the three thinkers' conception of the pertinence of historical studies. An excursus on the mutual relations of Foucault and the *Annales* school is appended to the chapter.

BRAUDEL, ELIAS, AND THE PRESENT

Braudel and Elias have many things in common in the way they treat matters of the relation of the present to the past. They both conceive the present as a development of the past and the studies in which they are engaged are unifying or synthetic of the human or social sciences. In this sense, they form part of the mid-twentieth century historical consciousness that repudiated the legacy of nineteenth century narrative history unified by reference to political events – the history of Ranke and his followers (Burke 1990: 7). There are, however, important differences. Whereas Braudel, particularly in his methodological writings, is concerned to provide a 'presentist' justification for history, Elias, perhaps paradoxically, rejects the presentism of sociology. Such different attitudes toward the present stem less from the idiosyncrasies of each author than their position in relation to the contingencies of their respective disciplines.

To start with Braudel. He liked to quote the words of Lucien Febvre, his mentor and the co-founder (with Marc Bloch) of *Annales* in 1929, in words echoed by Foucault's claim to the history of the present: 'History, science of the past, science of the present' (Braudel 1980: 37, 69). But how can this be so, how can the science of the past be also one of the present? This formula is certainly not a self-evident equation presupposing as it does a fundamental relation of identity of present and past. To understand the relation, at least as Braudel conceives it, it is necessary to understand his conception of history and historical time.

Braudel argues for a highly sociologised version of history. In fact he wrote on the unity of the human sciences even with the full acknowledgement of the practical and institutional reasons for their diversity (especially Braudel 1980: 55–63). More to the point, in his inaugural lecture at the *Collège de France* in 1950 (1980: 6–22), Braudel spoke of the fundamental reality of humanity as *social* reality and argued vigorously that history must tackle this reality, one which encompassed collective life, economies, institutions, social structures, and civilisations. It is clear that this 'new kind of history', as Febvre had dubbed it (1973: 27–43), was one which presupposed the intellectual, if not the practical, union of the human sciences.

For Braudel, if not for the major *Annales* practitioners, such unity would appear to come from historical time itself rather than the object of the human sciences. It is well known that Braudel introduces the possibility of a multiplicity of temporalities, working at different speeds and in different directions (e.g. 1980: 64–82). He first distinguishes a short-term history of events, *l'histoire événementielle*, a fecund and contingent history of actions and happenings, a 'micro-history' with its own 'micro-times'. Secondly, he distinguishes a conjunctural history, such as that most often studied by economists, a history of economic crises, cycles and intercycles, following a broader and slower rhythm than that of events. Finally, over and above this is a vast, stable history, bordering on immobility, the history of centuries, of civilisations, and of humanity's relation to the earth itself, the history of what he called in a famous article of 1958 the *longue durée* (1980: 25–54). This latter history and its time are not simply one level, but the all-embracing totality of historical time itself. He spoke of it as an 'anonymous history, working in depths and most often in silence' (ibid.10), a 'slow-paced history of civilisation, a history of depths, of the characteristics of their structure and layout' (ibid.11). This vast, slow-moving, 'ponderous history' appears as the privileged domain of historiography, a history not only of civilisation but of one in which time stands almost still, an *histoire immobile*, the history of the earth, of the relation of humanity and the earth that bears and feeds it. This history of the *longue durée* is quite evidently something deeper than that which most English-speaking social scientists mean by the 'long-term'. It is in these depths that Braudel discerns the 'unity of history' that is the 'unity of life' itself and the grand tableau, one might suspect, of the unity of human sciences (ibid.16–17).

If Braudel's conception of history succeeds in pushing it into the inter-disciplinary communication with the human sciences that foreshadows their unification, then how can history be distinguished from sociology? For Braudel (1980: 69) sociology and history are the only two global sciences and one suspects he feels that it is their consequent 'inflated imperialism' that is at the base of their disputes. However, he argues (ibid. 49–59), what distinguishes them from one another, and is at the root of sociological resentment, is historical time, a reality which retains its violence despite all attempts to break it down. History is thus an activity which is bound by an historical time that cannot be reduced to regularity and synchrony.

Returning to the principal point of this discussion, Braudel's notion of historical time is at the centre of his understanding of the relationship of past and present. The present is shot through with a multiplicity of historical temporalities, proceeding at their own pace and in different directions. The connection of present to past is thus not a univocal one. Present and past are linked by a descent that is itself composed of many 'micro-descents'. As Braudel puts it (1980: 39), 'a descent following the onward stream of time is conceivable only in terms of a multiplicity of descents, following the innumerable rivers of time'. However, at the levels of greatest depth detected by structural history, those of the *longue durée*, there lies a temporality that erases all discontinuities observable at the level of events and action, and that establishes a continuity of material civilisation, of humanity in its relationship with the landscape and the earth, its tools, technologies, and customs. On the one hand, the present can be temporalised at different levels. On the other, the significance of the present and the rupture it introduces recedes in the face of this deep history. It is at this deep level, that of structural history and the *longue durée*, that Braudelian history becomes a total or global history (he later preferred the term *l'histoire globale*) for it is here that the differential temporalities are synthesised to grasp the unity of life. It is only within such a history that the present can be situated. If history raises questions about society as a whole and the movement of time which ceaselessly carries life along, then the present cannot escape it, even if as an instant on the surface of a deeper movement, that present is always destined to be erased before it occurs.

Braudel's writings in many ways typify the problem for history in the mid-twentieth century: to open itself to the advances of the social sciences and to seek its justification in the intelligibility of the present. The writings of Norbert Elias start from the opposite problem, the involvement of sociology in the present, its lack of engagement with historical materials and appreciation of historical process.[2] Elias claims (1987b; Kilminster 1987) there has been a retreat (*Ruckzug*) of sociologists into the present since World War II. He regards this retreat as a symptom of a double problem: first, the politicisation of social theory, and, secondly, its isolation from the legion empirical inquiries of this period. Taking up the former, Elias argues (1987b: 225) that the division of theory into Parsonian functionalism and neo-Marxism represents 'an attenuated version of the class struggle within the setting of an academic discipline'. He suggests that this situation is in many ways analogous to earlier struggles (e.g. over the Copernican Revolution) of the natural sciences to free themselves from extra-scientific, especially religious, beliefs and ideals. In this sense, Elias' position should be understood in terms of his broader under-standing of the dialectic of involvement and detachment in human societies and in scientific endeavour (1987a: 3–41). The proliferation of empirical inquiries divorced from theory indicates for him a high degree of emotional involvement of sociology in the social issues and problems of the present, and the lack of detachment which would allow sociologists to appreciate the position of the present within the 'vast stream of humanity's development' (1987b: 224). For Elias, this involvement is a sign of the immaturity of the social sciences as compared to the natural sciences. It is also, more funda-mentally, a result of the nature of the social or human sciences in which the objects of study (persons) are also its subjects (Elias 1987a: 12). This, of course, is a variant on the familiar neo-Kantian theme of the ontological basis of the separation of the natural and social sciences. According to Elias (1987a: 14–16), social scientists, by virtue of their position in relation to a world of groups engaged in struggle for position and survival, face the limits to detachment imposed by their own participation in collective social life.

Elias is, of course, not arguing that sociologists should retreat *from* the present but simply that a certain degree of detachment and autonomy is necessary before sociology can contribute to the handling of social and political problems. However, because this detachment is limited by the peculiar nature of sociology, Elias draws the conclusion that the involvement and participation of sociologists is a condition of sociological knowledge. The solution for Elias is to postulate the need in the human sciences for a unifying framework built around 'universals of social development' such as the economic function, the control of violence, the transmission and acquisition of knowledge, and patterns of self-restraint (1987b: 226–31). These universals are used to derive 'process models', a term by which Elias seeks to distinguish himself from sociologists' 'static typologies and static concepts of structure and function' (ibid. 226). History becomes the ground from which these models arise, and by which they are refined and tested. The present may be understood more clearly by comparison with the conditions of the past, but contemporary social requirements and structures of self-restraint form an obstacle if they are projected into the past (ibid. 236–7). Elias thus argues for a degree of detachment from political and emotional investments in the present in order to understand the universal features of humanity that are revealed in the framework of developmental history. Elias, like Braudel, suggests that an understanding of present problems and issues can only be had within the project of a total history of humanity. Yet, where Braudel seeks to turn history toward our involvements in the present, Elias renounces that involvement to establish the historical credentials of sociology.

There are indeed fundamental tensions and problems in both these con-ceptions of history and its relations to the human sciences. For Braudel, there is the tension between the multiplicity of historical temporalities and the structural or unifying instance of the *longue durée*. For Elias, there is the call for detachment together with the recognition that involvement is one of the conditions for social scientific knowledge. In both cases there is the supposition that only some version of a total or global history can be of assistance in understanding the present. By contrast, Foucault's conception of the history of the present suggests a quite different stance in relation to these same problems. This is a stance that rejects a globalising perspective and a unifying instance of historical time and does not seek to suppress the involvement in the present which all parties accept is a condition of historical study itself. Foucault's thought deliberately thematises this involvement in its own constitution, particularly in relation to its understanding of the role of critical thought since Kant, examined in the next chapter. For the moment, however, let us examine how it poses the problem of the relationship between such involvements and the practice of historical writing.

FOUCAULT AND PRESENTISM

Foucault's conception of his historical studies and their aims and purposes is both distinctive and consistent. Despite relentless changes in formulation and the development of new methodologies and approaches, it is possible to discern a coherent conception of history and its relation to the present. Moreover, his fundamental and remarkably constant understanding of the relationship between 'genealogy' and 'archaeology' provides a way of resolving these problems – of involvement and detachment, of scholarly erudition and critical perspective – that can address the historiographical problem of 'presentism' and yet derive its pertinence as a history of the present.

Several commentators have noted that Foucault seeks to break with the 'presentism' of historical studies. In one account (Dreyfus and Rabinow 1983: 118), he thematises a problem common to all historians. Here, presentism is the unwitting projection of a structure of interpretation that arises from the historian's own experience or context onto aspects of the past under study. For example, the notion and practice of *police* as a condition achieved within a well-governed polity in seventeenth and eighteenth century continental Europe cannot be understood through a twentieth century understanding of police as a force of officers charged with the maintenance of law and order. Nor can eighteenth century 'political oeconomy' be understood in terms of a twentieth century concern with the laws of economic science. A 'history of the present' must avoid the 'writing of the past in terms of the present' (Foucault 1977a: 31).

In another account, that of Habermas (1987a: 249–51, 276–8), Foucault seeks to break with the presentism that is 'modernity's consciousness of time' only for it to return with a vengeance that will sabotage his genealogical project. Here, he undertakes something rather more than a methodological move. He rejects modernity's privileging of the present and its future-orientation and consequent narcissistic relation to the past. Presentism is thus diagnosed as a historiography which cannot break free of the vicious circle of its own forms of consciousness and can only function to provide assurance of contemporary forms of identity. However, this criticism holds, because genealogy is the relativist unmasking of the truth-claims of all knowledge, it is forced to instrumentalise the past in terms of the needs of the present (ibid. 278). It thus becomes a species of the presentism it seeks to avoid.

The first account of Foucault's criticism of presentism may be a little abridged in that it appears to reduce it to a purely methodological problem. This second account is quite mistaken and overblown in relation to what it can sustain with regard to Foucault's writings. The problem of presentism is undoubtedly a methodological danger. As such, it preoccupies 'archaeology' as a mode of analysis and description of discourse that seeks to avoid the presentist foibles of the history of ideas. More importantly, it is an ethical and political question concerning the various uses to which history is put. We have shown that Foucault sought to raise these problems in his engagement with the uses of history isolated by Nietzsche. If, then, we are to understand how a self-styled history of the present can avoid presentism, we must turn to the relation of archaeology and genealogy.

As for the second critique of Foucault's historiography as presentist, three points can be made. First, a rejection of historians' presentist narcissism does not entail a forsaking of a relation between historical knowledge and the future. Such an assertion would imply that the only 'responsible' relation to the future is one that affirms the present as an instant of the progressive movement of enlightenment and seeks to discern the utopian element within that movement. Indeed, historical thought can be responsible to the future by issuing warnings concerning the dangers inherent within certain modes of thought and institutional practice, including ones which present themselves as progressive, utopian, or even, simply, modern. Secondly, the characterisation of genealogy as an unmasking of truth claims is highly dubious, as I argue throughout this work and particularly in Chapter 7. Finally, to suggest that the attack on presentism is a break with 'modernity's time-consciousness' is itself the form of narcissism of a mode of reading that invokes a grid of inter-pretation preoccupied with discovering and attributing stances in relation to modernity in order to ascribe implicit political and normative positions.

If Foucault is first making a methodological critique of presentism, then what is its basis? An indication of this can be had from the distinction he draws between different types of the history of the sciences in *The Archaeology of Knowledge* (1972). Foucault has often been loosely grouped with the French school of thought concerned with the history of the sciences (e.g. Gutting 1989: 9–54; Descombes 1980: 110–117). Indeed, as he noted (Foucault 1980d: 52) in his essay on the thinker of this school with whom he has the closest filiation, Georges Canguilhem, there had been in France since World War II a line of division between two varieties of philosophical reflection, one grounded on experience, meaning, and the subject, the other on knowledge, rationality, and the concept. The first broadly encompasses the phenomenological tradition of Merleau-Ponty and Sartre, while the second the tradition of conceptual philosophy and the history of the sciences, and figures such as Jean Cavailles, Alexandre Koyré, Bachelard and Canguilhem. The archaeological methodology Foucault developed and employed throughout the 1960s can be understood within this latter horizon of the history of science and knowledge, of rationality and concepts. However, unlike the writings of other thinkers of this genre, archaeology sought to define a method capable of dealing with forms of knowledge which were both of increasing prestige but of a relatively low level of formalisation, the human sciences. Viewed as a methodology designed with this field of study in mind, archaeology is a form of history that suspends the norms of particular disciplines or established sciences as the filter through which to treat particular bodies of knowledge. Such a method is germane to the human sciences not only because of their lower epistemological status but also because of their immersion in other non-scientific, political, and ethical discourses, and the close relation between their contents and a whole range of institutional practices and the wider social and political field in which they are located.

In the chapter of *Archaeology* called 'Science and knowledge' Foucault distinguishes several different thresholds across which 'discursive practices' move, and the type of study that can be located at each of these thresholds. They are: a threshold of *positivity*, when a single system of forming statements can be discerned; a threshold of *epistemologisation*, when a dominant way of validating and verifying statements is achieved; a threshold of *scientificity*, when this dominant function fulfils formal criteria for the construction of propositions; and a threshold of *formalisation*, when that discourse is able to define its own axiomatic structure (Foucault 1972: 186–7). Corresponding to a science that has achieved formalisation, Foucault argues, there can be a *recurrential* form of historical analysis. This is a history, such as one that mathematics might recount about itself, of a highly formalised science from the viewpoint of the current epistemological structures of that science. Bachelard, for example, spoke of a recurrential history that takes the certainties of the present and writes the past as the progressive formation of the truth (Gutting 1989: 19).

Foucault then distinguishes an epistemological history of the sciences for which Bachelard and Canguilhem have provided models. Here, located at the threshold of scientificity, history is concerned with how a discourse was constituted as a science, the obstacles overcome, the breaks made, and the acts performed. It is thus written from the norms of present-day science but is not a completely internalist history. This is because such a history must distinguish between the relationship of scientific knowledge to its outside. It may be noted in these passages that for Foucault (as for the history of the sciences) it is quite legitimate to engage in a recurrential or epistemological history, to distinguish between what lies forever at the margins of science and what is valid in terms of the internal norms of the presently constituted sciences. In this sense, this tradition may be described as *positivist*, in so far as it does not bring philosophically conceived standards of truth and meaning to bear on scientific knowledge. It accepts a subordinate role, if one likes, for philosophy, in terms of the clarification and internal development of the concepts at work in any particular science or domain of knowledge.

If, however, Foucault places himself within this positivist domain, it is to discover a level of analysis which is indifferent to the norms and validity claims of science. This is evident in his discussion of the third type of historical analysis, that of his own archaeological history. This is a type of history situated at the threshold of epistemologisation, the point at which a discursive practice becomes unified into a single system. Here, 'scientificity does not serve as the norm' because one is concerned with 'discursive practices in so far as they give rise to a corpus of knowledge, in so far as they assume the status and role of a science' (Foucault 1972: 190). Archaeology takes the viewpoint of the regularity and organisation of a 'discursive formation', a regular system of the dispersion of statements, and on this basis it is able to chart the movement of a particular discursive formation across the various thresholds of epistemologisation and scientificity. Archaeology is not simply concerned with the criteria by which a discourse may assume the status of a science but with the rules which govern the production of statements in particular discursive formations, irrespective of whether or not they have crossed the threshold of scientificity. At this level, then, it may be possible for a discursive formation to give rise to practical, political, aesthetic, or ethical knowledge and not to undergo the same processes of epistemologisation that occur in other bodies of knowledge. Archaeology can thus address the human sciences not only on the basis of their systematisation but also in relation to adjacent fields of other systematic (scientific and non-scientific) forms of discourse. Its focus is not on particular disciplines, corpora, or branches of knowledge (*connaissance*) but the various conditions of formations which govern the emergence of objects, concepts, theories, and forms of subjectivity within knowledge (*savoir*) (Foucault 1972: 15n).

Archaeology does not provide a privileged access to the 'archaic', the discovery of the lost foundations of a culture or civilisation. It does not find a secret passageway by which we can gain access to the past as we nullify our involvements in the present. There is no complicity here with antiquarian, romantic or conservative conceptions of history. Rather what is discovered is another point at which the regularities of discourse can be described and analysed, one which refuses to take the standards of validity of established knowledge as the filter or framework for the organisation of history. The point of attack is one of the regularity of statements within discursive formations, when the totality of actual statements within a given discourse are subject to a system of formation which delimits the statements that can be

made, the relations they have with one another, their modes of transformation, and so on. Archaeology attacks presentism not by asserting an
impossible escape from its own presentness but by defining a level of analysis
that protects it from the claims of present-day sciences and disciplines and the
truths they have established.

It is also important to note that archaeology does not address the everyday
language and patterns of implicit and explicit communication and knowledge
arising in what German philosophy has called the *Lebenswelt* (life-world).
Nor is it primarily concerned with the abstract, highly formalised languages
of, say, mathematics or physics. Rather, it is defined in relation to the
constitutive rules of any systematised body of knowledge and discourse.
Archaeology concerns *veridical* discourses, to use Canguilheim's term (Foucault 1980d: 56), those discourses charged with the task of self-rectification
and self-elaboration with the aim of finally reaching the truth. Archaeology is
thus not a form of conversation analysis, an analysis of everyday encounters,
nor even an analysis of the encounters between various specialists and their
clients. Rather it is an approach to all those discourses that seek to rationalise
or systematise themselves in relation to particular ways of 'saying the true'. Its
principal focus would be a broad middle range (between spontaneous speech
and abstract scientific theory) occupied by the human sciences, medicine,
psychiatry and other 'psy' discourses, social work and counselling, sexology
and sex therapy, political discourses and ideologies, systems of ethics,
programmes of government and so. Archaeology can deal with scientific
knowledge in so far as it is situated within the broader terrain of discourses
and is subject to particular rules of its formation. It is able to address everyday
conversation in so far as the discursive formations it reveals are a condition of
informal communications.

Archaeology is not a magical device to help us reconstruct the past despite
present involvements. It can, however, help us in the organisation of definite
veridical discourses given to us within particular temporal–spatial co-
ordinates. It does this not by the impossible rejection of our place in the
present but by a suspension of the norms of already constituted sciences or the
claims of other forms of veridical discourse, e.g. various forms of normative
theory and philosophy. Foucault rejects presentism not to discover a deeper
truth hidden within the past but to break with the presentist imaginary various
veridical discourses seek to uphold as true, given, natural, foundational, and so
on. If one can detect a criticism of presentism in Foucault's archaeology it is to
guard against those procedures that would undermine attempts to make
intelligible the human sciences and other systematic discourses.

From the early 1970s Foucault places his studies under the new heading of
genealogy. However, in his inaugural address to the *Collège de France* (1981a)
this term describes a domain not fundamentally different from his earlier
studies. However, he does speak of a 'critical' section of the analysis that
alternates, supports, and complements the genealogical description of the

formation of positivities, the domains of objects of discourse (ibid. 70–3). The critical section addresses the external and internal constraints, and institutional systems that envelop discourse and subject it to forms of exclusion, rarefraction, and appropriation. Foucault speaks here of a 'morphology of our will to know' (ibid. 71). Indeed, he argues that all earlier forms of exclusion – such as prohibition and taboo, or the division and rejection he studied in relation to madness – have tended to drift toward a 'will to truth', the historically modifiable, institutionalised ways of creating oppositions between true and false statements that exert a power over the field of discourses and practices (ibid. 54–6). It is here critical description has a style of learned detachment (*la désinvolture studieuse*), while the genealogical mood is one of a fortunate positivism (*un positivisme heureux*). Where archaeology had earlier addressed the rules of formation of discourses, the new critical and genealogical description addresses both the rarity of statements and the power of affirmation. Genealogy will uncover a positive and productive form of power underlying every movement of institutional or discursive delimitation of statements. If Foucault remains a 'fortunate positivist' it is because he treats the formation of the objects of discourse as a distinct and knowable component of reality, while, at the same time, regarding these objects as ones shaped, fashioned and applied within social, political, and institutional spaces.

Genealogy emerges as a 'history of the present' because it is able to undertake an analysis of those objects given as necessary components of our reality. It isolates a form of analysis which suspends contemporary norms of validity and meaning at the same time as it reveals their multiple conditions of formation. In a 1976 lecture, Foucault defined genealogy (1980i: 81–3) as a union of two different forms of 'subjugated knowledge': the erudite knowledge and its historical contents present but masked within the smooth functionalism of global theory and its history; and the popular knowledges and local memories regarded as unqualified or actively disqualified within the hierarchies of scientificity. Such a union is thought in presentist terms: it 'allows us to establish a historical knowledge of struggles and to make use of this knowledge today'. But genealogy can only do this on the basis of archaeology. This historical knowledge of struggles, and the entertaining of the local, discontinuous, illegitimate forms of knowledge disqualified in the course of such struggles, can only be analysed because archaeology provides the point of attack on discourse we defined above. 'If we were to characterise it in two terms,' Foucault clarifies (ibid. 85), '"archaeology" would be the appropriate methodology of this analysis of local discursivities, and "genealogy" would be the tactics whereby, on the basis of the descriptions of these local discursivities, the subjected knowledges which were thus released would be brought into play'.

The roles of genealogy and archaeology appear complementary, the latter performing analyses that are a necessary condition of the former. If, from the perspective of the production of a knowledge of discursive formations, archaeology remains the indispensable methodology, from the practical, polemical and strategic perspective of the use of historical analysis, genealogy holds the key. However, beyond the language of complementarity, genealogy is clearly dominant. It connects the empirical analyses revealed to concerns activated in light of particular contemporary struggles.

It would seem, then, that the two methodologies and perspectives are more than contingent components of an intellectual biography. They are necessary components of the one evolving framework. Despite Foucault's aside in 1983 that he did not use the term archaeology any longer (1983b: 203), the distinction between it and genealogy is again activated even as his project metamorphoses in the introduction to *The Use of Pleasure* (1985). Foucault proposes a genealogy of the 'desiring subject' from classical antiquity to early Christianity (1985: 5, 12). Archaeology is concerned with the 'problematisations', by which human beings question what they are, do, and the world around them; genealogy with the changing conditions of formation of such problematisations in particular 'practices of the self'. Again archaeology is the systematic and analytical description of particular discourses, while genealogy not only introduces a serial component, but places such analysis in relation to the contemporary concerns of the self, its true nature, and the revelatory power of sexuality.

In a body of work so liable to internal reshaping and change, it is quite remarkable the fundamental relation of archaeology to genealogy remained relatively constant throughout this period. One could describe Foucault's historical studies in terms of his own recurrently constructed discontinuities and continuities. Thus, in this introduction, we find not only a reminder of methodological perspective but a recasting of the entire project in terms of successive theoretical shifts (Foucault 1985: 6). The first entails the analysis of discursive practices of the human sciences, the second, the analysis of the relations, strategies and techniques of the exercise of powers, and the third, the forms and modalities of the relation of the individual to the self. What is continuous is the concern for the historicity of truth. Here Foucault talks of his interest in the 'games of truth' involved in each of these three broad domains. This is a new term, no doubt, but one consistent with the earlier variations on the theme of discourses rationalised according to criteria and procedures for stating true propositions, such as the 'will to truth' (especially 1981a), or 'regimes of truth' (1980h). For this introduction the basic continuity is thought as a concern for the history of truth as a history of the 'games of truth and error through which being is historically constituted as experiences; that is, as something that can and must be thought' (Foucault 1985: 6–7). But even here there is a disjunction with an almost contemporary programmatic text in which Foucault describes the 'general theme of my research' as the ways in which 'human beings are constituted as subjects' (1982: 208–9). In fact, there is more continuity in his reworkings of historical approach than in his formulation of his general themes and objects. While the former is our immediate concern here, let us note that, although Foucault came to admit three phases of his work, one can discern varying degrees of concern for and balances between issues of power and government, truth and rationality, and subjectivity and ethical practice.

Archaeology is a highly developed version of the history of the sciences. It is a form of the systematic description of the organisation of statements into discursive formations. While it does not claim privileged access to the past, it remains a sophisticated approach to the uses of historical documentation that finds a level of the analytical description of statements in their rules of formation. The archaeological level of analysis avoids the retrospectivist accounts which take established sciences, their internal norms, and validity criteria, as the organising principles of the history of thought. Archaeology does not thereby claim to offer a reconstruction of the past but only to suspend the operations of the history of discourse as the progressive realisation of an already-given truth in order to define the rules governing what counts as truth within any particular discursive order.

The major problem of archaeology, and the fundamental reason for the shift toward genealogy, is not, I would suggest, the need to supplement the former's relatively 'internalist' account of the history of truth with one of the non-discursive contexts of discursive formation. In a practical sense, Foucault had already opened the issue of the relation between discursive and non-discursive practices both in his empirical studies of medicine and psychiatry and in several of his methodological statements. The problem Foucault's work addresses at the beginning of the 1970s is that he had undertaken analyses already implicitly deploying certain criteria of relevance of historical study. For example, the history of madness could not be understood without the development of oppositional discourses and struggles in and around the institutionalisation of those considered to be insane. Yet these criteria of relevance were not spelt out. One might do so, then, by introducing the history of the present as the third term which overrides and combines both genealogy and archaeology. A history of the present is concerned with that which is taken-for-granted, assumed to be given, or natural within contemporary social existence, a givenness or naturalness questioned in the course of contemporary struggles. This is certainly the case for madness, incarceration and imprisonment, sexuality, the hegemony of medicine, and so on. This does not mean these 'liberation struggles' give rise to genealogy or that it is conducted on behalf of those affected by some system of domination. It means simply that genealogy is conducted in the presence of certain issues problematised by contemporary social struggles. Beyond this, one can say that genealogy is a way of linking historical contents into organised and ordered trajectories that are neither the simple unfolding of their origins nor the necessary realisation of their ends. It is a way of analysing multiple, open-ended, heterogeneous trajectories of discourses, practices, and events, and of establishing their patterned relationships, without recourse to regimes of truth that claim pseudo-naturalistic laws or global necessities. As we shall see, the history of the present is, above all, a new form of criticism, able to induce critical effects and new insights without grounding itself in a system of values exterior to the domain and object under analysis. Rather than this being Foucault's Achilles' heel, as Nancy Fraser claims, it is this which constitutes the radical power of this form of critical and effective discourse.

Elias and Braudel, like Foucault, both thematise the problem of the present as a component in constructing criteria of relevance for historical–sociological study. Elias, like Foucault, argues that critical historical study must take into account our involvements and our capacity for detachment. However, whereas Elias thinks of involvement as a condition of social scientific knowledge from which we need to detach ourselves, Foucault presents methods allowing us to work with both involvement and detachment. The notion of a history of the present seeks to use our involvements and those of our contemporaries to problematise dimensions and regions of social existence and personal experience. It directs attention to potential positivities for analysis. Genealogy, while rooted in involvement, guards against presentist effects by locating those positivities as the historically contingent outcome of trajectories of ensembles of discursive and non-discursive practices. Archaeology is a method of detachment, suspending or bracketing the norms and criteria of validity of established sciences and disciplines in favour of the internal intelligibility of the ensembles so located, their conditions of emergence, existence, and transformation. A history of the present is thus doubly fortunate: it can maintain the connectedness of critical histories to engagements and experiences within the limits of our present while possessing methods for the positive analysis of historical ensembles and trajectories.

Braudel is, in many ways, closer to Foucault, operating a parallel displacement within social history to Foucault's displacement of the history of knowledge. Again, however, interesting contrasts can be made. The only way in which Braudel can conceive of criteria of relevance is to understand the present as a moment within the duration of historical time and movement of civilisation. The present is one moment that is traversed by the flow of multiple temporalities and the descent of the multiple processes which are traced by serial histories. Whereas Foucault uses these serial histories to suggest how trajectories of genealogical descent can be constructed which are multiple and dispersed, Braudel returns us to a total history in order to conceive how a science of the past may be a science of the present. For Braudel, historical study establishes a pertinence to the present because social reality is the fundamental reality. Foucault uses the present to construct serial histories and so establishes a pertinence no longer reliant on the underlying unity of time and social reality. In the next chapter, we follow this notion of a history of the present as Foucault sketches it in his writings and lectures on Kant and enlightenment.

EXCURSUS: FOUCAULT AND *ANNALES*

It is difficult to specify the somewhat complex and shifting relations of Foucault and the 'school' of history associated with the journal widely-known as *Annales*. This is due to three reasons. First, it is hard to distinguish references between one party and the other that are instances of collegial cordiality from those with more serious intellectual intent. Second, the *Annales* school has almost become synonymous with historical study in France and, in this sense, is sometimes held to extend to encompass eminent Marxist historians such as Ernest Labrousse and Pierre Vilar, Foucault himself, and figures like the historical sociologist of antiquity, Paul Veyne (cf. Burke 1990: 1). Although Foucault (like Veyne) clearly lies outside the boundaries of the school, this increasingly vague membership does create difficulties for establishing his relation to it. Third, even if we allow the employment of the terms of intellectual history, such as 'influence', it would be difficult to tease out influence one way or the other when both parties are very much a part of the same broad intellectual and discursive terrain.

The best way of approaching the problem may be to follow some of the explicit references of each to the other. If we do, the impression on the side of *Annales* is a sense of appreciation of Foucault's achievement, perhaps a mistaken identification of earlier works with a history of mentalities *à la* Lucien Febvre, a growing reflection on his methodological writings, and an increasing incorporation of Foucault's themes around the body, power, and micropolitics during the 1970s. In a prominent 'third generation' member of the school writing in the mid-1980s, Roger Chartier (1988: 53–70), we find a profound reflection on the relations between philosophy and history. Here, Foucault's methodological writings and engagement with the practice of earlier generations of historians are taken as something of a guide. On Foucault's side, the *Annales* figures most prominently in his deliberations on method in the late 1960s, and there we find a tremendous sense of the intellectual vocation of historians that goes far beyond that normally found in the work of philosophers. Let us start with Foucault's references for they are somewhat more easily dealt with.

The introduction to *the Archaeology of Knowledge* (1972: 3–11) is the *locus classicus* of Foucault's specification of his relation to *Annales*. One must say that this text is immensely complimentary to the achievements of *Annales*, to the point where Foucault even adopts its language, writing of 'general history', 'total history', and 'serial history'. Indeed, Foucault seems to do the impossible here, to reconcile the notion of the *longue durée* with his own apparent emphasis (which is also that of the history of the sciences) on discontinuous history. He claims both types of history are effects of the same epistemological mutation in historical thought, one that brings a new continuity to the history of material civilisation while it discovers new forms of discontinuity in the history of thought.

These apparently divergent movements are resolved, in an interesting way, through the notion of a 'serial history', a concept Braudel (1980: 91–104) had taken up in the early 1960s following the work of Pierre Chaunu. It is not too much to claim that to understand the language of Foucault's introduction, it is necessary to understand Braudel's own language and its evolution. In his 1950 inaugural *leçon*, Braudel had rejected a 'general history' as merely the combination of many narrative histories, the crossing of the 'exceptional destinies' of great beings (ibid. 11). Instead he spoke in favour of a 'total history of man in all its aspects' as being on the agenda of a history open to social reality and the findings of the human sciences (ibid. 21). He later substitutes 'global history' for this term (ibid. 93) and commends Chaunu's 'serial history' (ibid. 91–104).

There are no doubt some important shifts of position associated with these moves. If *l'histoire totale* placed Braudel near Marcel Mauss' description of his discipline as concerned with the 'total social fact' and Marxist concerns for totality, *l'histoire globale* may express some disquiet about this project. One commentator suggests that total history was too 'totalitarian' in its tendency to remove people from a scene dominated by the history of the *longue durée* (Stoianovich 1975: 115). Whatever disquiet he felt, however, Braudel continued to use the term total history in the conclusion to the second edition of his *Mediterranean* (1972/3, 2: 1238–44). There he wrote of a 'total history' but distinguished the 'historian's structuralism' from that of the human sciences: 'It does not tend towards the mathematical abstraction of relations expressed as functions, but instead towards the very sources of life in its most concrete, everyday, indestructible and anonymously human expression' (ibid.1244). Later, however, he will implicitly oppose global and total history. Thus, in 1978, Braudel said: 'Globality is not the claim to write a complete history of the world [*histoire totale du monde*] . . . it is simply the desire, when one confronts a problem, to go systematically beyond its limits' (quoted in Burke 1990: 113). In any case, these two terms are roughly equivalent in several ways: they discard the event as a discrete and tangible historical atom for a notion of historical facts as a construct of the historian; they indicate the need for a notion of structure, which would none the less remain somewhat vague and undefined; and, finally, they suggest the undertaking of the three-level history that Braudel envisaged.

If, however, instead of regarding the event as a discrete atom, we placed it in a series of similar, homogeneous events, so that we followed its repetition over a long succession, what type of history would we have? This is precisely the question Chaunu's serial history poses for Braudel (1980: 91). A series is a 'coherent succession', or at least one rendered so, one that both thinkers conceived in terms of mathematical series. It could deal with data on economic and agricultural phenomena (price fluctuations, harvest times and yields), biosocial ones (deaths, births, longevity, etc.), even the occurrence and observance of religious rituals and festivals (e.g. First Communion dates).

Such series could be 'a function of historical time whose progress has to be patiently established and then its meaning deduced'. For Braudel, it is clear that these series would confirm the perspective of the *longue durée*. For others, however, it may be that serial history would undermine the *longue durée* to the extent that the longer the series are extended the less likely they are to be homogeneous (Stoianovich 1975: 198).

Turning to Foucault's use of these terms, we find he rejects a 'total history' as seeking to reconstitute the overall form of a civilisation or reduce a society to the emanations of a single principle. He advocates, instead, a 'general history', the latter defined in terms of the establishment of relations between series. The problem of this general history is to constitute series, define the elements of each, set its limits, formulate its laws and, finally, to establish the relation between series, the 'series of series' or tables it is possible to construct (Foucault 1972: 7–10). Foucault concludes: 'A total description draws all phenomena around a single centre – a principle, a meaning, a spirit, a world-view, and overall shape; a general history, on the contrary, would deploy the space of a dispersion' (ibid. 10).

A striking passage on history in Foucault's inaugural address in 1970 (1981a: 68) – at which Braudel was present (Eribon 1991: 213) – takes up the theme of the relation between *l'histoire événementielle* and the *longue durée*, the event and the long duration. He argues here that there is no inverse ratio between the two, it is by 'pushing to its extreme the fine grain of the event' that historians arrive at the outline of 'massive phenomena'. This history does not deny the event but defines its series, specifies the mode of analysis that reveals the series, discovers regularities and limits of probability, and maps variations. What is problematic is not the focus on the event but understanding events 'by the action of causes and effects in the formless unity of a great becoming' (ibid.68). It is in relation to such themes of the philosophers that Foucault sought to replace notions of 'consciousness and continuity' with 'the event and the series' and concepts of regularity, discontinuity, dependence, transformation.

Foucault evidently upsets earlier *Annales* conceptions of a shift from a general history to a total history. His target is probably less Braudel's somewhat ambiguous relation to total history than a Marxist philosophy of history and, beyond that, any mode of explanation that partakes the totalising and teleological structure of the Hegelian philosophy of history. Nevertheless, if Foucault is playing with Braudelian categories, it is in an affectionate manner and with the *Annales* tools of series, functions, limits, and so on. Foucault here seems to be pondering the possibility of a history that generalises the careful specification of historical succession found in serial history, and even considering his own work on discourses and discursive transformation to be of a piece with this method. Foucault addresses the *Annales* school at the least interpretive, most 'positivist' – a better term perhaps than 'structuralist' – phase of his work and celebrates in it the sophisticated techniques of positive historical knowledge.

This playful manipulation of *Annales* categories, none the less, should not be construed as simply an embrace of their technical success. There is serious philosophic intent here which becomes clear in interviews around this time and in the inaugural lecture. In Foucault's hands (e.g. 1989a: 12–13, 41, 47–9, 59–60) the *Annales* school instances the gap between the history of the historians and history of the philosophers. The latter is the last refuge of dialectical thought, particularly of the dialectic between individual subject and the social totality suggested from the young Marx to the old Sartre. In the philosophy of history, historians find little that resembles their problems, practices, and methods. By contrast, an examination of the new ways in which historians pose fundamental problems of periodicity, of continuity and discontinuity, of series and function, and of the relation between history and the human sciences, reveals a new kind of history no longer ensnared in this dialectical philosophy. At the time, Sartre and others had reproached Foucault and those they designated structuralists as having contempt for history. Foucault is able to respond by pointing to the work of Bloch, Febvre, Braudel and *Annales* as long before having put an end to the myth of History in this dialectical philosophy of history. Foucault finds in *Annales* a practice of history which raises important philosophic problems. If indeed Foucault remains a philosopher throughout his career it is this respect for, and willingness to participate in, the practices of the historian that most sets Foucault apart from the dialectical philosophies of history of the twentieth century, not only from those of Sartre but also Lukacs and the Frankfurt School. The lesson of this engagement with the *Annales* school and other historians is that while Foucault may be a 'philosophic historian', using effective historical methods for philosophical ends such as the critical analysis of forms of rationality, he is definitely not a philosopher of history, for whom history is of interest to the extent that philosophy confers a meaning on it. As Foucault puts it, his analysis is 'articulated, not on the traditional thematics which the philosophers of history still take for "living" history, but on the effective work of historians' (1981a: 68).

On the side of *Annales*, the relationship is more complex and I cannot pretend to document its complexity. No doubt Braudel's characterisation of Foucault as 'the most brilliant and likeable' of the philosophers who 'speak out on history with the greatest vehemence' (1975: 16–17) should not be taken lightly. Braudel's personal and intellectual admiration is well documented as, too, is the role of Philipe Ariès in the publication of Foucault's history of madness (Eribon 1991). Braudel's 'note' appended to the *Annales* review of *Folie et déraison* (the first edition of Foucault's history of madness[1]) is fascinating for it seems to contradict the view that this book was received by *Annales* scholars as a 'psychological history' (Major-Poetzl 1983: 217). Indeed, Braudel rejects the view that it 'is merely one of those studies of collective psychology so rarely attempted by historians' (Eribon 1991: 118).

This magnificent book tries to pursue – apropos a specific phenomenon: madness – what the mysterious progression of a civilisation's mental structures may be; how it has to free itself from and give up on a part of itself, separating out those things it means to keep of what its own past offered and those things it hopes to repress, ignore, and forget.

(Braudel, quoted in Eribon 1991: 119)

This is clearly an appreciative reading, and Braudel continues by noting the synthesis of the human sciences required to undertake such a method, a synthesis he expected of history itself. Braudel reads the book in terms of mental *structures*, i.e. components of historical reality irreducible to collective mind and perhaps with the same importance as material structures. What he may fail to grasp is that this is an account of the conditions of emergence of a human science, psychiatry, and as such is as much concerned with institutional practice and the history of concepts as 'mental' structure. In other words, the location of this archaeology within the history of the sciences may not have been altogether clear to Braudel. This may be the reason why one commentator (Major-Poetzl 1983: 217) has suggested that later works of Foucault's archaeological period either left historians baffled, were regarded as metaphysical, or were ignored. However, this is certainly not the case for at least one prominent third generation *Annales* scholar, Roger Chartier, whose essay on the relation of philosophy and history (1988: 53–70) is, in major part, an extended meditation on Foucault's statements of archaeology and genealogy.

By the 1970s, Foucault and the newer members of *Annales* were travelling over very similar terrain, and the ground broken by Foucault was being incorporated into historical study generally. There is evidence that Foucault's methodological statements of the late 1960s and early 1970s did play a central role in shaping debate on inclusion and exclusion within discourse and history, and on the way in which an exploration of the 'other', of that which is marginalised, can bring into focus the limits of a culture and social organisation (Stoianovich 1975: 205–11; Major-Poetzl 1983: 15–18, 217–18). *Discipline and Punish* appears to have had a major impact on *Annales*, which began to incorporate themes of the history of the body and its relation to a history of power (Burke 1990: 84, 88). Such historians as Le Roy Ladurie (e.g. 1978) and Roger Chartier have displayed evident debts to Foucault's themes of micropolitics and his methodology in forming a 'cultural history of society'. There are also some signs that a re-thinking of the problem of events may be at work in *Annales* scholarship in this period, at least tempering the earlier generation's complete rejection of *l'histoire événementielle* (Burke 1990: 89–93). At this time, Foucault was describing his method as one of 'eventalisation', a construction of events in order to breach self-evident continuity and teleological schemas (Foucault 1981b: 6–7). To establish any firm relationship between these theoretical moves would require much more investigation than I am able to provide here. What is well established is that the project for a new history in the 1970s and 1980s (*une autre histoire*) was one which drew upon Foucault's themes and methods as models.

This is perhaps what one can say without equivocation: that there is much admiration and a good deal of borrowing on both sides. For Foucault the *Annales* scholars are exemplary historians whose practice, and reflection on that practice, opens up the positive field of historical knowledge that had been conventionally foreclosed by philosophers' dialectical and synthetic views of History. For *Annales*, Foucault's writings brought new themes and styles to historical writing that were compatible with and extended their own practice. He certainly affected the way in which the third generation of *annalistes* conceived their 'new history', and the themes and problems it could approach. It also seems likely that his rejection of 'total history' and his call for a renewed attention to the event left a deep methodological mark on this school. Above all, perhaps, it was Foucault who changed the French historians' relation to intellectual history, not only introducing a new rigor to its analysis, but also changing irrevocably what would constitute the real.

Chapter 3

Questions of enlightenment

I shall not make my head into a parchment and scribble old, half-effaced information from archives onto it.

I. Kant[1]

One might wish to regard the Enlightenment less as an event, period, or movement, than as the mentality given clearest form in the synthetic philosophies of history of the eighteenth century. Undoubtedly the pinnacle of this type of philosophical history is Condorcet's *Sketch for a Historical Picture of the Progress of the Human Mind* of 1794 (1955), but its principles – with certain reservations and modifications – are also found in the great systematic and stage-developmental theories of the eighteenth and nineteenth centuries, such as those of Adam Smith and Comte. The Enlightenment philosophy of history of the eighteenth century was not simply a form of the 'progress thinking' that had been in existence since the Renaissance, but a version of history in which the present is determined by the movement of linear time towards an open, and indefinitely perfectible, future. Thus, although history has no final state so that it is not teleologically limited in advance, this philosophy of history is a teleology that infers a direction and purpose in each moment of the historical sequence (Falk 1988: 377–82).[2]

The version of progress of this Enlightenment philosophy of history finds its model in the progress of the sciences. Indeed, science is both exemplar and motor of enlightenment. As the former, it is the product of the unimpeded operation of the human mind conquering the obstacles to knowledge present in nature. As the latter, it has the public responsibility for generalising enlightenment and overcoming prejudice. The progress of the mind entails a double consequence: by means of the natural sciences, the increasing mastery of the natural world; with the development of human sciences, the tendency toward perfection of political and social institutions correlative of the tendency to moral perfection of human beings (cf. Habermas 1984: 145–51). The philosophy of the Enlightenment entails the emergence of the moral and political sciences, including something we would today recognise by the name of sociology.

This philosophy of history certainly bears some basic affinities with older Christian eschatology, and acts as a legitimation myth for a type of civilisation that it helps to constitute, that of Western modernity. It is, in this sense, Lyotard's '*grand récit*', but with two qualifications Falk points out (1988: 381): first, the philosophy of history is extremely ambivalent about the role of humankind in history and, secondly, the end is not necessarily a perfect state. Human beings are makers of a history in which they are made. They make history on the basis of given conditions, to paraphrase Marx, but in the course of history the capacities and attributes of human beings are subsumed under the autonomous processes of the development of reason and science, technology, politics, the economy, and so on. In the twentieth century this ambivalence will become the basis on which philosophies of history sketch the existential dilemmas of 'modern Western' humans.

Secondly, even at the end of the eighteenth century, there was no guarantee against the discovery of a principle which would subvert the direction of this teleological movement. Condorcet may have envisioned a society without crime, misery, and sickness, so 'that the day will come when death will be due only to extraordinary accidents' (1955: 200).[3] However, he also posited the far-distant time in which population would grow beyond what it was able to extract as its subsistence from the earth. This would send humankind into an oscillation between progress and regress, good and evil, thus opening the way for Malthus' celebrated principle of population, so central to the history of poverty and poor policy. One might be led to say that no sooner had the internal teleology of the Enlightenment been discovered, than a *dialectic* of enlightenment would be initiated, a movement in which shadows of darkness would dance in the light of reason, in which perfection could be realised and then dashed, in which wealth brought poverty, and reason domination.

Kant's writings on history and the meaning of enlightenment must be understood as a contribution to this type of philosophy of history. Of great importance in themselves, these writings seek to apply the major themes of his philosophical work to a set of ideas which were current in the synthetic philosophies of history of the eighteenth century. They are a source of reflection on the purpose and meaning of history, the existence of progress within history, the role of critical reason and the uses to which it is put, and the relationship of the critical thinker to the present. It might be said, using the language of twentieth century social theory, that these writings focus political reflection upon the nature of rationality and its relation to modernity and the modernisation of societies. They are of continuing pertinence to current debates concerning the legacy of the Enlightenment and the forms of reason associated with modernity.

If, however, Kant's writings on history have a particular poignancy some two centuries later, it is no doubt in part due to the increasing attention paid to them by Michel Foucault in the last decade of his life (e.g. 1980d, 1986b, 1986i). In these texts, Foucault uses Kant's essay, 'What is Enlightenment?', to elucidate his own critical project in terms of what he calls an 'ontology of the present' (1986b: 96) inaugurated by Kant's essay, and found in the work of critical theory from Hegel to the Frankfurt School, including Max Weber and Nietzsche. An examination of Foucault's position on Kant and enlightenment now must also take into account the response by Habermas who suggests that such a position is profoundly self-contradictory, both in his memorial for Foucault, and later in his lectures on the philosophical discourse of modernity (Habermas 1989, 1987a).[4] I want here to examine Kant's philosophy of history itself, the position adopted by Foucault in relation to it, and Habermas' commentary on this encounter. In conclusion, I shall draw out the implications for what l shall call the 'critical history of rationality' (Foucault 1983b).[5]

KANT: ENLIGHTENMENT AS THE NECESSITY OF LIMITS

It is perhaps true that one can imagine nothing further from Foucault's genealogies of power–knowledge than Kant's writings on universal history, a political constitution of freedom, world citizenship, perpetual peace, and revolutionary enthusiasm as a sign of progress. Indeed, the type of philosophical history envisaged by Kant in his essay, 'Idea for a Universal History from a Cosmopolitan Point of View', first published in December 1784 in the *Berlinische Monatsschrift*, a principal organ of the German Enlightenment, could be made to stand as the antithesis to Foucault's historical perspectives and analyses, at least at first glance.

This essay, published a month after the one on enlightenment in the same journal, proposes the task of a universal history to be undertaken by a 'philosophical historian'. Kant commences (1963: 11) by suggesting that, despite the complex and chaotic appearance of human actions when considered from the perspective of the individual free-will, attention to the freedom of will at large reveals the actions of humans to be determined by universal laws, evidenced by the fluctuations in marriage, birth, and death rates. Kant's philosophy of history therefore proposes the existence of necessity over human events as much as over natural events. The existence of this determination in history, however, does not thereby undermine or overcome individual free-will. Rather, it is the existence of an anthropological teleology inherent his conception of human beings as free, rational subjects, willing and attempting to realise their purposes in the world, that guarantees the teleology of history guided by these specific rational ends.

Kant's philosophy of history discovers this teleology within the course of human affairs that takes the following form (1963: 12–16). All natural capacities evolve toward their end. In humankind these capacities are those directed to the use of practical reason. The use of this reason defines what is specifically human, for by it is created all that goes beyond the merely animal. But the final purpose of world history is given by the status of human beings as subjects of reason. That purpose or end is the full realisation of this natural capacity to use reason found in humankind, i.e. the installation of the sovereignty of rational 'man' under a 'perfectly just civic constitution', legislating and obeying moral law.

However, why universal history should move toward such an end is not simply given by the practical capacity to use reason. Universal history tends to the provision of a universal civic society because it must operate through specific means. These means are the actions of free subjects seeking to realise their diverse ends. These means determine the form in which this practical reason will be fulfilled. If humans are conceived as centres of free-will, then the individual attempts to realise such will creates antagonisms between individuals. These antagonisms lead to what Kant calls the 'unsocial sociability' of human individuals that binds them into society with mutual opposition (Kant 1963: 16).

Here we are arriving at the most delicate and important element in Kant's philosophy of history. The notion of individual free-will presupposes the possibility of antagonisms between the individual wills seeking to realise their purposes. But as the pursuit of self-interest binds free individuals together in market exchanges according to Adam Smith, so too the actions of free subjects bind individuals together in civil society for Kant. For freedom is both the means and the obstacle to the realisation of a rational society. While such a society is achieved by subjects pursuing their own purposes, there must also be necessary restrictions on freedom. Thus the goal of history is the achievement of a society that sets *limits* on freedom most consistent with the freedom of others by establishing lawful relations between individuals both within the state and among the different states (Kant 1963: 16–19).

History – most definitely with a capital 'H' – traces the movement from a creature of nature endowed with reason and will, at first subject to the antagonisms of wills, to one who, through the free use of that reason, can come to lead a creative existence as a member of a universal civic culture, a being who can know and do what she or he ought to do. But this movement displays a profound ambivalence concerning freedom. For Kant's philosophy of history, freedom can only be realised on the condition that it accepts the necessity of its own limitation. If we are used to thinking about enlightenment as the free use of reason, Kant's philosophy of history reminds us that freedom, like reason, can only be exercised under strict conditions. No doubt enlightenment shares a kinship with freedom, but it also presupposes a certain form of domination.

Now, according to Kant (1963: 24), the task for the philosophical historian is this: to take the 'Idea' of the natural plan or purpose of history and its movement toward its final realisation in achieving a global civic union as a 'guiding thread for presenting as a system . . . what would otherwise be a planless conglomeration of human actions'. This task would be realised by following such a thread through Greek, Roman, and barbarian histories in Europe, and so on until the present day, together with other known national histories, so 'one will discover a regular progress in the constitution of states on our continent' that will have universal implications for all other nations. Kant makes plain he does not mean to displace empirical history with such a universal one, but only to bequeath to later generations an account of the various contributions and damage done to the goal of universal citizenship (Kant 1963: 25–6).

This essay gives us a broad sense of Kant's philosophy of history, with its notions of causality, its teleology, and its optimism concerning the prospects of humankind when it takes up the use of its critical and practical reason. The earlier essay in the same journal, however, takes the quite different form of a response to a question put to him by its readership, 'What is Enlightenment?' The answer is direct, if not entirely straightforward:

> Enlightenment is man's release from his self-incurred tutelage. Tutelage is man's inability to make use of his understanding without direction from another. Self-incurred is this tutelage when its cause lies not in the lack of reason but in lack of resolution and courage to use it without direction from another. *Sapere aude!* 'Have courage to use your own reason!' – that is the motto of enlightenment.

> (Kant 1963: 3)

The slogan *'sapere aude'*, 'dare to know', then, is the foundation of Kant's answer. Here, Kant's attitude towards limits appears contrary to the one we have already noted. Here enlightenment surpasses limits. It consists in the overcoming of those obstacles, such as laziness and cowardice, that lead one to allow a book to do one's understanding, a pastor to be one's conscience, and a physician to decide one's diet. (Kant, we might note here, reproduces the division of the three critiques by these examples.) Enlightenment is a type of maturity. Such maturity consists of throwing off the 'fetters of an ever-lasting tutelage' embodied in 'statutes and formulas' and taking an 'uncertain leap over the narrowest ditch' even when one is not used to such free motion (ibid. 3–4). Moreover, this enlightenment will follow if a simple freedom exists, the freedom to make *public* use of one's reason, that is, the freedom of a scholar before the reading public. But even here this use of freedom is not unconditional. For the public use of reason is shadowed by a private limitation on it, a restriction of the private use of reason in one's civil post or office. Even at his most enthusiastic about the free use of reason, Kant is ready to accept this necessary limitation.

Kant's answer to the question put to him by this journal, then, is consistent with the inner end of history inscribed within human nature. This end is a universal civic culture and rational society, i.e. a society that fosters freedom by accepting the necessity of its limitation of freedom. Such a society follows from the enlightenment attendant upon the free public use of reason. The present age, in so far as it allowed such a freedom by the wisdom of the sovereign, suggests Kant (1963: 8), is not an *'enlightened age'* but *'an age of* enlightenment'. This is a critical distinction that allows both the affirmation of the primacy of the present but resorts to a teleology in which the present is located as a necessary moment oriented to the future. For Kant, the present is not the age to come, that is to say, the age of the fulfilment of reason that would follow its prolonged free public expression. Rather it is a kind of dawn, an age in which there is a general awakening of the capacity for reason. If these two essays published in the same journal a month apart are read together, the inescapable conclusion is that Kant situates the present as a moment within the progress leading to the accomplishment of universal goals by the development of critical reason. The same progress that depends on and makes possible freedom also, however, requires a careful specification of the necessary limits of freedom and reason.

This problem of the present, of limits and necessity, is at the heart of Foucault's interpretation of this essay. I want now to argue that this interpretation is only available if the definition of the enlightenment in terms of the present can be divorced from the teleological movement in which the events of human history are caught, if 'What is Enlightenment?' can be divorced from 'Idea for a Universal History' and, more generally, from Kant's critical philosophy. The above argument may suggest that this move by Foucault is somewhat problematic. However, there are good reasons for thinking this is not the case, ones that follow from the difficulties of Kant's position and the peculiarity of Foucault's perspective. More problematic, however, is the very notion of 'the present' itself which Foucault relies upon to save a pro-enlightenment position. Having deprived historical time of an internal teleology, the next step would be to reconceive the present outside a teleological structure of a moment that is manifest in separate and inter-dependent elements.

FOUCAULT: ENLIGHTENMENT AND THE LIMITS OF NECESSITY

In his first lecture of his course at the *Collège de France* in 1983, Foucault suggested (1986b) that the essay on enlightenment poses the question of the present in a way distinct from that of Kant's broader philosophy of history, from its concern for the form in which history is fulfilled and its inner finality approached. In fact, this lecture appears to bracket out or suspend the philosophy of history in which this notion of enlightenment is embedded, or at least only to allow its existence as an incomplete, and perhaps archaic, logic. The idiosyncrasy of this move is underlined when Foucault's lecture turns from this essay to Kant's deliberations on the question of 'Is there a constant progress of the human race?', dated fourteen years later in his *Conflict of the Faculties* (Kant 1963: 137–54).

In his lecture, Foucault argues (1986b: 88–9) that Kant is the first to problematise the meaning of the present for philosophical reflection, and hence to realise his position as a part of a 'we' which corresponds to a particular, contemporary, cultural ensemble. This '"sagital" relation to one's own present-ness' characterises the philosophy and discourse of and on modernity, itself a singular cultural process which comes to self-awareness through naming itself (ibid. 90). Elsewhere, Foucault emphasises again the separation of this concern with enlightenment from the synthetic philosophy of history immersed in the search for origins and the internal teleology of historical process when he reinterprets Kant's problem as one of 'contemporary reality', the present understood neither in terms of totality nor future achievement, but in its specific difference from what has preceded it (Foucault 1986i: 33–4). Enlightenment is, he suggests (ibid. 35), an 'exit' or 'way out' of immaturity, a phenomenon of which humankind is a part, but also a task and an obligation for each individual. It may be that the Enlightenment situates this contemporary reality with respect to the 'internal teleology of time', Foucault continues, but it is also about the responsibility of the individual for this process of overcoming immaturity and tutelage (ibid. 38). What appears to interest Foucault most in these reflections on Kant is the sharpness with which the latter brings the nature of the present into focus, the open-endedness of the present as a project and an arena of individual and collective experiment, the role of contingency, of events and the play of the undefinable space of freedom in the formation of the future.

This is clearly the case in Foucault's understanding on Kant's answer to the question of the constant progress of humankind. Kant's answer to the question was an affirmative one, but it is the way he gives such an answer that most intrigues Foucault. Kant looks for an experience or event that would act as a sign of the tendency of humankind 'to be the cause of its own advance toward the better' (Kant 1963: 142). He finds this historical sign in the French Revolution, not among the momentous deeds or crimes of humankind but in the attitude of the spectators displaying a 'wishful participation that closely borders on enthusiasm' (ibid. 144). Kant links this attitude to what he understands as a moral predisposition of the human race toward the provision of a constitution within a nation that appears good to its people, and is both good and just and can avoid offensive war.

There is, however, something contradictory, or at least paradoxical, about this way of answering the question of progress. Kant seeks to confirm progress by calling on an event that vitiates his own teleology. He seeks to demonstrate the ordered directionality of history by means of the most ruptural event imaginable, the Revolution! This is precisely Foucault's point. He says of Kant's demonstration (Foucault 1986b: 91): it is not sufficient to simply follow 'the threads of a teleological fabric . . . it is necessary to isolate, within history, an event which will have value as a sign'. In short, Foucault finds in Kant's demonstration of progress something more akin to the anti-teleological perspective of his genealogies. His own historical studies eschew teleology and the search for origins, and remain suspicious about the existence of necessity in history. As such, it is true Foucault's genealogies could not be further from the positions of Kant. However, this does not stop him finding in Kant's historical writings an element that affirms the primacy of the present, of the event, of the contingent, and of the freedom thereby possible. Thus, Kant's position does contain an internal torsion between a teleological history and the Revolution as sign of progress that permits Foucault to make an interesting, if novel, reading. However, his own genealogical perspective gives that reading its pertinence.

From this perspective Foucault insists that the legacy of Kant's thought on enlightenment, progress, and the Revolution is of a different order from that embodied in his three great critiques. While these minor texts inaugurate a form of critique, this critique is not concerned with establishing the necessary limits of our freedom, judgement or knowledge, or the conditions under which the uses of reason are acceptable. Rather than seeking the necessary and universal conditions of the use of reason, these texts suggest and foreshadow a critique concerned with the limits of contemporary forms of life and identity. This critique consists in distinguishing between what is necessary and what is contingent, the universal and the singular in contemporary life. It is a practical and perspectival activity that poses the ever-present and mobile possibilities of transgression of the limits of these forms of life.

It is only in this sense that Foucault discovered in Kant the emergence of two critical traditions in modern philosophy. He distinguished, first, an 'analytic of truth' that takes up the quest to define the conditions under which knowledge is possible, acceptable, and legitimate. This 'analytic of truth' is similar to that which is made intelligible in *The Order of Things* (Foucault 1970: ch. 9) as the 'analytic of finitude': the paradoxical proposition in which the limits of human existence (of 'Man') form the basis of true knowledge in the human sciences. However, secondly, Foucault discovers another, relatively unknown Kant in these apparently minor texts on history and enlightenment. From these have followed an 'ontology of the present, an ontology of ourselves' that interrogates 'the contemporary field of possible experience' (Foucault 1986b: 96). This critical ontology of the present forms a project 'in which the critique of what we are is at the same time the historical analysis of the limits that are imposed on us and an experiment with the possibility of going beyond them' (Foucault 1986i: 50). It should not be thought, however, that Foucault is here simply juxtaposing an 'analytic of truth' to an 'ontology of the present' as unrelated and divergent components of Kant's philosophical reflection. Rather, Kant's diagnosis of the present moment as one of enlightenment, as one in which 'humanity is going to put its own reason to use, without subjecting it to any authority', makes necessary the determination of the legitimate use of reason and critique (Foucault 1986i: 37–8). In Foucault's account, the analytic of truth undertaken in Kant's three critiques already presupposes our self-constitution within a specific historical moment.

This could be read as a re-working and broadening of the fundamental problem Foucault had earlier discovered in Kantian epistemology. He had argued (Foucault 1970: 318–22) that this epistemology was inherently unstable because the subject that was the transcendental condition of knowledge is already among the various empirical objects of the field of knowledge, formed under determinate conditions of life, labour, and language. Later, Foucault is concerned not simply with Kant's subject of knowledge, but also his moral–political and aesthetic subjects. It was by these subjects that Kant sought the universal conditions of knowledge, ethical life and citizenship, and judgement. However, for Foucault this universalism contains a kind of paradox: the possibility of seeking universal rules to guide our actions, judgements and understanding, only arises at a particular juncture, a specific, historically-given, locus of self-constitution. Indeed, the attempt to recognise oneself as a universal subject can be viewed as a particular form of ethical practice, as Foucault points out in an interview in 1983. Here Kant's thought is reinterpreted as a form of asceticism in so far as it 'introduces one more way in our tradition whereby the self is not merely given but is constituted in relationship to itself' (Foucault 1986d: 372). Enlightenment is another form of asceticism.

It is indeed this problem of self-constitution Foucault used to redefine his own project in the introduction of the second volume of his history of sexuality, *The Use of Pleasure* (1985: 6; cf. Poster 1989: 53–69). In that introduction, we can see the fruit of the recasting of his critical concerns so he now suggests that, after having examined 'games of truth' in relation to knowledge and, later, power, he 'felt obliged to study the games of truth in the relationship of self with self and the forming of oneself as a subject'. This is consonant with the notion, elaborated in the pieces on enlightenment, of a practical, historical critique concerned with analysing and reflecting upon the limits under which *we* have been led to constitute ourselves as subjects of knowledge, as moral subjects, and as subjects within power relations (1986i: 47–9). The historical-theoretical project Foucault's writings on Kant implies, and which the rest of his work can be shown to exemplify, is not directed towards an objectivistic, comparativist, science of history, nor to metaphysical philosophy of history as humankind's journey to a higher goal or search for the recovery of its lost origins, but to the political and ethical issues raised by *our* insertion in a particular present, and by the problem of action under the limits establishing the present. This is indeed a critical theory but one that forms its critique of institutions, practices, and forms of knowledge, not by postulating a glorious endpoint which recedes as one advances toward it, but by an historical analysis of what is superable and insuperable in the conditions of specific identities and current forms of life.

Has Foucault taken his criticism of the philosophy of history far enough to dispel the lasting effects of teleology in this notion of the present? Before answering this, it is first worth asking who are the 'we' constituted in the present by relations of knowledge and power, and ethical practices of the self.

In response, it can be discerned that 'we' are those whose ontology is of the present and who are thus subject to contemporary forms of experience. Yet, the boundaries of inclusion and exclusion are not clear here: the contemporary experience of all human life is of course immensely various. To speak of a 'we' is always indeterminate. Where does this 'we' stop and its outside begin? For Foucault (1986b: 89), this 'we' are those who 'correspond to a cultural ensemble' characteristic of the philosopher's contemporenity, that is, those who live in a particular culture, and share in a certain understanding. If this is so, then the present is a particular present, a present for a specific community, one capable of practising a certain philosophical ethos or adopting an attitude of modernity. The problem here would seem that there are a multiplicity of presents and a multiplicity of versions of 'we' which themselves do not cohere into a unitary reality, whether one calls that 'contemporary experience', 'modernity', 'humanity', and so on. In other words, to follow Foucault's annexation of the present from the teleology of historical process and time, it is necessary to break with a teleological conception of the present itself as a unity of discrete but interdependent elements which are manifestations of the historical moment. If Kant's essays help define the relation of philosophy to the present, Foucault's lectures on enlightenment force the very notion of the present as a unity of inter-dependent elements into focus. As a consequence, I would suggest, the very notion of the present as equivalent to or a surrogate for 'the modern West' must fall. This, at least, would appear to be the consistent implication of his stance toward enlightenment.

The problem of the present may be that which Foucault discovers in Kant: 'What difference does today introduce with respect to yesterday?' (Foucault 1986i: 34). But this problem is radically incomplete unless the further questions are asked: which today and yesterday, and for whom? Genealogy constructs specific lineages of difference, and so constitutes historical series. These series, however, are always conducted within specified parameters and at particular levels and temporalities. The relations between such series cannot be reduced to successive moments coherent in themselves. Rather these relations themselves form a kind of meta-series. If Foucault was led to argue that *Discipline and Punish* (1977a) formed a 'history of the present', it was because the present was conceived as one traversed by revolts against the prison as a material instrument of power. He said: 'That punishment in general and the prison in particular belong to a political technology of the body is a lesson that I have learnt not so much from history as from the present' (Foucault 1977a: 30–1). This present, then, is simply a mode of struggle over specific instruments and discourses of power, and a mode of self-constitution. It can neither be an arena for an exhaustive understanding of a unitary age, epoch, moment, period, or society, nor a present that excludes other experiences, struggles, and modes of self-constitution.

At several points, Foucault situates himself as working in a form of reflection initiated by these 'minor' texts of Kant, one with a lineage 'from Hegel to the Frankfurt School by way of Nietzsche and Max Weber' (1986b: 96).[6] But is *this* really the case with respect to the Frankfurt School? Or is it an example of a continuing intellectual generosity? For while Foucault may have discovered he held the problem of enlightenment and modernity in common with the Frankfurt School, he gives it a different treatment and appreciation from German critical theory and its use of the Weberian theme of instrumental rationalisation. This difference is highlighted by the degree of incomprehension of proponents of critical theory when faced by Foucault's declaration of intellectual filiation.

To illustrate this, consider the memorial Habermas made for Foucault, in which he responds to the latter's lecture on Kant and enlightenment. In this piece, Habermas suggests (1989: 176) that Foucault is either caught in a 'productive contradiction' or has finally reconciled himself to the 'philosophical discourse of modernity'. The productive contradiction is this: on the one hand, Foucault espouses an 'affirmative' understanding of the role of theory toward the present, and places himself within the tradition of the Enlightenment; on the other, he maintains a critique of modernity, and the form of knowledge characteristic of it. Habermas cannot reconcile Foucault's interest in Kant's philosophy of history with his earlier archaeologies of discursive formations and genealogies of power relations. Nor can Habermas link what he sees as Foucault's newly favourable position on the Enlightenment with the aporias of the cognitive subject he discovered in Kant, and following him, the human sciences, in which the self-referential subject, defined by its own finitude, is overloaded with a task which requires infinite powers. Was Foucault himself caught in an endless theoretical trap, Habermas suggests, or did he finally realise, at the end of his life, that he must rejoin that discourse of modernity which he tried to explode?

Habermas' criticism here is clearly unsustainable. Foucault sought to detach Kant's reflection on the present from the teleological philosophy of history in which it is encased. His interest in this Kantian philosophy of history is not as a philosophical justification for the emergence and destiny of a yet to be completed *enlightened age*, but for its attempt to specify what enlightenment means at a particular moment for a particular community engaged in forms of social and cultural practice. Enlightenment is a multiplicity of attempts to go beyond the limits set for reason and action by that philosophy of history. Indeed, there can be no equivalent to a notion of modern society in Foucault's genealogies. Their objects are historical forms of rationality and their inscription within systems of practices, not the characterisation of a single present – modern society – that is the outcome of processes of cultural and societal rationalisation in the West, as in Habermas' blend of neo-Weberianism, neo-Marxism, and neo-functionalism (Habermas 1984, 1987b). Moreover, by contrasting the critical ontology of the present with the Kantian analytic of truth, Foucault clearly signals he has not retreated from his earlier characterisation of the Kantian form of knowledge and the project it inaugurated in the shape of the human sciences. Further, if Foucault was occasionally led to align himself – and indeed the French school of the philosophy of science (Foucault 1980d) – with the critical post-Enlightenment German tradition, it is not because the latter forms a canonical circle to which he is petitioning admittance, but because it represents a continued pre-occupation with the critical examination of forms of science, knowledge, and rationality that traverse contemporary social relations and institutions, and the issues of power and domination that these forms raise.[7] Finally, it is doubtful that Foucault can be characterised as the trenchant critic seeking to explode the discourse of modernity (and thus a representative of post-modernity), particularly given his sceptical stance on the explanatory capacity of such concepts, and his conception of modernity not as period, but as attitude, following Baudelaire.

Foucault's characterisation of the attitude of modernity is both subtle and complex and too clearly expressed in his essay 'What is Enlightenment?' to be repeated here. Nevertheless there remains one key point. Foucault notes (1986i: 42–3) that this mode of philosophical interrogation which 'prob-lematises man's relation to the present' must refuse what he calls the blackmail of the Enlightenment, the necessity to be for or against the Enlightenment. Yet then he goes on to characterise the attitude of modernity as a 'limit-attitude'. Here the question is no longer of the limits which found true knowledge (as in the analytic of truth) but of 'a practical critique that takes the form of a possible transgression' (ibid.45).

Let us be clear about Foucault's position here: it is not a matter of being for or against the Enlightenment, for or against a unitary and totalising form of reason, but of working at limits in accord with an attitude of modernity. This means sorting out the contingent and singular from the universal and necessary. Transgression thus works at the limits that have defined ways of being, doing, and thinking, seeking the ever-present possibility of the 'un-defined work of freedom' (Foucault 1986i: 46). It is not a matter of a once-and-for-all break with a universal and total form of reason, but an 'experimental' attitude that crosses and recrosses the limits of our forms of rationality. Transgression, then, is not a residual equivalent of the global emancipation of the subject, but a possibility arising from the work of criticism, an option emerging through trenchant historical and theoretical work. There can be no a priori that favours either transgression or the maintenance of the present *status quo*. This is a form of critique which uses the knowledge of limits to establish political options without prescribing resolutions.

This theme of the reciprocal dependence of limits and transgression was present in Foucault's thought as early as his 1963 essay on Georges Bataille: 'The limit and transgression depend on each other for whatever density of being they possess: a limit could not exist if it were absolutely uncrossable and, reciprocally, transgression would be pointless if it merely crossed a limit composed of illusions and shadows' (1977c: 34). Foucault's histories stand in such a relation to modernity, enlightenment, and reason. Their attitude is historical, critical, and experimental, marking a zigzag path at the limits under which the present is constituted for various modalities of contemporary experience. Just as it is problematic to speak of a Western reason or a modernity that is universal and totalising, it is equally problematic to imagine boundaries established under such terms can be crossed forever into a postmodernity. The attempts to label Foucault a total critic of modernity and rationality resemble nothing as much as the empty shadow-boxing of a child's puppet. If Foucault does presage a postmodernity, it is neither as a new attitude nor an attitude in favour of the new – the adoption of both is resolutely modern. Nor is it a new periodisation of socio-cultural evolution. Foucault's postmodernity would be found instead in the restive 'problematisation' of what is historically given.

CONCLUSION

The synthetic philosophies of history of the eighteenth century rest on the supposition of a teleological unfolding of the natural, rational capacities of humankind. For Kant, for example, history is the sphere of the evolution of the capacity of reason toward a final purpose of a fully 'rational man' living under rational political arrangements of his own creation. But in these philosophies of histories, there is a double ambivalence with regard to the human actor. First, history is the stage of a human drama precisely because it is both made and not made by human actors. Indeed, the movement of time in such philosophies concerned the realisation or retardation of these capacities by the opportunities and obstacles presented by history.

Secondly, and perhaps more importantly, the realisation of the subject in history presupposes necessary limitations on the use of the subject's attributes, in particular, a necessary limitation on freedom. Kant's teleological philosophy of history parallels his critiques of reason in proposing the limitation of freedom as necessary to the coming of a universal civic society.

Foucault's work on Kant's philosophy of history seeks to detach the notion of enlightenment from teleological history. This is both a methodological and perspectival manoeuvre. The methodological implication of Foucault's position is the need to abandon all conceptions of reason or rationality that regard them as features or faculties immanent to human actors within history. For Foucault, it is necessary to reject this understanding of history, so pervasive since the eighteenth century, in terms of the evolution of the natural attributes of the rational subject as social-historical actor. It is further necessary to maintain a vigilance regarding all the attendant themes of such a history which express the ambivalence noted above: those of the loss, repression, deformation, alienation, and division, of the capacities and attributes of the subject and their promised reconciliation, redemption, transcendence, and emancipation. Only by breaking with such themes is the space opened for what might be called a 'critical history of rationality'.

Such a position is not that of the 'death of the subject' attributed to Foucault by those such as Agnes Heller (1990: 24). One could hardly imagine a philosopher for whom the subject was so alive! Rather, what is rejected is this romance of the voyage of the subject within a philosophy of history. The supposition that social-historical actors can be identified as possessing a capacity of reason, and action is the mechanism by which the purposes of reason are realised within the world, returns us to the search for the scenes of the perpetual human drama. By contrast, a critical history of rationality cannot start from such a supposition because it is concerned with the variation of forms of specification of human beings and their capacities under definite social, ethical, political, and cultural conditions. Such forms of specification are not necessarily those of the subject, a unique being replete with reason, consciousness, will, and so on.[8] To suppose that they are would be to undermine the central task of a critical history of rationality to examine the way in which such forms of specification have particular discursive conditions presupposed by and necessary to various forms of social, legal, political, and economic practices and techniques.[9]

There is also a reversal of perspective here. Rather than posing the problem of reason and freedom in terms of a necessary and universal limitation, Foucault's writings on enlightenment, and his historical studies, start from the actual limits to forms of rationality and action. The point is not to seek the universal conditions that make it possible to speak and act, and to enshrine them in foundational moral codes and epistemologies, but to discover what it is possible to think, to say, and to do under various contingent conditions. This is not to say anything is possible in an irrationalist or libertarian fashion, but that there always remains to be determined a space of contingency and freedom within the conditions of experience and identity.

This is a delicate and subtle position to maintain since, while 'anti-humanist', it does not entail a rejection of all notions of the subject. On the one hand, it demonstrates the *necessity* of notions of rights, freedoms, duties, and obligations attributed to subjects within particular social relations and discourses. As a consequence, political ideologies that draw upon norms and values associated with the subject (e.g. in discourses on human rights, democracy, etc.) cannot easily be abandoned. If concepts and suppositions concerning the subject (or the person or the self) are formed and specified within particular social relations and discourses, then they cannot be simply written out of them or legislated out of existence. Notions of the subject, person, self, etc., are not the less 'real' for having particular conditions of existence. On the other hand, these notions should not be raised into the necessary and insuperable universals of human existence. Foucault's critique consists precisely in an analysis that seeks to discover what can be surpassed and what is no longer necessary. From such a position, Heller's definition of the subject (1990: 37) as 'the idiosyncrasy of the interpretation of human world-experience and self-experience under conditions of modernity' pre-supposes that the conditions of experience are given as a unity of inter-dependent elements which are manifestations of the single present that is modernity. Foucault's lesson, it seems to me, is a contrasting one. It is this: only by the dual problematisation of the actor as subject and the present as a unified modernity can an horizon for a critical and effective history of reason – or a historical sociology of forms of rationality – be established.

The key implication of Foucault's later work on Kant is located in its retrieval of the notion of enlightenment as independent, critical activity from its identification with an ideal of reason, whether formal, substantive, or even procedural. Cutting across the assumptions of subject-centred social-theoretical traditions, Foucault's work locates rationality not within the attributes of the actor or the features of action, but within the discursive and practical conditions of action, which he variously calls 'discursive formations', 'regimes of truths', 'games of truth', and 'power–knowledge' relations. This has important implications for how we read the central historical–sociological master-key of Weber's notion of rationalisation. If we are to retain this term, it cannot be understood as unified by reference to a type of social action (such as purposive–rational action, or communicative action). Nor can it be understood as a unified process coherent or consistent across all specific facets and instances of rationalisation. It follows that it is not particularly insightful to characterise historical processes in terms of increasing or decreasing rationality. What emerges is an understanding of plural, non-unified, systems of rationality, possessing no necessary coherence amongst themselves, and having specific, and analysable conditions of existence. It is this and not the teleologies of the rational subject or of rationalisation which provides the terrain of a critical history of rationality.

Having understood this much of a critical history of rationality we can now turn to an examination of the concept of rationality at work in Max Weber's historical sociology.

Chapter 4

Weber, rationality, and the subject

Addressing the question of rationality in his historical studies, Foucault commented:

> One isn't assessing things in terms of an absolute against which they could be evaluated as constituting more or less perfect forms of rationality, but rather examining how forms of rationality inscribe themselves in practices or systems of practices ... it is true that 'practices' don't exist without a certain regime of rationality. But, rather than measuring this regime against a value-of-reason, I would prefer to analyse it according to two axes: on the one hand, that of codification/prescription ... and on the other, that of true or false formulation.
>
> (Foucault 1981b: 8)

The object of such an analysis is not reason, considered as an 'anthropological invariant' (ibid. 8), a universal feature of humanity, but the relation between forms of rationality and the practices to which they are linked. The object, in other words, is a plural one, rational*ities* or, to be more precise, the processes bringing forms of rationality into relation with systems of practices.

The general argument of this and the following chapter is that the term 'rationalisation', often identified as the masterkey to Max Weber's historical sociology, should be used only in a restricted sense of the diverse processes by which particular forms of knowledge come to be connected to 'regimes' or organised systems of heterogeneous social practices. This may be thought of as a minimalist conception of 'rationalisation' in so far as it seeks to restrict the number of assumptions concerning the nature of rationality. Above all, such a definition excludes universalist themes of a rationality grounded in the structure of the human subject and revealed or realised in the broad movements of the history of civilisations. This argument is sketched against the background of a reflection upon Weber's concepts of rationality and rationalisation and the body of commentary which seeks to identify the 'central theme' of his work. The alternative approach to a critical history of rationality represented by Foucault's work is drawn upon in the course of the discussion.

Remarks such as those quoted have given rise to attempts to specify

Foucault's relation to Weber's themes of rationality and rationalisation. Yet such attempts neither quite resolve this relation nor reach a consensus on what we should draw from it. Foucault's own scant comments (1981b: 8–9) on rationalisation and the methodology of the 'ideal type' seek to contrast his own position with that of Weber. Some draw the implication that there is a clear distinction between the two based on Foucault's rejection of an overarching process of rationalisation (Smart 1985: 138–9). However, from different perspectives, both Dreyfus and Rabinow (1983: 133, 166) and Dews (1987: 151–2) argue that Foucault's historical studies can only be properly understood in terms of the Weberian concern of rationalisation. The former characterise Foucault's approach as a 'finer-grained' advance within the general Weberian problematic. Dews contends, on the contrary, that Foucault's account of power lacks a Weberian framework and only becomes intelligible given the historical dominance of the highly rationalised forms of administration and social organisation with modernity. Both these accounts also have in common the fact that they situate Foucault and Weber upon the intellectual terrain shared by Nietzsche, Heidegger, and the Frankfurt School, all of whom are said to be concerned with the application of rationality in modern society.

Both Gordon (1987) and Turner (1987b) have advanced this debate by suggesting axes for a meeting of Weber and Foucault that emerge if we suspend an interpretation of rationalisation as a uniform, continuous, monolinear process of rationalisation. Drawing on the work of Wilhem Hennis (1983), Gordon (1987: 293–4) suggests a more specific ground for comparison, that of government and the 'conduct of life'. Turner (1987b) shifts attention from the conventional preoccupation with the rationalisation of forms of consciousness for an historical sociology of the rationalisation of forms of regulation of the body. Such interpretations of Weber are clearly ones which only become available through a Foucauldian focus on knowledge, power, and discipline. Indeed, rather than Weber's general methodological protocols and metahistorical narratives, they emphasise the historical rupture central to Weber's account of Protestantism (Weber 1985) and Weber's study on the origin, meaning, and spread of discipline (Weber 1970: 253–64).

While accepting the validity of such approaches, the general tenor of my argument is to accentuate the obstacles to any rapprochement between the two thinkers. Indeed, Weber's notions of rationality and rationalisation, and his conception of the cultural sciences, rest upon a philosophical anthropology which is fundamentally alien to Foucault's genealogy and its status as a counter-science working against the grain of the human sciences. Moreover, this anthropology clearly separates Weber from Foucault's conception of forms of rationality as depending on distinctive historical formations made up of heteromorphous discursive and non-discursive dimensions. For Foucault, forms of rationality depend on and operate through particular social and historical institutions, and the practices, techniques, strategies and modes of calculation that traverse them. Rationality is a feature specific to ensembles of social practices and inscribed within relations of 'power–knowledge' and not a general capacity or need of human subjects or a feature of their purposes. While specific social analyses may constitute points of contact and overlap between Weber and Foucault, at a methodological and meta-historical level their positions are not simply different but fundamentally incommensurate.

While Weber continues to be a central focus of historical–sociological characterisation of modernity (e.g. Whimster and Lash 1987), these deep-seated conceptual problems are rarely acknowledged. On the one hand, there are problems around the identification of rationality with the attributes of the human subject in his models and typology of social action. The typology of social action refers us to a specific philosophical anthropology, a conception of the invariant features of human existence and the structure of rationality. This philosophical anthropology underlies Weber's conception of the field of sociological knowledge and forms what he calls the 'transcendental pre-supposition' of his conception of the spiritual or cultural sciences (*Geistes-wissenschaften*). There are specific problems with the acceptance of such a basis as the subject/object of knowledge, and as the key to approaching issues of rationality. Such problems throw into relief the contrast between Weber's project for the cultural sciences and Foucault's use of genealogy as forming a 'counter-science' of 'anti-science' to those very cultural sciences. I shall argue that an effective history is one that deprives the cultural sciences of the very entity for whom they are preparing a safe resting place. It is these issues which occupy the present chapter.

On the other hand, there are aspects of Weber's historical analyses that do not directly employ a reduction to the attributes of constituent subjects. Yet these analyses in many ways mirror the problems of his approach to social action by employing the notions of 'Western rationalism' and 'civilisation'. Such notions often collapse heterogeneous instances of rationalised social practices into the spurious figure of the West. Against the grain of lesser themes of the social-historical conditions of forms of rationalised life-conduct and the regulation of the body, Weber's overall account manages to construct and privilege Western rationalism, and fails to overcome certain elements of a teleology of reason. What can be called Weber's 'occidentalism' and his philosophical anthropology present the dual limits of the capacity of his analyses to do what I take to be the core of what I have been calling a 'critical history of rationality', viz. to constitute the fields of dispersion which characterise forms of rationality and modes of subjectification in relation to governmental techniques of the body, self, and life of individuals and populations.

The next chapter situates Weber's historical–sociological studies within his general philosophy of history and indicates its major features. Taken together Weber's philosophies of humankind and of history indicate the limits to a critical and effective historical sociology of rationalities presented by the specious unities of the founding subject or of the comparative history of civilisations from the viewpoint of the West.

RATIONALITY AND THE SUBJECT

Weber's discussions of rationality appear in both his specific historical analyses of religious and secular rationalisations and in his typology of social action. Despite, or perhaps because of, the great weight of recent commentary on these aspects of Weber's thought, the relation between these diverse discussions remains unclear. In this section, however, I shall argue that if Weber's understanding of rationalisation is based on this typology, then there are serious limits to its contribution to a critical history of rationality.

For a substantial and influential body of Weberian scholarship, rationality and historical processes of rationalisation can be characterised in terms of the *types* of rational social action and/or legitimate domination. Here, the rationalisation characteristic of modernity concerns the dominance of a particular type of social action, instrumentally rational or purposive–rational (*zweckrational*) action, and its institutionalisation in formal bureaucratic administration based on the rational–legal type of domination.

Take the famous 1932 essay of Karl Löwith (1982). This is perhaps the classic statement of the 'rationalisation thesis'. Here rationality sums up 'the particular problematic of this reality of ours', and Weber's critical concern is the irrational consequences of the 'general process of the rationalisation of our whole existence' (ibid. 40–1). Löwith identifies rationality with 'freedom of action' in that the latter is a form of 'teleological rationality', the pursuit of purposes through the free conscious choice of adequate means (ibid.45). Rationalisation, which brings about the unique 'original' totality that is the 'occidental ethos', concerns the manifestation of such a purposive–rational action in the many spheres of social life. Yet the 'paradox of rationalisation' (e.g. Schluchter 1979) is that the institutionalisation of this form of rational action raises the very possibility of its extinction, in the form of the domination of means over ends (Löwith 1982: 48). In a move which reverberates through the entire conceptual apparatus of the Frankfurt School, Löwith establishes the theme of the irrational consequences of the peculiar rationalisation of the West, and of the devastating transmutation of the history of the progress of reason into one of the intensification of the domination of instrumentalism. In doing so, he reveals the problematic form of Weber's narrative of rationalisation as one in which the heroic value-driven action produces an outcome obliterating the possibility of such a heroism (Turner 1987b: 231). The Protestant quest for salvation thus results in an iron cage of capitalist bureaucracy undermining all moral values. This resignation to the fate of a rationalisation that is also a disenchantment of the magical features of the world indicates the embedded tragic and philosophical nature of this discourse.

This fatalism of rationalisation is also noted by other influential commentators. Wolfgang Mommsen makes clear how the principal direction of rationalisation can be summarised in terms of types of social action:

> Weber points out that the process of rationalisation has often been initiated by revolutionary action, either of the value-rational or charismatic type . . . Weber makes the further allowance that the process of 'rationalisation' may, in particular cases, retain its original association with particular value-attitudes. As a rule, however, it almost always takes a different direction, inasmuch as it paves the way for the universal advance of purely instrumentally-oriented social institutions, to the detriment of all value-oriented forms of social conduct.
>
> (Mommsen 1974: 80–1)

We can ignore for a moment the question of why these different types of action almost always 'pave the way' for the advance of instrumental rationalisation, or why that should be an irrational or pathological form of rationalisation, as interpreters from Löwith to Habermas urge. It is interesting that Mommsen, like Löwith, characterises Weber's concept of rationalisation as entailing the advance of instrumental rationality, at least under conditions of modernity. It is perhaps more interesting here that both these Weber interpreters view his account of societal processes at the level of social institutions in terms of rational social action.

Classically, then, this 'rationalisation thesis' has been regarded as the key to the implications of Weber's approach to matters of rationality for social theory and sociology. But this approach is complicated by its coexistence with one which shifts the focus from the subjective rationality of individual conduct to supra-individual, institutionalised, rationality, i.e. forms of rationality embodied in different institutional practices and techniques. The relation between these two different foci is discussed in the celebrated 'Author's Introduction' of 1920:

> though the development of economic rationalism is partly dependent on rational technique and law, it is at the same time determined by the ability and disposition of men to adopt certain types of practical rational conduct. When these types have been obstructed by spiritual obstacles, the development of rational economic conduct has also met serious inner resistance.
>
> (Weber 1985: 26–7)

The second sentence is extremely important and I shall return to it later. There are, then, two 'levels at which Weber seeks to address the problem of rationality.[1] On the one level, rationality can be identified with the individual subject and its conduct, as Weber does not only in his typology of forms of

social action in *Economy and Society* (1968, 1: 3–62) but also, more am-
biguously, in *The Protestant Ethic and the Spirit of Capitalism* (1985). On the
other level, when Weber talks of the rationality of the capitalist economy,
modern law, and administration, he is addressing features of objective social
structures which are supra-individual and form external conditions of action.
However, because of his commitment to viewing social relations ultimately as
relations between subjects, as intersubjective relations, Weber needs to show
that the rationalisation of social relations and social structures presupposes a
prior rationalisation of the inner existence of individuals and, as a consequence, their conduct (Brubaker 1984: 9). This is the purpose of the essay on
Protestantism and his sociology of religion in general, in particular the
typology of forms of rationalisation in salvation religions contained in the
'Intermediate Reflections' (Weber 1970: 323–59). The rationalisation of 'objective' social structures presupposes the prior 'inner' rationalisation of the
ethical conduct of human actors and its conflicts with the various spheres of
action or 'life orders' (ibid. 323).

One way of characterising the most general object of Foucault's genealogies
would be the analysis of the historically specific modalities within which
diverse practices of self-formation take place (e.g. in 'The subject and power',
Foucault 1982). Such an analysis is concerned with displacing notions of the
founding rational subject by way of an analysis of the means which seek to
establish and promote particular human capacities – including those we might
wish to regard as 'reasoning' – within bodies of knowledge and types of
rationality, forms of power and government, and ethical practices. The
possibility for a meeting of Weber's historical sociology with Foucault's
genealogies would appear, then, to depend on a reading of Weber's notion of
rationalisation as a term describing the formation of the ethical conduct and
inner existence adequate to particular social relations in disciplinary and other
governmental practices and discourses (Hennis 1983, 1987; Gordon 1987).
Here, however, I wish to pursue the limits placed not only on this dialogue but
also on the usefulness of Weber's positions by his suppositions concerning the
role of the social actor as human subject in the genesis, first, of meaning, and
secondly, of rationality.

Weber's position assumes as its starting point a classical philosophical
conception of the human subject as a free and rational being, a centre of
consciousness and will (Hindess 1987). This entails the postulation of a realm
of freedom, of a subject who has the capacity to represent the external world
to itself in ideas, value, beliefs, and to act according to these representations. It
also involves the postulation of a realm of determination, the material world in
which action must occur, and which sets limits to and defines the sphere of
freedom. In Weber, the two realms are those of culture, subject to the
teleological causality of the subject's purposive action, and nature, the realm
of mechanical necessity, (e.g. throughout the essay '"Objectivity" in social
science and social policy', Weber 1949: 49–112). The 'neo-Kantian' division

between these two ontologically given realms of nature and culture establishes the specific domain of the cultural sciences. While recognising the complex interplay of mechanical and teleological causality in any given phenomena, Weber insists on the strict analytical separation of the two classes of determination and restricts the role of sociological knowledge, and the cultural sciences generally, to the interpretative understanding of the purposes of teleological action. The cultural sciences are sciences of understanding the human subject's freedom to act according to the ends it chooses within the limits of a material world of the scarcity of means and the conflicts between subjects seeking their freely chosen ends.[2]

The reasons why this account of the cultural sciences is disabling have already been mentioned in earlier chapters but they bear repeating here. First, social relations and institutions, discourses and forms of rationality, are strictly irreducible to the potentials, attributes and capacities of free, creative subjects. At some level, all critical historical studies of reason, in so far as the intelligibility appropriate to them is one which seeks to constitute the maximum difference betwen the forms of rationality implicated in social practices, must implicitly recognise this. Secondly, the notion of the universal human subject as the unique site in which consciousness and will are coincident does not stand up to anthropological scrutiny, as has been known at least since Mauss' seminal essays on notions of the self and person and techniques of the body (Mauss 1979). Thirdly, as Hindess' work (1989) demonstrates, an account of social action as the action of human subjects not only assumes a universal form of specification of individuals as subjects but also excludes the consideration of diverse non-human actors, including corporate actors, as forming loci of decision-making. Finally, and perhaps most importantly from the perspective of our present concerns, issues of the (governmental, ethical, and discursive) practices and techniques of self-formation and the constitution of capacities for action, choice, or reasoning, cannot be thematised by such a cultural science, or, if they are, only by following these capacities back to a primordial origin such practices merely help realise. To varying degrees, Weber's historical–sociological studies implicitly assent to each of the above propositions. However, his statements of method and epistemology depend on a definite conception of the universal features of the social actor as human subject, a philosophical anthropology. This can be illustrated by Weber's conception of both the cultural sciences and the nature of social action and sociological knowledge.

In the former, Weber suggests that the cultural sciences are founded on a 'transcendental presupposition,' that we are *cultural beings* endowed with the capacity and will to take a definite attitude toward the world and lend it *significance*' (Weber 1949: 81, original emphasis). This implies two interrelated sets of propositions concerning both subject and object of knowledge. The first concern the significance attributed to the object of the cultural sciences by the knowing subject. Weber's position here is a thoroughgoing perspectivism.

The subject of knowledge, the cultural scientist, is, above all else, a meaning-giving subject. This subject chooses from an inherently meaningless universe containing a 'multiplicity of successively and coexistently emerging and disappearing events' in terms of 'cultural interests' which give a segment of reality its 'value-relevance' (Weber 1949: 72, 76–82). 'All knowledge of cultural reality . . . is always knowledge from *particular points of view*' (ibid. 81, original emphasis). Having established the role of values in the constitution of cultural scientific knowledge, Weber immediately returns to a positivist conception of the nature of empirical knowledge based on the sharp separation of fact and value and a nominalist conception of knowledge (ibid. 85f.).

Turning to the object of knowledge, Weber argues that sociology is concerned with the interpretative understanding of social action (1968, 1: 4). Action occurs 'insofar as the acting individual attaches a subjective meaning to his behaviour – be it overt or covert' (ibid. 4). This action is social, moreover, to the extent that it takes into account the behaviour of others or of objects. Like his account of the unity of the cultural sciences in terms of the attributes of the subject of knowledge, Weber's definition of the object of sociology assumes the existence of a meaning-creating and bestowing being, capable of representing the world and its own or others' behaviour to itself and freely orienting that behaviour according to its purposes. No account of the various attributes of this constituent being can be given by such a science. Take the capacity for subjective meaning. Such a capacity is merely a part of the transcendental presupposition. It simply happens to exist as a pre-social attribute of human individuals. The possibility that it is given within language and social and discursive practices, or cultivated by forms of ethical or ascetic practice, cannot hence be contemplated by such a framework. This rules out the possibility of anything like the 'structural' study of language descended from Saussure entering into the cultural sciences or a study of the modes of formation of such subjects in various form of discourse. Language is reduced to the vehicle or instrument of the subject to create or express meanings. No account is possible of a conception of sense as arising from structured systems of signification, whether of a spoken or written language or other types of cultural practice (Hirst 1976: 69–70).

The dilemma of language in Weber's conception of the cultural sciences is posed by Foucault's account of the relation of the study of language to the human sciences in *The Order of Things* (Foucault 1970: Ch. 10). On the one hand, language appears as a fragmented and objective materiality the study of which, together with biology and economics, forms one of the planes which define the space of the human sciences. Philology, as the study of the objective structure and development of language, however, is not a human or, to use Weber's term, cultural science. Only when it is animated from within by the speaking subject, and hence becomes something to be interpreted, does language enter the hermeneutical region occupied by the cultural sciences. The cultural sciences are interested in language as the means for the expression and transmission of values, animated from the outside by the human subject as a cultural being and meaning-giving entity. For the cultural sciences, language is a dead collection of meaningless sounds and marks awaiting the animation of this being. But language always exists within the cultural sciences as a kind of unacknowledged general condition of their existence: the objects, as well as the concepts of the cultural sciences, in the form of meanings, values, representations, etc., are only available through language and its structuring systems. Given this, the cultural being of the 'transcendental presupposition' cannot be understood as lying behind or beyond the linguistic means to which it lends significance but is itself a site within a particular discursive practice. This strange entity, a subject radically exterior to the form of knowldge of which it is an object, is constituted discursively. The problem with Weber's conception of the cultural sciences is that it prevents that which is a condition of its knowledge (i.e. this subject which is also object) from becoming a topic and an avenue of investigation and theorisation. Fortunately, there are other ways by which this investigation is secreted into his work. As we have noted above, much of his sociology of religion can be said to be concerned with the way various types of self-formation occur within diverse ethical rational-isations of the conduct of life. Moreover, one perspective of his sociology of capitalism is concerned with the way in which discipline and the government of the body unleashes a process of self-formation with an elective affinity to capitalist social relations.

A similar and related set of points can be made in relation to rationality. In Weber's typology of social action, rationality is assumed to inhere within the subject and to follow from its status as a meaning-creating being. As such, the problems of Weber's conception of rationality follows the hazardous path of his anthropology: the rationality of the knower and the rationality of the known reflect each other in an act of mutual confirmation across the space of typological sociological knowledge. Sociological knowledge can only properly know that of which it is a part, the purposive–rational action fulfilling the potentialities of the human subject. It can only know other types of conduct, and other forms of rationality, as deviations from this structure of thought and action. It cannot constitute forms of rationality in their radical specificity or otherness, i.e. it cannot fulfil the minimum requirements for a critical history of rationality. Let us consider these points in more detail.

For Weber, action is rational in so far as the actor attaches subjective meaning to its behaviour. This may happen in one of two ways. The actor may rationally pursue and calculate ends by means of expectations about the behaviour of objects or of others, in instrumentally rational or purposive-rational (*zweckrational*) action, or the actor may consciously act in accord-ance with some absolute value, in value-rational (*wertrational*) action (Weber 1968, 1: 24–5). Now, while not all or even most of human action is rational (ibid.6–7), Weber contends that for a typological social science 'it is convenient to treat all irrational, affectually determined elements of behaviour as factors of deviation from a conceptually pure type of rational action' (ibid.6). It is possible to interpret the meaning of social action with 'the highest degree of verifiable certainty' when such an actor 'tries to achieve certain ends by choosing appropriate means', i.e. when the actor acts in an instrumentally rational fashion (ibid. 5).

But why should forms of action be treated in such a way and why should this yield such a degree of validity? The answer is clear if we compare Weber's definition of sociology and social action in general with his definition of instrumental action in particular. The latter is not merely one case of the former. Rather, instrumentally rational action undertakes what all social action does, but with the maximum degree of clarity, caculability, systematicity, and consistency. In social action, the actor attaches meanings to its behaviour, and takes account of the behaviour of others. In rational action, of either type, the actor consciously attaches meaning to its behaviour. But only in instrumentally rational action does the actor do so on the basis of expectations about the behaviour of others and of objects. Thus value-rational action is understandable in terms of the rationality of the means to achieve absolute values, while instrumentally rational action is comprehensible in terms of the choice of alternative means, the taking into consideration of their secondary consequences, and calculations about the ends to be pursued (Weber 1968, 1: 26). Instrumentally rational action realises the constitutive elements of social action in general in their most clear contours. Because of its consistency and clarity about choice of ends and means, such action is most readily accessible to a form of analysis which works backwards from social action in order to understand the motive or 'complex of meaning' embodied in it (ibid. 11).

The problems of understanding action directed toward ultimate ends and values arise from the degree to which such forms of action are oriented to ultimate values different from those of the sociologist. In the case of the other two types of social action, affectual or traditional action, the problems are infinitely greater. These forms of action stand on the borderline between meaningful action and mere behaviour, between culture and nature, in so far as they are close to automatic reactions to external stimuli or unconscious patterns of habit (Weber 1968, 1: 25). Such forms of action can be understood to the extent to which they exhibit the features of rational action, e.g. when an actor self-consciously follows a tradition, or consciously sublimates emotions. To the extent to which habit or affect determine behaviour, it is irrational, i.e. it is subject to forces interfering with the capacity of the actor to attach meaning and purpose to its behaviour. This behaviour can only be understood by comparing actual behaviour with what would have happened had action been of a conceptually pure type of rational action (ibid. 6).

Social action is thus not necessarily rational because it is also subject to the realm of mechancial determination of nature, in the form of external stimuli of a psycho-physical nature, or because it is subject to the force of habit. To the extent that mechancial behaviour gives way to social action, it becomes rational. In so far as behaviour is rational, it is social. It is important to underline here the elision between the rational and the social. Talk of rational social action is close to tautology. Corporeal, affectual or traditional determinations, unless they exhibit features of purposive and calculated choice, are understood as obstacles to properly rational conduct, and thus to social action itself.

For Weber, then, a certain type of rationality is given methodological privilege because it replicates in the most explicit fashion the structure inherent within social action itself. Sociological knowledge is an act of recognition by the subject of knowledge of the anthropological structure shared with the objects of knowledge. Because this structure is most clearly expressed in rationally purposive action, it is this form of action which can most clearly be understood. In this case, the act of recognition is not mediated by the need to take into account unfamiliar ultimate value commitments, patterns of habit, the interference of emotions, or of psycho-physical phenomena such as fatique, euphoria, or reaction-time and precision. Weber's sociology prepares a resting place, at the centre of a world of arational values and irrational bodies and affects, for a potentially rational, self-possessed being, in full control of its body and emotions, capable of giving meaning to that world, of deliberately choosing its ends, and finding the most appropriate means to them. Despite an attempt to provide a full account of the complexity of the determinants of individual human action, Weberian sociology continues to provide a haven for the autonomous, affectless, disembodied, universal, subject. The realm of the freedom of this subject is one of the conscious choice between ultimately irrational values, and the capacity to orient action toward ends by the formal characteristics of rationality, by a deliberate calculation of means, by clarity over ends and values, and by anticipating the consequences of action.

We cannot leave Weber's account of the relation between rationality and social action without noting that in it the relation of values to rational social conduct is somewhat ambivalent. On the one hand, ethical ideals derived from religious or other sources act as obstacles to fully rationalised conduct. This is illustrated by the sentence already cited: 'When these types [of practical rational conduct] have been obstructed by spiritual obstacles, the development of rational economic conduct has also met serious inner resistance' (Weber 1985: 26–7). Systems of values are obstacles not to the choice of means to a specific end but in the more fundamental sense that action is fixed onto specific ends. They restrict action to the realisation of an absolute value inherent in the way of acting, and thus prevent the orientation of action towards the achievement of ends which are external to that action. Forms of rationalisation of systems of absolute value are possible but these are particular, not universal, rationalisations. Only when such values are undermined in favour of a form of rationality able to serve any ends, does rationalisation have universal implications.

On the other hand, values are conditions of rational action and are hence also a necessary component of practical rational action in modern societies. In 'Politics as a vocation' (Weber 1970: 77–128), Weber argues that there is no rational way to reconcile competing forms of substantive rationality having different value commitments. This is the thesis of the 'ethical irrationality of the world' (Weber 1970: 122; Brubaker 1984: ch. 3). He also argues that an 'ethic of responsibility' is most appropriate to modern politics. Such an ethic pursues deliberately chosen irrational values in a calculated and systematic manner, fully taking into account the means chosen and the consequences of the use of such means (Weber 1970: 120–7). Similarly, Weber's moral philosophy rests on the idea that 'meaning and moral dignity derive from the systematic integration of individual actions into a unified life pattern based on certain fundamental values' (Brubaker 1984: 94). Moral conduct, like political action, exhibits both instrumentally rational and value-rational features. Rational practical conduct is thus a combination of these two types of social action. The meaning-giving capacity and rational potential of the actor, derived from Weber's philosophical anthropology, become translated into an essential component of irrational practical conduct. The deliberate choice of ends in terms of rational values, together with their maximum degree of calculation and consistency over the choice of means and consequences of action, constitute the necessary components of integrated moral conduct and responsible political conduct in the modern world. The most highly developed forms of personal conduct replicate what is assumed in the structure of the subject with its absolute autonomy in respect of values and heteronomy with regards to technicised means and its own embodiment.

Where does this ambivalence with regard to values leave Weber's account of rationality? Values are both obstacles to and conditions of rational action. Rationality transcends values in that its formal qualities (e.g. its clarity, consistency, calculability, rule-governed nature etc.) are independent of any substantive ends. Yet it is dependent upon values in so far as all rational action, including practical rational action, seeks ends that are freely chosen and for which there can be no rational criteria. This ambivalence gives rise to the distinction between *formal* rationality involving calculability and consistency of means and ends and *substantive* rationality concerning the value of actions and their consequences. As is well known, this distinction is called to account for a critque of modernity as a social order increasingly governed by the formal rationality embodied in the impersonal norms of the market, bureaucracy and law, but which is substantively irrational from the viewpoint of values of egalitarianism, fraternity, and *caritas* (Brubaker 1984: 35–43). The conflict between substantive and formal rationality in modern society, however, is already inherent in the structure of the social actor as having the capacity of attaching meaning to behaviour and pursuing specified ends by a calculation of means. Again, this philosophical anthropology is at the base of

Weberian distinctions but, this time, it provides the means for the portrayal of the modern drama.

On the one hand, the choice of values, of substantive rationality, is always an irrational one, depending as it does on the unconditioned freedom of the human subject. On the other, tensions and conflicts between value spheres are reconciled by the drive to greater consistency, to a greater degree of formal rationality. The main theme of the 'Intermediate Reflections', for example, is the way tensions between various value spheres are interconnected with the exposure of both religious ethics and other spheres to the 'imperative of consistency', pressing 'towards making conscious the *internal and lawful autonomy* of the individual spheres' (Weber 1970: 324, 328, original emphasis). Schluchter (1979: 17) locates the basis of Weber's account of this rationalisation of 'world images' in the structure of human needs which include needs for greater calculability of the world and for a unified attitude toward a defined place within it.

Despite Weber's position of 'value-neutrality' with regard to types of rationality the distinction between substantive and formal rationality gives a dual priority to the latter. First, as we have already shown, those forms of action displaying formal rationality yield the greatest degree of validity for the method of interpretive understanding. Secondly, formal rationality, when applied to ends themselves, is raised to universal significance. In a striking formulation, Brubaker argues (1984: 37) that the end of maximum calculability is not really an end but in modernity 'a *generalized means* that indiscriminately facilitates the purposeful pursuit of all ends'. Formal rationality has a universal significance because it is used to achieve any human purposes, i.e. it reproduces the teleological structure of action itself. Its extension and intensification in modernity reproduces the human drama in tragic mode as the narrative of the drive for greater formal rationality fatally undermines the very possibility of the values it originally serves.

WEBER AND FOUCAULT ON METHOD

The preservation of the autonomous subject as both creator and creation of the cultural sciences is fundamentally problematic from the perspective of a form of historical study of rationality which seeks the dispersion of forms of rationality and the analysis of the historically specific practices (of the body, power, self, and knowledge) having the formation of the subject and subjective capacities as their aim. As a heuristic guide, such a form of study should suspend propositions concerning the invariant nature of actors and the location of rationality as a universal capacity of them. Moreover, in its creation of a positive science founded on the capacity of the human subject for rationality, Weber's position is found at the opposite end of the spectrum of approaches to the critical history of rationality represented by Foucault's archaeology and genealogy. For these latter fields of study are most definitely not cultural sciences in Weber's sense but, rather, 'anti-sciences', or 'counter-sciences'. In this respect, Foucault's description of psychoanalysis, ethnology, and linguistics, as 'counter-sciences' may be applied to his own project:

> In relation to the 'human sciences', psychoanalysis and ethnology are rather 'counter-sciences'; which does not mean that they are less 'rational' or objective' than the other, but that they flow in the opposite direction, that they lead them back to their epistemological basis, and that they ceaselessly unmake that very man who is creating and re-creating his very positivity in the human sciences.

(Foucault 1970: 379)

While Weber's cultural sciences presuppose the metaphysical existence of a meaning-creating being as their necessary condition, the critical history of rationality seeks to problematise its given nature by constructing lineages of the historical emergence of its attributes and capacities within discursive, governmental, and ethical practices. In other words, the 'transcendental presupposition' of the cultural sciences becomes a key avenue of investigation for both archaeology and genealogy.

It may be observed that Foucault shares with Weber a radical perspectivism and a normalisation of knowledge. In Weber's case, however, that perspectivism takes the form of a radical *subjectivism*. It is grounded in an account of the subject and its capacities as representing a rational fold within the greater irrationality of the world. For Weber, nominalism is appropriate to a realm in which meaning is projected by the subject into a meaningless world. The cultural world is a world of given facts: the knowledge of this world consists in the establishment of connections between such facts by the investigator.

For Foucault's counter-science, archaeology, the positions of the knowing subject are governed by particular discursive and institutional conditions, and cannot form a stable foundation for the establishment of a definite form or realm of knowledge. Foucault's perspectivism is thus not rooted in the innate capacities of the subject but in the relation between forms of discourse, the historical struggles in which they are immersed, the institutional practices to which they are linked, and the forms of authority they presuppose. He describes his genealogies as 'anti-sciences' which, on the basis of the analysis of domains of knowledge and discourse (archaeology), use such historical knowledges in the course of struggle over the status and role of knowledge, particularly those forms of knowledge seeking to function as organised scientific discourse (Foucault 1980i: 82–5). Further, nominalism is not the form of knowledge appropriate to an essentialised cultural reality composed of meaningless facts. Rather, it is used as a new style and kind of critique. As Foucault points out in 'Questions of method' such a critique is not concerned with the delineation of a new field of positive knowledge, a cultural science, but with disarming that science, by problematisating the givenness of its contents and suppositions, and showing the process of emergence and formation of that which the cultural sciences take to be their empirical domain (Foucault 1981b: 14).

Weber's account of social action, of practical political and ethical conduct, depends on a straightforward decisionism. This is to say there can be no rational grounds for choosing between particular value positions. His account of social scientific knowledge links this decisionism to a positivist separation of fact and value in which sociology is limited to a hermeneutical role of reading back from action to its purposes, and to the technical roles of assessing the degree of appropriateness of the means chosen to given ends and the clarifying of ends. Such a position could hardly be further from that of Foucault. Against the reign of the arbitrary decision, we find in Foucault the immersion of critical analysis in struggles over the functioning and effects of knowledge. Against the positivist fetish of fact, we find the breaching of the self-evidence upon which the human sciences rest. Where nominalism is used in Weber to constitute cultural scientific knowledge, in Foucault it takes the form of an analysis of the historical conditions of formation of the concepts and objects of knowledge. And where Weber reserves a tiny fissure where the rational subject faces a meaningless and irrational social reality, Foucault discovers an historically given real traversed with multiple and contingent rationalities inscribed within heteromorphous relations of power, strategies and forms of calculation, and institutional practices and techniques.

It is true that Weber and Foucault can be located within a common domain of twentieth century thought which interrogates the role of rationality in modern societies. Yet they face opposite horizons: one toward the being of humankind, its experience of the world, its potential for a kind rationality, and its dilemmas in a world that cannot be delivered, even by the use of that potential, from its irrationality; the other to the multiple forms of rationality inscribed in heterogeneous and irreducible systems of practices through which the various identities of humankind are ceaselessly made and unmade, and in which its capacities are formed and transformed. In one, reason inheres in human conduct and is a necessary part of it. In the other, it is located within the forms of discourse, social arrangements and institutions, practices and techniques, that form conditions of conduct. From the perspective of Weber's presuppositions about the nature of social action and social science, it is clear that this anthropological structure of the subject forms an obstacle to a critical approach to rationality if by that we mean a strategy for grasping the intelligibility of specific and diverse forms of rationality, their conditions of emergence and existence, and their consequences for the subjective attributes, corporeal deportment, and ethical forms of life adequate to particular social relations.

The effect of treating rationality as an intrinsic feature of the human subject is to foreclose an analysis of the discursive conditions of sense and the dependence of forms of rationality on specific discursive forms, modes of calculation, and particular social techniques, practices and conditions. By reducing social action to the invariant potential of the subject, Weber imposes a spurious unity on diverse agencies and predisposes analysis toward the assumption of consistency on the part of the social actor as human subject. Affectual and traditional forms of action cannot be derived from Weber's model of social action because the latter assumes an intrinsic rationality on the part of the human subject. They become merely residual categories comprehensible only to the degree to which they share the features of rational social action. They exist, at least for the purposes of sociological knowledge, as deviations from the ideal model of rational action. Rationality is able to become manifest in the absence of irrational interferences. The meaning of rationalisation, whether of the value-rational type witnessed in the development of world religions, or the secular instrumental rationalisation of modernity, gains a problematic coherence because of its anchorage in the attributes of the subject. It is tempting to see both religious and secular rationalisation as processes simply fostering the realisation of the anthropological character of humanity by overcoming the obstacles presented by tradition and by other irrational factors. It is tempting, furthermore, to see secular rationalisation as the process allowing the subject to exercise its calculation of ends as well as means which is prevented by the adherence to absolue values of religions. It is precisely the exercise of this formal rationality that undermines all substantive ends turning Weber's historical sociology toward a philosophy of history resigned to the fate of a modern humankind in nostalgic search for an unrecoverable meaning.[3]

An 'effective history', according to Foucault's rendering of Nietzsche, 'places within a process of development everything considered immortal in man' (Foucault 1977b: 153). It is directed against the very identity Weber places at the heart of his enterprise and towards what may be called an analytic of diverse modes of subjectification. We shall address this issue of the modes of self-formation in later chapters. But Weber's historical sociology, and its central concept of rationalisation, seek to save another entity dear to the philosophy of history, the universal destiny of the West. It is to that we now turn.

Chapter 5

A 'specific and peculiar rationalism'?
Beyond the rationalisation thesis

> What is that fear which makes you seek, beyond all boundaries, ruptures, shifts and divisions, the great historico–transcendental destiny of the Occident?
>
> (Foucault 1972: 210)

The comprehensive unity of Max Weber's historical sociology has usually been sought in the problem of the origins and development of Western rationalism, and in the concept of 'rationalisation'. Conventional sociological wisdom attributes to Weber a 'rationalisation thesis', the thesis that both the unity of the development of Western civilisation and of Weber's own project are given by this notion. This thesis has more recently been subject to scrutiny and qualification, particularly following Tenbruck's (1980) seminal reappraisal of the themes of rationality, rationalisation, and disenchantment, and their place in Weber's *oeuvre*.

The bulk of this recent literature, however, reaffirms the centrality of the theme of rationality for Weber and for the social science he founded. In so doing it interrogates the nature of the historical framework in which that theme is situated and seeks to define more closely the status and scope of rationalisation. Of particular concern is the relation between the analyses of the religious rationalisations both within the West and within non-Western world religions, the secular rationalisations of modern economy, administration and law, and the delineation of definite 'value spheres' and 'life orders' (e.g. Mommsen 1974, 1987; Schluchter 1979, 1981, 1987; Roth 1987; Brubaker 1984; Habermas 1984).[1] Indeed, if recent commentary has effected any broad shift of emphasis, it is toward placing Weber's sociology of religion at the heart of his project and reinterpreting his concern with rationalisation in a universalistic and evolutionary fashion.

In this chapter, I would like to explore two themes of this 'return to Weber': first the universalisation of the notion of rationalisation and, secondly, what might be called its 'dispersion'. I shall argue that, while evidence for each of these interpretations can be found in Weber's work, neither resolve its considerable problems. These, instead, are linked to the place of the theme of rationalisation within the labyrinth of a particular philosophy of history.[2]

Perhaps the most striking legacy of this 'return to Weber' is the shift of rationalisation from a culturally specific phenomenon of the West to one of universal–historical significance. To this end, Tenbruck (1980: 323–6) criticises earlier scholars, such as Bendix (1966), for understating the provenance and significance of Weber's comparative studies in religion and for misunderstanding the key processes of rationalisation in all world religions, and, consequently, for identifying rationalisation with Occidental development. He declares: 'Today "rationalisation process" is taken to be synonymous with occidental development but, for Weber, this was a particular case of a more general class of events' (Tenbruck 1980: 321).

Such an assertion gives the tenor of much of this recent debate and what we might call the 'neo-evolutionary' view of rationalisation that has come to a wider social–theoretical audience through the writings of Habermas (especially 1984: 143–271). This view assumes that in the course of his life-work Weber acquired a universal–historical perspective built around the evolution of rationality (Tenbruck 1980: 332–42). However, we should also recall that there are important dissenting interpretations of Weber, particularly the previously noted one put forward by Hennis (1983, 1987), which, by refocusing analysis on the shaping of life-conduct through ethical practices and its implication for the 'characterology' of humanity effectively displaces this concern for rationality and its development.

If the matter of a shift in the field of application of the concept of rationalisation is relatively straightforward, its dispersion is rather less so. In order to accomplish his purposes, for example, Tenbruck (1980: 322) establishes a terminological distinction between the 'rationalisation process' as the whole sequence, religious rationalisation as 'disenchantment', and the post-religious rationalisation as 'modernisation'. Nevertheless, the dispersion of the concept is not simply a matter of breaking it down into phases and stages. Rather this dispersion goes to the origins, pace, direction, and ends, of a *multiplicity* of rationalisation processes, thus going to meet at least one dimension of the Foucauldian position on rationality. Accordingly, rationalisation is a 'multiplicity of distinct though interrelated processes arising from different historical sources, proceeding at different rates, and furthering different interests and values' (Brubaker 1984: 9). Further, this dispersion even contains relativist elements, well summed up in Weber's statement: 'Life may be rationalised from very different basic points of view and in very different directions' (1985: 77–8). One can, no doubt, with Nietzschean flourish, speak of a *genealogy* of rationalisation processes. Thus, Tenbruck (1980: 339–41) argues that the ideal type of the disenchantment–rationalisation process should be understood as a 'genealogical tree' in which there are several possibilities at each point, some of which may prove blind. Thus there are possibilities of partial rationalisations in various spheres (e.g. economic, technical, military, administrative), which can and do remain stuck and protected from comprehensive rationalisations.

Mommsen and others attempt to find a counter-principle by invoking the dialectic of charisma and rationalisation, in which disenchantment sets off the search for charisma that in turn initiates multiple religious rationalisations (Mommsen 1974, 1987; Tenbruck 1980: 337–9). Schluchter's influential interpretation (1979, 1981, 1987) seeks to displace a monolinear, teleological view of history and rationalisation by means of an evolutionary model in which different processes of rationalisation are components of a developmental sociology of world-history. In an allied move, Roth (1987) argues that Weber should be read as disaggregating German historicism, intricately linking a form of developmental history with a complex historical sociology in a combination of horizontal and vertical typologies. For him, Weber posited no simple rationalisation thesis, and 'modified the tradition of unilinear progress by viewing socio-cultural evolution along various dimensions and directions' (Roth 1987: 76).

In recent commentary, then, the unitary nature of rationalisation is dispersed, and the identification of rationalisation with Western modernisation is broken. It argues for a Weber without a 'rationalisation thesis', and with a concern for rationalisation in complex and recurrent relation to forces of charisma in all world religions. Moreover, the secular rationalisation of modernity is dependent on the prior processes of religious rationalisation, and all major world religions appear to have been effected by drives toward consistency and systematisation characteristic of the Judaic-Christian development. Rationalisation, and rationality, cannot be solely identified with the forces which have resulted in modernity in the West. At best, one can speak of a genealogy of rationality, together with wrong turns and blind alleys, and a limited, inner necessity of rationalisation, rather than an overriding unitary teleology of reason. Rationality itself is multidimensional and multidirectional, dependent on particular ethical and value standpoints.

These reinterpretations of Weber's notion of rationalisation arise from critical impulses: an anti-teleological one and an anti-relativist one. The first desires to reaffirm the centrality of processes of rationalisation, both in Weber and in all historical–sociological understanding, while rejecting a realisation thesis, viz. that rationalisation is the realisation of the constituent features of social action or forms of consciousness. These are, however, two incompatible goals. If rationalisation is not conceived as the realisation of the social and/or human capacity for rationality under favourable conditions, then its significance as a unifying theme for the understanding of historical development must fall. Conversely, if it is to act as a unifying theme for the comparative analysis of different cultures, then rationalisation must refer back to some universal or invariant aspect of social existence. The only candidates for this for Weber lie in the structure of the actor, its capacities and needs, or forms of historical consciousness. Thus each of these commentators is forced to locate some type of invariant which accounts for rationalisation, whether in the 'antimonic structure of human existence with its separation between objective and subjective worlds' (Schluchter 1987: 96), 'a constant and universal anthropological problematic' (Tenbruck 1980: 338), or 'a formal stock of universal structures of consciousness' (Habermas 1984: 180).

The anti-relativist impulse brings out these tensions in another form. Here, recent commentary makes claims that are both universalist and comparativist. First, it regards rationalisation as a process, or set of processes, of universal significance, rooted in the anthropology of needs or structures of consciousness. Secondly, it claims that there are highly divergent paths, objects, and directions of rationalisation. But in order to reconcile these two propositions, it must raise one form of rationalisation to the status of a norm by which all others can be compared and analysed. Thus, despite the universalisation of the notion of rationalisation, a special status is granted to what Weber called the 'specific and peculiar rationalism' of the West. Thus, these two sets of claims, in principle incompatible, can only be reconciled in a synthetic philosophy of history, a form of 'occidentalism'. It is this philosophy of history, and the ambiguous status it grants to the trajectory of the West, which allows the theme of rationalisation to gain its multiple senses and play its several roles.

The argument in the last chapter suggested that there are limits to introducing a minimalist notion of rationalisation as a set of heterogeneous processes with no necessary source, direction, or end, within a framework dominated by Weber's philosophical anthropology. Another limit to that dispersion is provided by occidentalism. The argument will now be completed by showing how the limits set by this philosophical anthropology are played off against those of occidentalism. Weber's historical sociology is defined by both of these problematics and is hence incapable of detaching notions of rationality from the spurious unifications of the human subject or the form of modern Western rationalism. This is perhaps why, despite his own efforts and those of interpreters, Weber's position on rationality can never approach the level of adequacy necessary to grasp different forms of rationality and their inscription in ensembles of social practices.

The examination of Weber's concept of rationalisation in light of these recent debates has its intrinsic worth as an examination of one of the 'master-concepts' of an historical sociology. But there are also two, rather more polemical points, which can be made within the present context of assessing Foucault's relation to historical sociology. The first is to ask whether the notion of rationalisation can be understood in such a way as to promote a possible fruitful engagement between these thinkers as key sources of critical historical studies of rationality. My answer is that for such an engagement to occur, Weber's specific historical–sociological studies, of religion, economy, state and law, must be divorced from the philosophy of history which inspires his metahistorical framework.

The second is to open up the investigation of the legacy of Weber's thought on rationality within critical theory. In the next chapter, I shall show that, in its appropriation of Weber's thought most clearly instanced in *The Dialectic of Enlightenment* (Horkheimer and Adorno 1972), the Frankfurt School understood Weber's notion of rationalisation precisely as the teleological realisation of instrumental reason in the modern West. It could neither envisage the use of Weber's work as a source of complex themes of rationality nor sketch an historical sociology of rationality. I shall also argue there that the resolution of the difficulties over the contemporary appropriation of Weber's *œuvre* is not, as Habermas contends, to rework and expand the concepts of action on which such notions of rationality depend, but to abandon the notion of rationalisation as a universal process of evolution, consistent amongst its various components, with a specific, unitary direction and set of imperatives, and ultimately intelligible in terms of types of social action. In other words, we must follow the anti-teleological impulse of recent commentary but not its anti-relativist one. This is not to argue that the Frankfurt School has fundamentally misread Weber. Rather, it is to suggest that its attempts to develop a critical historical approach to rationality have foundered on their Weberian heritage.

From this perspective, recent reworkings of Weberian notions of rationalisation have not gone far enough. If the notion of rationalisation is to be retained, it can no longer be the master-key of historical explanation. The notion of rationalisation should be used in a far more restricted sense of the processes in which formalised, sanctioned and systematic knowledge and institutional practices become mutually embedded. It thus opens up the question of what Foucault might have called the relation between 'regimes of truth' and 'regimes of practices' (1980h, 1981b). Foucault's critical analysis of forms of rationality displaces the concern common to both Weber and the Frankfurt School with the all-pervasive domination of instrumental reason in modernity which results in progressive bureaucratisation and a 'totally administered society'. This displacement is particularly clear in Foucault's studies of 'governmentality', i.e. the heterogeneous, non-subjective processes in which practices and techniques of governance have come to depend on discursive representations of their fields of intervention and operation (see, for example, Chapters 9 and 10 of the present study, and Foucault 1979a, 1982, 1988g, 1988h; Burchell, Gordon, and Miller 1991).

Let us now consider the way in which Weber's ambiguous oscillation between cultural particularism and universalism bedevils his understanding of rationalisation, exposes his position to ethnocentricism, and forecloses the possibility of a critical history of rationality.

OCCIDENTALISM AND UNIVERSALISM

In the celebrated 1920 'Author's Introduction', Weber (1985: 25) poses the problem: 'Why did not the scientific, the artistic, the political, or the economic development there [in China or India] enter upon the same path of rational-isation which is peculiar to the Occident?' His answer to this is quite straightforward. Weber claims that it is 'spiritual obstacles', in the form of 'magical and religious forces, and the ethical ideas of duty based upon them', that have obstructed the path to economic rationalism and the 'dispostion of men to adopt certain types of practical rational conduct' in the East (Weber 1985: 26–7). This answer thus strongly suggests the presence of a 'realisation' thesis of the progressive unfolding of practical rational conduct that was present in other of his formulations.[3]

However, my interest here is not so much in the answer, which reproduces certain of the problems of the types of rational action, but the nature of the question itself and the means with which Weber proposes to answer it. For he suggests that this is 'a question of the specific and peculiar rationalism of Western culture' (ibid. 26). It is this rationalism which Weber claims needs to be explained: 'It is . . . our first concern to work out and to explain genetically the special peculiarity of Occidental rationalism, and within this field that of the modern Occidental form' (ibid. 26). But why does this rationalism need to be explained and why is it so special?

The answer I propose is this. For Weber, the intelligibility of the concept of rationalisation is given within a definite philosophy of history. This is not the philosophy of history of the Enlightenment in so far as Weber is concerned to distance himself from notions of necessary progress, increasing reason, monolinear development, and so on. Moreover, it no longer takes the natural sciences and technology as the model of that progress. His is a rather more equivocal philosophy of history, although it retains the assumption that the modern development of Western rationalism poses questions fundamental for all human existence. Indeed, this is among the explicit themes of 'Science as a vocation', particularly where Weber discusses the relation of science and the development of Occidental culture (Weber 1970: 138–42). Weber's social theory remains within the terrain opened up by eighteenth century phil-osophies of history due to two fundamental presuppositions: first, it is possible to identify a definite conception of rationality with 'the West' and, secondly, this rationality has 'universal significance', i.e. for all other 'civilisa-tions'. These tenets in turn rest on the idea of 'civilisations' as unified cultural totalities with definite traditions consistent in themselves and heterogeneous to one another. Thus 'civilisations' are the quasi-naturalistic, given units of analysis and comparison.

The name which is most appropriate to this philosophy of history is 'occidentalism'. Occidentalism may be understood as a form of history, or rather a philosophy constructed on the basis of historical interpretation, that is written from the perspective of what it constructs as the 'modern West', and which detects in Western history something of universal significance. As such, it can take several forms. It might take the form of a teleology linking the West's modernity to the development of other civilisations as the endpoint of a necessary sequence of successive stages. This position, associated most recently with ideas of modernisation, is not Weber's mature one, although there are teleological implications of this kind implicit in his discussions of types of rational action. Occidentalism might also propose an evolutionary framework in which the development of the West reveals the secret of societal development in general, even where other civilisations have evolved in different directions. This is the position of much recent commentary on Weber, from Schluchter to Habermas. Finally, it might simply be the discovery within the West of an element of universal–historical significance, such as Karl Löwith's 'Western ethos' as the generalisation of purposive–rational action. In so far as Weber claims to find such an element within Western rationalisations, he partakes of this position, particularly in the retrospective account contained in his late synopses.

In any case, how the West's universality is established matters very little. Occidentalism basically construes diverse historical trajectories as the history of an unproblematic entity, Western civilisation, and then proceeds to claim universal–historical significance for the development of this civilisation. That occidentalism is an unproblematic feature of Weber's historical sociology is presupposed by virtually all recent commentary. Moreover, that same commentary assumes occidentalism as the given terrain for historical sociology. The main area of contestation in such commentary is the relation between Occidental history and universal history, which we shall now examine. Indeed, universalism is not a solution to occidentalism, as much contemporary Weberian scholarship and critical theory imagines, but its symptom.

A key target for current disputes is Bendix's 'intellectual portrait' which states more than once that 'Weber was preoccupied throughout his career with the development of rationalism in Western civilisation' (Bendix 1966: 9, 471), and the aim of his studies of China and India 'was to delineate religious orientation which contrasted sharply with the West' as a means to identify the specific character of the West (ibid. 268). Bendix portrays Weber's work as unified by a process immanent to the development of Western civilisation, discernible in its origins in Ancient Judaism, but being more recently motivated by secular forces resulting in the rationalisation of economy, law, and state in the modern West.

By contrast, in keeping with the universalisation of the notion of rationalisation, recent commentators no longer conceive Weber's mature approach to non-Western cultures, particularly in his sociology of religion, as merely marginal to his principal focus on the trajectory of the West. Thus a recent authoritative collection of essays on Weber begins by identifying the principal questions he pursued. First among these is 'how Western civilisation came to modernity, why other civilisations progressed in different directions, and the consequences of the attainment of modernity for the world as a whole – what Weber referred to as its "universal–historical significance"' (Whimster and

Lash 1987: 1). In this, these authors are at one with neo-evolutionary understandings of the concept of rationalisation. Yet some interpretation remains somewhat closer to the 'rationalisation thesis' as a thesis about the West. Brubaker, for example, asserts that Weber was concerned with the distinctiveness of Western rationalism, but immediately notes that his methodological writings 'emphasize the universal capacity of men to act rationally' (Brubaker 1984: 1). I shall now consider how Weber's theme of rationalisation can accommodate this diversity of positions within its own 'thought-space' and one of the attempts to justify a universalist and evolutionary reading of Weber.

In Weber's philosophy of history, one civilisation, the West, has a dual and somewhat ambiguous place that departs from what he called 'charisma of reason' of the Enlightenment (1968, 3: 1,209). On the one hand, the world is as multi-rational as it is multicultural: the West is simply a particular form of civilisation with a specific form of rationalism. The rise of this Western rationalism, rather than possessing any necessity, is contingent upon the configuration of a range of factors. Consider the example of the capitalist economy and capitalist economic conduct. Its existence presupposes a multiplicity of contingent conditions: 'rational accounting', the 'appropriation of all physical means of production', 'freedom of the market', 'rational technology', 'calculable law', 'free labour', 'the commercialisation of economic life', the 'separation of household and enterprise' (Weber 1927: 276–8; 1968, 1: 161–4). Yet, by themselves, these general presuppositions are insufficient to account for the institutionalisation of rational economic conduct. Weber argues (1927: 354) in his lectures: 'Necessary and complementary factors were the rational spirit, the rationalisation of the conduct of life, and a rationalistic economic ethic.' The important problem is how rational economic conduct becomes institutionalised:

> If the economic impulse in itself is universal, it is an interesting question as to the relations under which it becomes rationalised and rationally tempered in such fashion as to produce rational institutions of the character of capitalistic enterprise.

> (Weber 1927: 356)

This rationalisation of economic life is accomplished through the effects of the ethic of conviction embodied in Protestantism and its notion of calling, and is reproduced through the Protestant sects. Yet, because this is an unintended consequence of Protestant asceticism, the rise and spread of rational economic conduct takes on an aura of contingency. Rather than understanding Western rationalism as a universal and necessary form of reason, following the model of the progress of the sciences, Weber shifts attention to its particular and contingent nature, and the central role of the rationalisation of ethical conduct and its implications for economic life.

On the other hand, this civilisation retains its 'universal–historical significance' but no longer because all other civilisations can be located at different developmental stages through which they are bound to pass. It does so for two related reasons. First, as demonstrated by Tenbruck, Weber breaks with German historicism to rediscover, somewhat reluctantly, that he has gone over to the 'camp of evolutionism' (Tenbruck 1980: 333). There is a unidirectional development, not toward the formation of scientific reason, but internal to the codes of moral and practical conduct found in religious ethics. In each of the world religions a similar process deriving from 'the need to possess a rational answer to the problem of theodicy' is followed (ibid. 333). Religion thus 'advances to its own laws' (ibid. 334). The universal–historical process is that of *disenchantment*, the de-magicalisation of the world, and, in each case, it starts from the same problem of theodicy, the experience of suffering and injustice in the world and its reconciliation with religious world-images. The process of religious rationalisation, or disenchantment, together with the search for charisma, are universal. Indeed, Tenbruck describes them as 'anthropological constants' (ibid. 338).

Yet this still does not establish the universality of Western reason. This arises because the process of disenchantment is brought to finality in the West, and its institutions, such as the economy, state administration, and the law, come to embody both purposive–rational action and legal-rational forms of domination. Such an eventuality thus establishes a form of institutionalised rationality that relativises the value orientations and cultural contents of all civilisations against a formal rationality which both undermines and can be used in the service of any ends or values. Western rationalism, while the result of a specific process of rationalisation, is the culmination of a process of disenchantment that both magnifies the efficiency and productivity of human action while threatening the capacities of the actor of Weber's anthropology. It massively enlarges the capacity of teleological action itself, the capacity to achieve ends, while undermining all specific forms of meaning the subject gives to its behaviour. Further, because Weber conceives freedom as the freedom of the subject to give meaning, the undermining of this capacity entails a loss of freedom. This rationalism is hence of universal significance because it optimises the capacities of the human actor while presenting the actor with insoluble dilemmas as to the choice of values. It is clear that this is a philosophy of history in the sense of a narrative of the subject and its capacities, possibilities and dramas within the great sweep of History.

The status of Weber's thought on Western rationalism as a philosophy of history has a number of consequences. Above all, because this philosophy of history is constructed around the dilemmas of the subject manifest within the historical trajectory of the West leading to its modernity, the issue of the status of the subject can never be posed. This may actually raise acute problems of the ethnocentrism of this type of discourse. I take up this issue below. In a more general sense, however, its status as a philosophy of history allows the projection of the aporias of its conceptual apparatus onto the field of investigation itself. Rather than construing history as a form of (historiographical) practice that constructs series and regularities out of the space of dispersion of discursive, social and institutional practices with particular temporalities and loci, we have History as an arena of the expression of questions that, it is claimed, are fundamental to human existence.

The problem with this is that such fundamental questions typically reproduce the conceptual dilemmas of the enterprise itself. Consider the issue of universalism. The different strands of interpretation of Weber do indicate something of the fractures along which the unresolved tensions of Weber's philosophy of history begin to open up. Thus, as Schluchter has noted (quoted by Habermas 1984: 179–80), Weber understands his problematic of rationalism in the following way: first, 'the rationalism of mastering the world is *our* perspective'; yet, 'modern occidental culture is at the same time of such a kind that *all* civilised men could take an interest in it'. Again it might be asked, who are the 'we' implied in the notion of 'our' perspective, and how is the more inclusive category of 'all civilised men' delineated? Such categories invoke specific principles of inclusion and exclusion that are never made clear. This philosophy of history is thus riven with myriad problematic assumptions about the nature of civilisation, of those who qualify as civilised subjects. Even assuming that 'men' is here used in a gender non-specific way, such categories cannot remain the taken-for-granted foundations on which to erect a form of cultural or historical science. In other words, the construction of both the 'we', the subjects participating in Western rationalism, and other subjects of civilisation must become an element of problematisation.

This problem of Weber's equivocal universalism is noted by Habermas. For him, Weber 'only appears to mediate between two opposed positions on the claim to universality of the modern understanding of the world' (Habermas 1984: 180). This is an accurate diagnosis of Weber's dilemma and there is nothing controversial about it as such. However, when Habermas tries to resolve this ambiguity in the direction of universalism, he merely reproduces a different account of these dilemmas:

If we do not frame Occidental rationalism from the conceptual perspective of purposive rationality and mastery of the world, if instead we take as point of departure the rationalisation of worldviews that results in a decentered understanding of the world, then we have to face the question, whether there is not a formal stock of universal structures of consciousness expressed in the cultural value spheres that develop, according to their own logics, under the abstract standards of truth, normative rightness, and authenticity.

(Habermas, 1984: 180)

It should be noted that, contrary to his own self-understanding as breaking with the 'philosophy of consciousness', Habermas here reproduces an account of rationalisation in terms of structures of consciousness. To move from a subjectivist account of consciousness, and Weber's methodological individualism, to the structures of intersubjectivity progressively manifest in the rationalisation of world-views, does not entail a crucial break with philosophical anthropology and the philosophy of history. Further, to undertake this shift away from purposive rationality and the orientations of the actor, Habermas resurrects (ibid.180) a distinction between the form and content of rationality and culture, so that universalism 'regards the multiplicity of forms of life as limited to *cultural contents*, and it asserts that every culture must share certain *formal properties* of the modern understanding of the world, if it is at all to attain a certain degree of "conscious awareness" or "sublimation"'.

This is why Habermas (1984: 195–8) follows Tenbruck (1980) and Schluchter (1991) in their accounts of religious rationalisation as a universal–historical process of disenchantment that starts, in each of the major world civilisations, from the same problem, that of theodicy. These rationalisations of religious world-views, however, according to Habermas and contrary to more relativist readings, *do* point in the same direction, that of the internal validity, differentiation, and autonomy, of different 'cultural spheres of value', and the development of the inner logics of these spheres according to universal standards of truth, right, and authenticity, grounded in the procedures of communicative action. However, it is only in the modern West that this religious rationalisation is brought to an end, and that the potential of rationalised structures of consciousness could be realised by their embodiment in domains of institutionalised social action, or what Weber calls 'life-orders' (in the 'Intermediate Reflections') and cultural rationalisation could thereby be transformed into societal rationalisation (Habermas 1984: 213–15).

This attempted resolution can be approached on both metahistorical and methodological levels. First, at a metahistorical level, it simply retains all the problems that necessarily accompany the conceptual baggage of occidentalism. Hence the following questions cannot be posed within occidentalism. What is the status and role of concepts such as 'civilisation' and 'rationality'? What places them in positions of theoretical privilege? What are the conditions of the rational and civilised theorist? What principle of coherence is presupposed by the positing of the trajectory of a civilisation and its homogeneity? What is the basis of the unity it possesses and the historical continuity that is claimed? Secondly, a series of methodological questions emerge. How do we distinguish between occidental and other cultures? What constitutes the unity of this entity, the West? On what basis is it possible to talk of a *Western* rationalism? How can a comparative analysis of civilisation be undertaken that adopts what it takes to be the standpoint of one?

Weber's problematic, and Habermas' attempted recasting of it, can never resolve the opposition of universalist and relativist elements but only displace it onto ever-multiplying conceptual pairs, e.g. purposive–rational and value–

rational action, formal and substantive rationality in Weber, or formal properties and cultural contents. Both Weberian and Habermasian accounts of rationalisation, it should be noted, tend towards a form/content division in order to save the universality of rationality, although what counts as the formal properties of rationality – consistency, systematicity etc. in Weber, and the adherence to the implicit norms of communication in Habermas – are quite different. In both cases, however, what is considered to be the formal properties of rationality are protected from relativist scrutiny and then linked back to a specific philosophical anthropology.

The resolutions of the universalism–relativism opposition characteristic of this occidentalist philosophy of history then suppose that the formal properties of rationality refer back to either a universal structure of social action (whether purposive or communicative) contingently revealed first in the West, or universal structures of forms of consciousness or communication which are implicit in the trajectories of worldviews but which first become fully manifest in the West.

The universal structures of actors, consciousness, and so on, then, need only be identified with what are considered the formal properties of rationality to produce a universalist position. Habermas' resolution or rectification of Weberian notions of rationalisation again rests upon some notion of the universal potentials and capacities of the actor or structures of consciousness realised – however imperfectly – in the Western trajectory. The fact that Habermas shifts focus from instrumental rationality to communicative rationality does not alter the thought-figure in which he is operating or the closure effected by it.

There are two perspectival implications of the above discussion. The first is that there is no necessity for a resolution of Weber's dilemma as Habermas imagines. Indeed, an alternative, and certainly more readily defended, position, would be to simply forsake this problematic, and quit its characteristic themes of the universal significance of Western rationalism in favour of an analysis of the functioning of forms of rationality within ensembles of social practices. This indeed would seem to be the option presented by various formulations of Foucault on the question of rationality. There is no necessity for a critical history of rationality to declare itself in an argument that only becomes pertinent within a problematic of occidentalism in which the question of the trajectory of the spurious unity of the West is posed and given unique privilege.

Habermas' account is instructive since it draws attention to the way in which cultural particularism and universalism coexist in Weber's thought. However, in regarding this as a contradiction to be resolved, rather than a feature of a specific discursive form, Habermas remains fundamentally tied to such an occidentalist framework and has, in this respect, not advanced beyond Weber's position. He merely displaces the universal element of Western development from teleological onto communicative action. The possibility of a critical history of rationality outside the opposition of universalism and particularism is not considered.

The second is perhaps more serious for it concerns the positive thematisation of that which occidentalism cannot pose, the position of the subject of knowledge and theory. In any account that assumes the universality of forms of consciousness and/or action no account of the conditions of existence of the theorising subject can be had because it is presupposed as a particular case of a more general universal nature. Thus Weber or Habermas claim the position of their respective versions of the universal rational social subject and, by implication, exclude all other versions of the position of the theorising subject. By contrast, as was shown in relation to Kant, Foucault argues that the central problematisation concerns the epistemic, political and ethical conditions that define the relation of the critical thinker to the present of a specific cultural ensemble, and the limits and potentials of that present. To ignore the latter option, and adopt the position of the universal social subject, is to risk a particular danger – that of ethnocentrism. I want now to examine whether this danger befalls Weber.

Ethnocentricism

It is this question of the self-constitution of the theorising subject that leads us to raise the sensitive question of whether this Weberian occidentalism entails ethnocentrism. This danger of ethnocentrism represents one of the less edifying pitfalls of playing the game of cultural relativism versus universalism constituting Weber's problematic. For the purposes of the following discussion, I would suggest that ethnocentrism can be understood in the following ways. First, any general preoccupation with the development and comparison of cultural groups (whether as ethnic groups, races, nations, or civilisations) as unique and homogeneous unities could be regarded as broadly ethnocentric. In this sense, Weber's thought on rationality, like a fair portion of the social sciences, is clearly – and for the most part inoffensively – ethnocentric. What is less clear is whether Weber is ethnocentric in a second sense of the term. Here, ethnocentrism consists in the presentation of the particular perspective of the theorising and knowing subject as a universal position.

To consider whether Weber's historical studies qualify in this second sense, it is worth carefully reading the opening sentence of the 'Author's Introduction':

A product of modern European civilisation, studying any problem of universal history, is bound to ask himself to what combination of circumstances the fact should be attributed that in Western civilisation, and in Western civilisation only, cultural phenomena have appeared which (as we like to think) lie in a line of development having universal significance and value.

(Weber 1985: 13)

This statement of the type of endeavour undertaken in his sociology of religion certainly falls within the bounds of occidentalism as I have defined it, despite its ironical qualification. The implication of this for the study of world, non-Western, religions, is clear. In the same piece, he states that the study of each of them 'quite deliberately emphasises the elements in which it differs from Western civilisation' (ibid. 27).

It has been suggested this passage indicates that Weber did *not* indulge in ethnocentricism (Schluchter 1979: 22n.). It is true that Weber did not see Western rationalism as the only possible product of processes of rationalisation, and argued that rationalisation applies to different objects and works in different directions. Yet neither of these moves protects Weber from the first sense of ethnocentricism stated above. A pervasive, and therefore somewhat taken-for-granted, characteristic of Weber's schema is the supposition that it is possible to understand processes of rationalisation as trajectories of cultural entities expressing particular inner principles remaining coherent over long durations, i.e. as civilisations.

Weber's position, however, goes further than the assumption of civilisations as the given units of comparative historical sociology. The claim of the 'universal significance' for the 'special and peculiar rationalism' of the West can only be distanced from a more explicit version of the second sense of ethnocentricism by irony or contradiction. Thus Weber's qualification, 'as we like to think', may be thought to take an ironical distance from ethnocentrist accounts entailing a universalist priority for Western development. However, the 'we' invoked here can only possess a unity in terms of the notion of 'product of modern European civilisation'.

It might be argued that this position is fully consonant with the distinction between 'evaluation' and 'value-relatedness' that Weber inherits from Heinrich Rickert (Hirst 1976: 52). Here, the 'value-relatedness' of the cultural sciences is thought in terms of the selection of subject matter and problems for empirical analysis in terms of supra-individual cultural values (Weber 1949: 22). In this case, however, the value-relatedness of Weber's problem of Western rationalism concerns the value that 'products of modern European civilisation' give to that rationalism. This path, however, leads only to an insoluble dilemma. On the one hand, the problem might be resolved by saying that Western rationalism has universal significance for Western subjects constituted in Western civilisation. Its universalism is thus only given from the value standpoint of Western subjects. If this is admitted, however, Western rationalism cannot make good on its claims of universalism. On the other hand, if instead the universalist claims are insisted upon, then the value-relatedness of Western rationalism must fall. Weber thus manages to commit himself both to the particularity of a Western perspective constructed as his own and to making universalist claims for that perspective. Weber seeks the impossible path of overcoming ethnocentricism within an occidentalist framework that asserts the universality of Western rationalism.

Weber's position fluctuates between universal and cultural relativism reflecting the unstable amalgam of his version of occidentalism. I would suggest that his incomplete relativism merely nuances, rather than overcomes, the ethnocentricism of his occidentalist vision. Consider all the adjectives used to describe what is rational in Weber's writings, such as 'systematic', 'deliberate', 'calculable', 'rule-governed', 'impersonal', 'instrumental', 'exact', 'quantitative', 'methodical', 'predictable', and so on – Brubaker (1984: 2) isolates sixteen on the basis of Weber's characterisation of modern capitalism and ascetic Protestantism. Despite the claim that the concept of rationality is evaluatively neutral, its characterisation by means of such terms remains open to the charge that what is rational for Weber necessarily encompasses qualities positively valued within a specific form of life. Such terms might be regarded as less descriptors of a formal rationality than as the discursive means to define the contours of a particular conduct of life and the attributes appropriate to it.

This form of life is built into Weber's methodology at the level of his social-action concepts, as I have shown in the previous chapter. Sociological knowledge as a product of Western rationalism can best understand those forms of action that most perfectly approximate the characteristics of instrumental reason. Other forms of action can only be understood from the perspective of such rationality and only in so far as they deviate from the ideal type of purposive-rational action. Moreover, at the level of comparative macro-historical sociology, as I have just mentioned, Weber's position is that the study of non-Western world religions deliberately emphasises the differences from the development of Western culture and society. Similarly, it is only in the modern West that theory and reality tend to coincide. In regard to economic conduct, for example, Weber argues (1975) that the understanding of the capitalist epoch is premised on the fact that the relation between the theoretical propositions of the marginal value theory and reality is one of constantly increasing approximation. When such methodological injunctions give priority to instrumentally rational action, occidental development, and capitalist economic action, it is difficult to see why the uniqueness of modern Western rationalism and the methodical conduct of life of rational capitalism are persistently emphasised in the absence of a conception that can only be called ethnocentric in a strong sense, one identifying the 'point of view' afforded by a particular form of life with the universal conditions of knowledge.

In sum, occidentalism, as the practice of reading diverse trajectories, conflict, mutation, and division, through the grille of the 'great historico-transcendental destiny' of the West, to quote *The Archaeology of Knowledge* (Foucault 1972: 210), does not simply form a fundamental obstacle to an effective critical study of rationality but – as exemplified by Weber – exposes its practitioners to the legion dangers of ethnocentricism. Indeed the very notion of a distinctive 'Western rationalism' or 'Western ethos' prevents the critical analysis of diverse forms of rationality both inside and outside the fluid, and usually unspecified, spatial and temporal boundaries of the West.

One can say that the type of comparative historical sociology envisaged by Weber does assume, like ethnology itself, 'the historical sovereignty of European thought and the relation that can bring it face to face with other cultures including as well as with itself' (Foucault 1970: 379).

The construction of a perspectivism around the notion of the West forecloses several avenues and arenas of investigation. For example, no account of the unity of Western history, or the form of its social, historical, or discursive constitution can be given. If the constituent subject imposes a spurious unity at the level of social action, notions of 'the West' and 'civilisation' repeat this unity at the level of the trajectories of social relations and forms of rationality. Such a position cannot account for the fluidity and contingency of the notion of 'the West', its lack of specificity, and how this term functions as a given within very different forms of discourse. Thus what is covered by such a category depends on its place in different geopolitical, diplomatic, military, historical and economic discourses. It is true to say that history of the occidentalism, as a social and discursive construction, with definite conditions of existence and effects, has yet to be written. The West – with the notable exception of Said (1985) and more recently Stuart Hall (1992) – has yet to become a domain of genealogical problematisation!

Further, if we understand Weber as writing an occidentalist universal history, it would severely circumscribe the usefulness of his analyses and bring them closer to the philosophies of history of the eighteenth century. Such analyses would seem to be mesmerised by notion of civilisation and the problem of the universality of the West. Rather than forming the basis for a critical history of forms of rationality and their inscription in regimes of social practices, his studies of religion would be limited to concerns with the origins, nature, and future of the modern West, and its special and peculiar rationalism. The study of non-Western cultures would be either to refine definitions of Western rationalism, or to decide the degrees of variation from and similarity to the modern Western form. If Weber is to be read as a variant within occidentalism, then the distance separating his history from the eighteenth century philosophies of history is not as great as might be imagined. In the reduction of historical trajectories to the unitary processes of the development of civilisations, and the placement of reason at the centre of those processes, Weber would appear only to have partially broken with the progressivist philosophies of histories of the eighteenth century, no matter how ambivalent is his concern with Western rationalism and Enlightenment rationality.

A minimalist account?

Weber's historical sociology is thus confined within a philosophy of history bound finally to a philosophical anthropology. I want now to consider whether it is completely disabled from the viewpoint of an historical sociology of rationality seeking to employ a minimalist account of rationality, such as that found in Foucault, and whether it is possible to detect another strand of Weber which saves his approach.

There are indications of such a minimalist account within Weber's writings. For example:

> There is, for example, rationalisation of mystic contemplation, that is of an attitude which, viewed from other departments of life, is specifically irrational, just as much as there are rationalisations of economic life, of technique, of scientific research, of military training, of law and administration. Furthermore, each one of these fields may be rationalised in terms of very different ultimate values and ends, and what is rational from one point of view may well be irrational from another. Hence, rationalisations of the most varied character have existed in various departments of life and in all areas of culture. To characterise their differences from the view-point of cultural history it is necessary to know what departments are rationalised and in what direction.
>
> (Weber 1985: 26)

This is from the 1920 'Author's Introduction'. The same point is made in the *Protestant Ethic* itself when Weber suggests the first proposition of any study of rationalism should be that one may 'rationalise life from fundamentally different basic points of view and in very different directions' (ibid. 77–8). Habermas suggests that such a position poses questions about the relation between cultural relativism and the universality of the rationalisation process (1984: 181). As I have shown above, such an interpretation would place Weber firmly within the irresolvable oppositions of occidentalism. But can a position be found which places Weber outside this philosophy of history? Is it possible to find an interpretation in which Weber acknowledges, against the grain of his principal themes and concepts, that his historical sociology requires only a minimalist conception of rationalisation and rationality?

For recent commentary, despite the attempted 'deconstruction' of the notion of rationalisation, Weber is still generally allowed an underlying universal–historical perspective that unifies the fragmentation and heterogeneity of his specific historical analyses. That perspective is rooted in the lessons of the form of rationalisation of the West culminating in Western rationalism (Brubaker 1984: 8). Tenbruck even suggests (1980: 344–6) that it was in this course of investigating the multiplicity of rationalisations in 'The Economic Ethics of World Religions' that Weber acquired a 'universal–historical perspective'. From this universal perspective is presumed to issue Weber's central theme: 'what is rationality?' (Tenbruck 1980: 343). However, it is precisely such an interrogation of the nature of rationality and its development in the West that lead Weber away from a minimalist version of rationalisation towards an account of rationality in terms of the capacities of the human subject and their problematic development in the universalising rationality of the West. The notion of the limited and partial rationalisations emphasised in this literature, varying in their objects and directions, and even their substantive ends, does not touch the unity of the notion of rationalisation in the structure of needs and capacities considered as an anthropological invariant. The imperatives to maximum calculability, certainty, and consistency, characteristic of formal rationality, return us to a humanist version of rationalism. The anthropological basis of Weber's historical and socio logical thought thus presents important limits to an analysis of a world traversed by a plurality of rationalities and an analysis of the ways in which such rationalities arise from, codify, and direct, forms of social practice. Weberian historical sociology is led away from the critical task of grasping the diverse and heterogeneous forms of rationality inscribed within socio-cultural practices and towards a philosophy of history that sketches the inner dilemmas of humanity in a modernity both realising and undermining its essential nature.

Weber's historical sociology has left us with a rich and diverse corpus of work which forms an ambiguous legacy. On the other hand, his empirical sociologies of religion, of law, the economy and the state, remain valuable resources for critical historical studies today. However, his approach to the pivotal issue of rationality is limited by its location in a philosophy of history constructed around the problematic term, 'rationalisation', and grounded within a philosophical anthropology.

As for the massive industry of Weber commentary, it is necessary to pass a severe judgement. On the positive side, such commentaries make us more sensitive to the dispersion of themes and concepts existing in Weber's thought and the heterogeneity between texts. However, the real failure of this industry has been its inability to learn from the dispersion it has revealed. Rather than capitalising on it, it seeks to deny it. Thus, and this may be a fundamental problem with much intellectual history, they remain committed to the search for the thematic unity of Weber's *oeuvre*. In doing so, and by presenting spurious candidates for this 'central theme', from rationalisation to rationality, the value of this scholarship is extremely limited.

WEBER AND FOUCAULT REVISITED

I began this discussion (at the beginning of the previous chapter) by noting the variety of positions on the comparison of Foucault and Weber on issues of rationality and rationalisation. In the course of the discussion of Weber's concepts and problematic, I have sought to indicate some obstacles to an easy assimilation. Of course, there are themes and analyses in Weber, such as those of discipline, administration, ethical practice, and asceticism, as well as rationality, that overlap with those of Foucault. Moreover, in a project so open to redescription and reformulation as Foucault's, it is to be expected that his paths should cross those of Weber. None of this is in doubt. Nevertheless, it would be difficult to conceive of approaches as different in terms of fundamental presuppositions and methodological precepts, and, indeed, styles of analysis.

I have already noted that the similarities of perspectivism and nominalism were only superficial. The aims of their methodologies, the grounding of their perspectives, and the uses of nominalism are vastly different. These differences crystallise around the nature of the social actor and the relation of rationality and the subject. At base, Weber's philosophical anthropology is fundamentally alien to the problematising discourse of Foucault's historical studies which set themselves against any such universalist premises.

In this chapter, I have shown that Weber's deliberations on rationality, no matter how finely nuanced and complex, finally return to a philosophy of history grounded in questions about the origin and nature of Western rationalism. Moreover, Weber's perspectivism claims a universal significance for itself and thus is imperilled by ethnocentrism. Here again, one could point to a host of similarities: the concerns to establish a non-reductive historical study of forms of rationality, to thematise the impact of religious practices, to consider the relation between discourse, practice and the human body, and so on (see Turner 1987b). However, Weber – despite his own debt to Nietzsche – reproduces in his philosophy of history the central vices Foucault found in 'continuous history' in *The Archaeology of Knowledge* and in the uses to which history is put in his essay on Nietzsche. Of the former, Foucault said:

> Continuous history is the indispensable correlative of the founding function of the subject: the guarantee that everything that has eluded him may be restored to him; the certainty that time will disperse nothing without restoring it in a reconstituted unity; the promise that one day the subject – in the form of historical consciousness – will once again be able to appropriate, to bring back under his sway, all those things that are kept a distance by difference, and find in them what might be called his abode. Making historical analysis the discourse of the continuous and making consciousness the original subject of all historical development and all action are the two sides of the same system of thought. In this system, time is conceived in terms of totalization and revolutions are never more than moments of consciousness.
>
> (Foucault 1972: 12)

For Foucault, then, a universal historical subject and continuous philosophy of history are the two sides of the one coin. On such an analysis it is unsurprising that Weber's appeal to the development of a civilisation and a rationalism with universal significance, i.e. the appeal to an occidentalist philosophy of history, returns us to a vision of history as a journey of the subject, a fateful one in which the increase of the subject's powers results in a loss of its freedom.

Moreover, in its presumption about the trajectory of civilisations forming the given or even natural units of analysis, Weberian history takes as its objects dubious cultural totalities and their process of totalisation. By binding historical sociology to both these metanarratives of subject and civilisation Weber's analyses foreclose the possibilities of an 'effective history' which introduces discontinuity, defines events in their uniqueness, uproots tradi tional foundations, and deprives itself of the reassuring affirmation of identity (Foucault 1977b: 152–7). To the degree to which rationalisation is a necessary process with roots in an essentialism of the subject, it becomes less a means for an historical sociology to analyse heterogeneous rationalities and their relation to the direction of conduct and modes of subjectification than a reassurance of the fateful necessity of the Western course of development. This is in sharp contrast to Foucault's pluralist approach to rationalities that requires us to divorce the analysis of rationalities from the putative attributes of human subjects. As we showed in relation to Kant, Foucault's work locates rationality not within the attributes of the actor or the features of action, but within the discursive, institutional, and practical conditions of action.

We might also invoke the difference, as Foucault saw it (1972: 9–10), between a *total* history and a *general* history as a means of thinking about the Weber–Foucault relation. A total history seeks a governing principle of a civilisation, epoch or society, which accounts for its coherence; it seeks to establish an homogeneous network of relations and causality across a clearly defined set of spatial and temporal co-ordinates; it imposes a totalistic form of transformation, and it is able to divide history into definite, cohesive, periods and stages. This is Weber's project, and in so far as users of Weber's work today seek to derive a characterisation of modernity as a period from Weber, or postulate on ineluctable process of rationalisation (not to mention its closely allied derivatives, modernisation, bureaucratisation, and so on), his torical sociology cannot be a critical study, or a problematising discourse, but rather a version, no doubt attenuated and deprived of the optimism of progress, of the philosophy of history in existence since the eighteenth century. If enlightenment poses the problem of the present, its singularity and the possibilities contained within it (as Foucault thought, following Kant), then the invocation of all these transhistorical schemas, all these 'isations', is an unenlightened submission to the tutelage of the formula. Sociology may be a child of the Enlightenment, but that does not means it automatically becomes an enlightened and mature adult.

A general history, on the other hand, is that form of critical history that exists in the space opened up by the double rejection of the themes of a philosophical anthropology and those of a synthetic philosophy of history. Foucault terms this 'a space of dispersion' (1972: 10). Rather than a generative principle, such a history seeks series, divisions, differences of temporality and level, forms of continuity and mutation, particular types of transitions and events, possible relations and so on. A general history would be a non-reductive, non-totalising, one which specifies its own terrain, the series it constitutes, and the relations between them. It is the introduction of this approach into the field covered by an historical sociology such as Weber's which opens up an attention to detail, grain, and complexity, and the specification of form of relation which is indispensable if that enterprise is to move beyond caricatures of historical periodisation passing for a science of social development.

Of course, the texts and statements we call 'Weber' reveal a divided being. Alongside the totalising, essentialist, Weber, discussed above, another Weber is revealed particularly by the commentary of Hennis (1983). For this Weber, his basic action concepts, and 'south-west German neo-Kantianism', are relegated to minor and even negligible contributions in comparison with a qualitative interest in humanity as an historical variable (in *Menschentum*). This Weber would indeed shift the focus from the significance of the general process by which rationality develops to problems of the social and historical constitution of the subject, its capacities and modes of conduct (the *Lebens-führung* or life-conduct). In this case, the historical studies of Foucault and Weber would indeed share a common terrain (Gordon 1987).

Nevertheless, there must be some doubt that we can dismiss the importance of the basic concepts in *Economy and Society*, the writings on methodology, and the retrospective synthetic synopses, so readily. However much we may like to liberate Weber's historical sociology from the positions of his epistemology and philosophy of history, we still must come to terms with the way in which Weber has been understood, particularly by sociologists. The Weber of these texts, and the Weber of received sociological opinion, defines the contours of his historical sociology of rationality against the proposed transcendental ontology of the subject on the one hand, and the concern for the destiny of the West on the other.

From the perspective of Foucault's Nietzscheanism, these contours of Weber's project form limits to an 'effective' history. On the one hand, Weber's histories confirm the presuppositions of the cultural sciences. Foucault, on the other, tells us more than once that his historical studies are conceived not as the basis for a cultural science but rather as 'counter-sciences' or 'anti-sciences' challenging the claims of established human science about the identity of the subject. He also informs us that the main theme of these histories has been the formation of the subject in modes of knowledge, techniques of power, and ethical practices (Foucault 1982). At this level, it is harder to imagine a project more opposed to a neo-Kantian cultural science premised on an anthropological invariant.

If Weber's historical sociology finds its inner limit in the notion of the potentially rational subject, it finds its external limit in the notion of the homogeneous totalities making up 'civilisations'. As I have argued elsewhere (Dean 1986), Foucault's own historical analyses, particularly the first volume of the *History of Sexuality* (1979b), are not entirely free from a preoccupation with the form of the West's modernity. There, Foucault occasionally took refuge in the notion of the West as something more than a metaphor. Nowhere is this exemplified more than in his opposition (later abandoned [Foucault 1986d] between a *scientia sexualis*, characteristic of the West and culminating in psychoanalysis, and an *ars erotica* said to flourish in ancient and Eastern societies (Foucault 1979b: 53–57). Given our present concern with Foucault's *methods*, we should simply note here that this apparently occidentalist orientation is fundamentally at odds with the methodological principles of his critique of cultural totalities and his embrace of effective history.

There is much in Weber which contributes to such an effective history, e.g. his analyses of Protestantism and its unintended consequences, his studies of discipline, and much in his sociology of religion. In his case, however, such an effective history was made despite, not because of, his basic orientations. For Foucault, despite lapses in the organisation of his historical studies, this effective history centrally defines his whole body of historical work.

Chapter 6

Absent history and enlightenment dialectics

... if I had encountered the Frankfurt School while young, I would have been seduced to the point of doing nothing else in life but the job of commenting on them.

(Foucault 1991b: 119–20)

Perhaps! Despite this startling confession, Foucault did not become a critical theorist. Indeed, it is possible to distinguish quite clearly between critical theory as practised by the Frankfurt School and the critical history that can be derived from Foucault's analytic practice. One way of reading the present chapter is as an argument for a critical history over a critical theory.

In this chapter, I address the account of rationality, domination, and subjectivity provided by Horkheimer and Adorno in the seminal statement of the Frankfurt School of critical theory of the 1940s, *The Dialectic of Enlightenment* (1972) (hereafter, *Dialectic*). It is important to consider this text and associated writings from the point of view of my concerns for a number of reasons. Above all, these writings pose the challenge of the rational criticism of reason, i.e. a critical approach to reason seeking neither the wholesale abandonment or destruction of reason. They are thus a part of a body of literature that does not give in to what Foucault called the 'blackmail of the Enlightenment' (1986i: 42–3), the requirement that one must declare whether one is for or against the Enlightenment for fear of lapsing into irrationalism.

Secondly, in seeking to accomplish this task, these Frankfurt thinkers move toward the terrain occupied by a critical historical sociology. However, rather than developing a critical and effective history, they announce a synthetic social theory that provides a transhistorical schema of social development. This social theory, reduced to its barest bones, attempts to combine Weber's notion of rationalisation with an Hegelian–Marxist critique of capitalist society in terms of reification and a Freudian account of civilisation as self-renunciation. The critical theorists are Freudo-Marxists who seek to achieve the integration of Freud and Marx via Weber.

Finally, the cornerstone of the critique of modernity undertaken in the

Dialectic is the sustained attempt to establish the identity between instrumental reason and domination. This move may be thought to anticipate the genealogical thematic of power–knowledge, or *pouvoir–savoir*, of Foucault's historical studies of the 1970s. Like Foucault, Horkheimer and Adorno show that reason, far from being universal, is in particular, rooted in systems of power and domination, and linked to historic processes of self-formation. Unlike Foucault, they undertake a critique of reason that *is* total because they regard instrumental reason as coextensive with Western reason. Allusions to an alternative or broader form of reason within this framework are largely gestural. For these theorists, reason cannot become multiple, and the diverse processes of self-formation are telescoped into the single theme of the renunciation of the self.[1]

In sum, the Frankfurt theorists address major concerns also animating the writings of Foucault and the effective history of rationality. In so doing, their work would appear to offer an opportunity for a critical historical inquiry into forms of reason and knowledge, power and domination, and self and subjectivity. This, however, is not the case. It is the failure to constitute an effective historical inquiry that may make the choice of this text, and critical theory more generally, appear misplaced from the point of view of our concern with historical sociology and critical history. Yet my concern is not the body of literature that has achieved the appellation, 'historical sociology', or applied it to itself. Rather, it is with the statement of the conditions for an historical sociology able to confront questions of rationality, selfhood, and power. The *Dialectic* bears heavily on these themes but falls short of anything that might resemble such a project. Nevertheless, the theoretical and conceptual reasons critical theory fails to provide a critical historical inquiry into rationality and subjectivity and a relational and strategic conception of power are most instructive.

I argue that this failure is not simply an oversight or lack of interest in this field of inquiry but arises from the constitutive features of critical theory, at least as it is enunciated by the Frankfurt theorists in their nodal statements of the 1940s. These features include its reliance on a philosophically conceived notion of the subject, a Hegelian notion of rationality, and, perhaps most importantly, an endorsement of a totalised version of instrumental rationality inherited from Weber by way of those such as Karl Löwith and Georg Luckacs. The very self-conception of the enterprise, condensed into the term 'critique', might also be called into question, as I suggest in a postscript.

Weber's concept of rationalisation becomes, for the Frankfurt School, a golden thread drawing together the diverse themes of a dialectical philosophy of history into an analysis and critique of Western development and modernity. This is as true for Habermas – discussed in the next chapter – as it is for Horkheimer and Adorno. For these thinkers, rationalisation becomes identified with the path of the progressive extension and deepening of *instrumental* rationality in the West. The *Dialectic*, as the central theoretical achievement of at least one phase of this school, would be unintelligible outside the framework provided by the Weberian themes of rationalisation and disenchantment. It is here we find the concept of rationalisation stripped of many of Weber's hesitations and ambiguities and forced into the service of an unremitting critique of the forms of reason and knowledge said to be characteristic of modern society. In what follows, I provide a critical commentary on the central thesis of this text and its implications, and then compare Foucault's critical history of rationality with the positions of this and related works along two key dimensions: first, the terrain of historical investigation and use of historical materials; and, secondly, the various conceptualisations of subjectivity and rationality and their consequences for critical historical inquiry.

The problem of the philosophy of history is again raised by the conceptualisation of these critical theorists. In both this and the next chapter, I argue that critical theory is unable to escape its status as a definite philosophy of history because domination and power are conceived in terms of the repression of the universal attributes of the subject and a totalised instrumental mastery characterising the whole trajectory of the West. In other words, the constitutive theoretical strategies of critical theory commit it to a philosophy of history that excludes the possibility of an effective historical study and thus of the type of historical sociology envisaged here. Rather than opening up the question of the constitution of forms of subjectivity, domination, and rationality to a field of critical and reflexive historical study, critical theory remains wedded to an essentialist conception of reason, an opposition between essential subjective capacities and domination, and an eschatological narrative of the loss and (somewhat deferred) reconciliation of the unity of humanity and nature. In so far as any effective historical analysis is a contingent effect of this framework, it is vitiated by an interpretation of the Weberian thematic of rationalisation that wraps the fateful dialectic of enlightenment and myth, reason and domination, in a blanket of irreversibility, completion, and finality. The narrative of Western Reason is how rationality as critique and autonomous subjecthood is lost in the instrumental domination of outer, and inner, nature. Horkheimer and Adorno unwittingly find themselves victims of a total critique of modernity with only the gestural politics of negation left as a vestige of uncontaminated reason. The theoretical gains in this manoeuvre cannot compensate for its analytic and empirical deficits.

By contrast, Foucault has left us with a series of critical and historical inquiries not into the nature of a transhistorical Reason but into the forms of rationality inscribed in a variety of institutional practices. Moreover, because these studies are not founded on a philosophical conception of the subject and its attributes they are able to undertake a manifold analysis of the formation of the subject and subjective attributes within systems of power and domination, knowledge and rationality, and ethics. From the viewpoint of an historical sociology concerned with issues of rationality and subjectivity, the suppositions of such studies warrant our attention as opening up a far richer terrain of inquiry. This chapter is written not primarily to undermine the claims of certain kinds of critical theory but to suggest why certain theoretical strategies have proved more fruitful than others in a domain that all sides would accept is of the utmost importance.

THE DIALECTIC OF ENLIGHTENMENT

The centrality of the problem of enlightenment in late-twentieth century social thought is undoubtedly largely due to this one key text of the Frankfurt School. Conceived and written in America in exile in the war years, published in Holland in 1947, and not officially republished until 1970, and only then translated into English, it is an uncompromising, multi-layered, dense, theoretical treatise of dialectical negation of what the authors took to be the path of reason which has culminated in its positivist, instrumental, form in modern Western civilisation. In it, the most prominent authors of the first generation of the Frankfurt School present a theoretical polemic against the instrumental form of reason they regard as characteristic of modernity, in which 'power and knowledge are synonymous' and 'enlightenment is totalitarian' (Horkheimer and Adorno 1972: 4, 6).

The critical core that is the first chapter of the work elaborates the thesis stated in its introduction, that 'myth is already enlightenment; and enlightenment reverts to mythology' (ibid. xvi). Yet this polemic takes the form of a *critique* of enlightenment, an act of negation leading to a purification of the irrational within reason, 'intended to prepare the way for a positive notion of enlightenment which will release it from entanglement in blind domination' (ibid. xvi). In a sense, the aim of the dialectic of enlightenment is the liberation of reason from itself, the recuperation of a truly rational reason from its present form.

To leave the notion of critique of the *Dialectic* at this point would be incomplete. For here 'critique' functions in both a conventional and also a far more radical way. Inherited from the German Enlightenment and Marx, this form of critique first aims to liberate the rational potential shackled by the immersion of reason in ideology, domination, and other non-rational dross (cf. Habermas 1987a: 116–18). In other words, the unmasking of the ideological content of reason is a step toward the revelation of emancipatory truth. Yet Horkheimer and Adorno, in an ambivalent relation to Nietzsche, extend the notion of critique to its own foundations. In accepting what they see as Nietzsche's 'merciless doctrine of the identity of domination and reason' (ibid. 119), the critique of enlightenment turns on the act of critique itself. The result is that the path of the original release of enlightenment from domination becomes rather a precarious one, with problematic consequences for the critical intent of critical theory.

What do these authors mean by 'enlightenment', and how do they defend a thesis of such sweeping generality? In the first few pages of the work, the authors treat enlightenment as the patriarchal sovereignty of the human mind over a disenchanted nature, as celebrated by Francis Bacon (Horkheimer and Adorno 1972: 3–4). The concept of enlightenment may be encapsulated in the writings of *the* Enlightenment but is not coeval with them. For enlightenment characterises the *whole* project of civilisation or, at least, Western civilisation, and is present at its origins. Enlightenment is an originary act grounded in an existential choice presented to humankind by its given relation to nature: 'Men have always to choose between their subjection to nature or the subjection of nature to the Self' (ibid. 32). Enlightenment is thus not an historical occurrence but the very presupposition of a (Western) history.

This story of enlightenment is not simply one of the instrumentalisation of external nature. It is also one of self-domination or self-sacrifice, what the authors call the 'introversion of sacrifice' (ibid. 46–56). The 'identically persistent self' (ibid. 54) arising in the quest for the instrumental domination of external nature at once subjects itself to the same mastery. Domination of external nature in the interests of self-preservation is only possible with mastery of internal nature. In a thesis reminiscent of both Nietzsche's and Freud's diagnoses of civilisation, Horkheimer and Adorno argue: 'The history of civilisation is the history of the introversion of sacrifice. In other words, the history of renunciation' (ibid. 55).

The concept of enlightenment manifests the features of a philosophy of history. It posits first a distinct state anterior to history, the subjection of humankind to blind nature. It proposes an act, enlightenment, in which history originates and that contains within it the teleology of history, the progressive mastery of nature. It further proposes an end of history, emancipation, as the realisation of that history and already present to the original act of attempted liberation from nature. The basis of enlightenment then is not a distinctive historical process but humankind's drive for *self-preservation* manifest as the rendering of nature into a calculable, manipulable entity. Within such a philosophy of history critique becomes total because there is no point of exteriority from which it can operate its enlightening moves. Critique, as a component of enlightenment, is identical to the very reason it wishes to transform. References to the virtue of 'determinate negation of the existing' can only ever be gestural (Jay 1973: 266).

The constituent features of Horkheimer and Adorno's approach to this history can be brought out through the dialectic of enlightenment and myth. They argue that enlightenment, while defining itself in relation to a myth, reproduces its key features, in particular, its anthropomorphism. On the one hand, enlightenment thought is simply the pure instrumentalisation of nature. It reduces the multiplicity of the qualities and forms of nature, and the intermingling of words and things characteristic of the magical attitude, to a passive, calculable, usable, predictable realm of matter and fact (Horkheimer and Adorno 1972: 9). It does this in its reliance on system and abstraction, most clearly in evidence in the primacy accorded formal logic and mathematics. For Horkheimer and Adorno, enlightenment thought reduces nature to a realm over which humankind is godlike

On the other hand, there is more than a hint of myth in humanity's heroic and tragic attempt to constitute itself as a subject whose command is virtually indistinguishable from the creative God of monotheism. Indeed, for the Frankfurt authors, the enlightenment view of myth is its own creation. The epic narratives of antiquity, of which the *Odyssey* is exemplary, already display the touchstones of enlightenment thought: a valorisation of discipline and power, an hierarchical cosmos, the gradations of sacrifice, and the crucial distantiation between sign and thing, concept and matter, existence and reality (Horkheimer and Adorno 1972: 8–9). Moreover, they suggest, these elements of the epic form are linked to the rise of the national state, kingship, territorial domination, a hierocratic division of labour, forms of unfree labour, and the emergence of fixed property (ibid. 13–14). What is called enlightenment is present from the beginning of the long process first apparent in the epic form at the founding of the state. The identity between social domination and intellectual mastery is a necessary and complete one. 'The universality of ideas as developed by discursive logic, domination in the conceptual sphere, is raised up on the basis of actual domination' (ibid. 14).

At one turn of the dialectic of enlightenment, then, there is no real discontinuity between enlightenment and myth, but between enlightenment and myth and the heritage of mimetic magic tabooed with the founding of the state. Here, the shaman can be opposed to the modern positivistic scientist (Horkheimer and Adorno 1972: 9–12). Both are concerned to gain control of forces in the world, but only the latter turns the totality of nature into an instrument. The former pursues his aims by mimesis, by specific representation in sacrificial ritual, rather than by a mastery that presupposed the distancing of subject and its petrified object, and the universal interchangeability of experimental elements reduced to meaninglessness. But even here the authors remain trenchant dialecticians, and the opposition between scientist and magician is not a complete one. The strategies of both archetypes show a certain symmetry: 'Animism spiritualised the object, whereas industrialism objectifies the spirit' (ibid. 28). The conventional view of their relation can be subject to reversal: Freud's ascription to magic of the '"unshakeable confidence in the possibility of world domination". . . corresponds to realistic world domination only in terms of a more skilled sciences' (ibid.11). In the final instance, there is the same configuration of rationality and domination: tribal magicians, by virtue of their access to the sacred, and professional knowledge of the territory of power, are able to establish social subordination through the submission to the norms of nature, no less than scientists with their technical world-view (ibid. 21). The hierarchy and order of the magical mode of behaviour and apprehension, as much as that of the positivist, reflects the state of domination in the division of labour. Against Durkheim, Horkheimer and Adorno claim that the social character of thought categories is not given by the fact of social solidarity, but by the 'inscrutable unity of society and domination' (ibid. 21).

In this presentation of the complex, no doubt dialectical, entwinement of myth and enlightenment, and enlightenment and the instrumental domination of nature, the outline of the target of critique becomes harder to discern. The further the elaboration of what is meant by enlightenment proceeds, the more difficult it becomes to draw its clear outlines, to identify it with specified temporal and spatial co-ordinates, and thus to grasp the historical terrain of the critique, let alone its target. There are at least two strands of historical reference interwoven in Horkheimer and Adorno's use of the term, enlightenment, and their coexistence, and mutual interaction, gives their critique an uncertain, even hallucinatory quality. From the first lines, enlightenment is a synonym for the 'progressive thought' that seeks to liberate humankind from fear of nature and establish its sovereignty (ibid. 3). It is thus something akin to the process described by Kant of humankind's emergence from immaturity and tutelage (ibid. 82–5). In this sense enlightenment is coeval with the programme of the 'disenchantment of the world' (ibid. 3), Weber's term for the process of putatively emancipatory demystification of the world that had characterised Western civilisation and reason over millennia.

Yet these authors also have in mind *the* Enlightenment, an event of relatively recent occurrence, which, together with the Reformation, the French Revolution and the Industrial Revolution, provided the historical co-ordinates of what they refer to as 'bourgeois society'. Here, enlightenment becomes a specific conception of reason characteristic of the bourgeois epoch, emphasising properties of system and order, *mathesis*, and logic (e.g. ibid. 82–3). The Enlightenment is thus a particular event bringing knowledge to the court of formal reason and signalling the intellectual ascendancy of the bourgeoisie. If the critique of enlightenment allowed the Frankfurt authors to entertain the Weberian themes of disenchantment and rationalisation, the critique of the Enlightenment allowed this to be inflected with themes redolent of Hegelian–Marxian thought, such as alienated labour, universalised exchange, commodity fetishisation, reification, and so on.

The central point to note here is that while the dialectic of enlightenment is worked out along the explicit dimensions of the relations between enlightenment and myth and reason and domination, there are also an implicit set of shifts which form, separate, and superimpose, 'Western civilisation' and its 'bourgeois form'. Indeed, one might be led to suspect that the seeds of the bourgeois form of technocratic domination can be found in Greek antiquity and before. It is this double historical sense to the dialectic of enlightenment that allows the authors to bring together a generalised Weberian critique of the 'long march' of instrumental reason with Marx's thesis of the alienated form of labour under capitalism and Freud's identification of civilisation with repression and renunciation. It must be said, however, that while capitalist commodity exchange intensifies and facilitates this rationalisation, capitalist social relations are rather more the symptom than the cause of the crises and pathologies of modern reason. The *rapprochement* of Freud and Marx sought by Horkheimer and Adorno is conducted under the auspices of a totalised Weberian account of rationalisation.

Indeed, despite the identification of bourgeois society and the positivist world-view, there is a strong sense in which the fundamental Marxist analysis of the regulation of social relations through the capitalist market and its law of value can no longer be said to apply to contemporary society. The objective laws of the market have been replaced by the conscious decision-making of the managing directors who continue to impose the law of value in a totally administered society (on the latter in twentieth century thought, D'Amico 1991). In place of the bourgeois entrepreneur, the technocratic manager and 'forest of cliques and institutions'; for the revolutionary proletariat, the union boss, on the one side, and the supernumerary mass, deprived of self-consciousness by the culture industry, on the other (Horkheimer and Adorno 1972: 37); and for the universal concepts of bourgeois metaphysics, the positivist fetish of number and fact. In fact the Frankfurt authors believed that market capitalism and the primacy of economic class rule had been the exception in the history of humanity. This is in keeping with the recurrent Frankfurt argument of this period in which the shift to an 'authoritarian state' represents a reversion to the primacy of class rule based on a political domination resting finally on physical force rather than on an economic exploitation achieved through market participation of the propertyless (Bogner 1987: 266–7).

The *Dialectic* does have a definite perspective on historical development and the threefold relation between rationality, the self, and power. Further, it holds to a model of modernity based on a transition from a market-exchange phase of capitalism to a totally administered monopoly phase of state capitalism. The question now arises as to whether this perspective on history, and the diagnosis of the times it leads to, can be said to offer the possibility of a critical historical sociology. Or, to put it more precisely, whether the Frankfurt authors can establish an effective history of reason despite their immersion in a philosophy of history that vitiates its very point.

Towards a critical history of rationality?

I have argued at several points that a requirement for an effective historical sociology would be the capacity to address the variation in forms of rationality and subjectivity under definite social and historical conditions. *The Dialectic of Enlightenment* does, at times, seem to suggest such an historical sociology, but the terms in which it casts it severely limit its capacity to deliver. Here I seek to construct what that historical sociology might look like and show how the basic concepts employed close it off as a fruitful avenue of investigation. The next section furthers this process of criticism in relation to a consideration of the genealogical themes of Foucault.

As the author's revision of Durkheim illustrates, there is indeed an implicit historical sociology at work in this text. It is one in which social organisation, considered as the succession of forms of domination in the division of labour, forms of rationality, considered as the organisation of categories of thought, and forms of personality, conceived in terms of a philosophical conception of the subject, would be linked across a tableau provided by the Weberian disenchantment of the world. The emphasis on the pivotal and perhaps determinate role of domination in the division of labour would appear to return the analysis to a form of historical materialism, or at least a material and historical account of forms of rationality. Consider the following passage:

> But of course the social character of thought is not, as Durkheim asserts, an expression of social solidarity, but evidence of the inscrutable unity of society and domination. Domination lends increased consistency and force to the social whole in which it establishes itself. The division of labour to which domination tends serves the dominated whole for the end of self-preservation. But then the whole as whole, the manifestation of its immanent reason, necessarily leads to the execution of the particular. To the individual, domination appears to be the universal: reason in actuality. Through the division of labor imposed on them, the power of all the members of society – for whom as such there is no other course – amounts over and over again to the realisation of the whole, whose rationality is reproduced in this way. What is done to all by the few, always occurs as the subjection of individuals by the many: social repression always exhibits the masks of repression by a collective. It is this unity of the collectivity and domination, and not direct social universality, which is expressed in thought forms.

> (Horkheimer and Adorno 1972: 21–2)

For Horkheimer and Adorno, then, domination is conceived as the process of the subjection of individuals by other individuals, the many by the few. Domination is primary and original for it is by means of it that property relations and the division of labour arise. This domination also determines the forms of social thought or rationality. It does so, however, in an indirect or mediated fashion. Domination is determinate because rationality is determined by forms of domination in the division of labour. It is indirect because this is mediated through forms of human consciousness expressing the social whole. Forms of rationality do not appear as the effects of forms of domination but as the manifestation of universal principles contained in the social whole. This is why reason itself takes a universal form. Thus the Frankfurt authors cite Vico's contentions that the concepts of Plato and Aristotle originated in the marketplace of Athens. They argue that the philosophers appropriated the conditions of domination they were used to and elevated them to universality and truth (ibid. 22).

This indirect or mediated historical and materialist account of rationality as a social product, however, is only one component in the Frankfurt theorists' account of rationality. For despite references to bourgeois society and to the universal equivalence of exchange within it, the capitalist economy has ceased to be the central focus of critique, as it had been in classical Marxism, and is now viewed as but one form of rationalisation, the 'autonomous dynamic of means–end rationality' (Dews 1987: 150). They thus agree with Weber that the threat posed by the administered society, in which all social forms come to be subordinated to instrumental rationality, is far deeper than those of capitalist relations of exploitation and class domination (ibid. 150–1). Perhaps one can extend this line of thought and say that Horkheimer and Adorno are too ready to identify instrumental rationality with the rationality of commodity exchange and thereby affirm an extremely continuous history. For even in Homer they rediscover forms of barter and gift-giving embodying the principle of equivalence characteristic of rational exchange (Horkheimer and Adorno 1972: 49–51).

The Frankfurt authors would thus concur with the Weberian analysis of the 'iron cage' of rational economic action of the calling as a degeneration of the conduct of life inscribed in Protestant asceticism (Weber 1985: 181). However, within their implicit historical sociology, they regard this as but one key episode in the world-historical process of disenchantment, in which instrumental rationality sought the subjugation of the natural world through deforming repression of the desires and pleasures of the self. History becomes the story of the originary refusal to accept humankind's domination by nature which leads to: the subjection of nature to the self in the interests of self-preservation; the attendant domination expressed in the division of human labour; and the necessary deformation of the individual this entails (e.g. Horkheimer and Adorno 1972: 31–2). The disenchantment and domination of nature and the repression of myth as animistic superstition mark the very 'turning points of Western civilisation, from the transition to Olympian religion, up to the Renaissance, Reformation and bourgeois atheism' (ibid. 31). The dialectic of enlightenment may contain the possibility of a linkage of forms of reason, domination, and self. However, the means of discrimination is collapsed in a unidirectional account of the West in terms of an instrumental rationality in which 'technology is the essence of this knowledge' (ibid. 4). Moreover the direction of human history is nothing more than the generalisation of this model of domination by rational knowledge. It can only be understood as the progressive subsumption of the particular, concrete, multiple, different and individual contexts of nature in the general, abstract, unitary, identical, comparable and calculable object of human knowledge. A critical history of rationality is impossible because of critical theory's preoccupation with what it understands as the onward march of instrumental rationality through history. Thus the account of history of the Frankfurt School here reveals a key characteristic of the philosophy of history – it totalises a model of reason, even if here it is reason as domination rather than reason as liberation.

The *Dialectic* proposes systems of historical classification and forms of historical explanation only to undermine them in this unidirectional story of progressive instrumental mastery. The clearest example of this is its highly suggestive account of what it calls the 'mode of apprehension' (e.g. Horkheimer and Adorno 1972: 6). There are four different modes of apprehension of the world mentioned in the *Dialectic* loosely corresponding to different collective forms of domination in the division of labour. They are the mimetic, the mythic, the metaphysical, and the positivistic, which correspond to tribal, monarchical, market-capitalist, and administered-capitalist social divisions of labour (see, e.g. ibid. 31). Each mode of apprehension has a specific relation to nature: moving from imitation, substitution and symbolisation, conceptualisation and universalisation, to one of logical formalism and petrified abstraction. Again the problem is that the narrative of rationalisation collapses each of these modes of apprehension of nature into a unidirectional process of tearing free from nature in order to dominate it. The mimesis instanced in the magic of the shaman seeks only 'specific representation' of the multiplicity of relations between existents with no necessary unity and thus does not unify the cosmos for mastery. However, every step away from magic is a phase in the divorce of words and things, of thought and reality, leading to the petrified scientific object become instrument before the universal, abstract self. Science prepares the end of this state of affairs, argue Horkheimer and Adorno: 'representation is exchanged for the fungible – universal interchangeability' (1972: 10). In so doing, the 'neutral sign' of enlightenment science consumes symbols and the universal concepts of metaphysics (ibid. 23). The modes of apprehension are not attempts to grasp the structure of forms of rationality but different moments in the unravelling of the subjection of humankind and domination of nature entailed in enlightenment. If archaeology can be understood as the attempt to define a level of analysis of discourse adequate to the intrinsic intelligibility of forms of structuring of statements or what we might call forms of rationality, then the archaeological level has been buried beneath an overblown critique that too easily totalises as it fails to allow empirical study.

There is only one panel left now of the triptych of rationality, domination, and selfhood. For these forms of domination that give rise to instrumental rationality themselves define a particular position of the individual and self. Again, it may be asked whether the outline of the history of the individual could form a possible basis for an historical sociology of the self. To answer this, the more realised version of the history of the self found in Horkheimer's other major work of the 1940s, *Eclipse of Reason*, can be examined (1974: 128–61). Here one finds traced the development of the individual from the pre-individuality of tribal societies 'living in the gratifications and frustrations of the moment', through the model of the Greek hero, the flowering and retreat of individuality in the city states with Platonic objective reason, Socratic conscience, and Stoic resignation. These are followed by Christian notions of the immortal soul later subject to a gradual humanisation and secularisation in the Renaissance, Reformation, and Enlightenment. The 'era of free enterprise' then undertakes the open proclamation of an individualism that proves to be evanescent under administered capitalism and mass culture. Again we find the totalised philosophy of history at work. The self is an historical product: it is transformed throughout different phases of historical development corresponding to different forms of domination in the division of labour. Yet behind this historical variation lies the problem of the subject as an identical, self-possessed self with attributes of autonomy, will, and consciousness. Historically existing forms of domination are all attempts to subjugate external and inner nature to this identical self. This self arises in the very act of seeking to control nature by cognitive processes and thus exists in one manner or another in every known phase of existing civilisation. It is the attempt at self-preservation, rather than any specific historical practices and discourses, in which the self is constituted.

Different modes of domination foster or retard different attributes of the subject. One can take the transition from bourgeois individual to the hyperconformity of managed subjectivity as a key example. The liberal individual, particularly the independent entrepreneur is sketched almost with a degree of affection. The subordination of individuality to self-interest characteristic of commodity exchange under capitalism encouraged independent thinking, and the management of inherited property across the horizon of an individual life-span provided foresight and sobriety. The bourgeois individual is characterised by a 'strong yet sober ego, maintaining interests that transcended his immediate needs' (Horkheimer 1974: 140). One might suggest it is this bourgeois individual that realises most perfectly the attributes of a self seeking the rational subjection of nature.

In contrast, the post-entrepreneurial bourgeois individual is a 'shrunken ego', tied to a changing tide of the short-term, dwarfed by the colossal organisations of national and international economic and political power, and subject to a perpetual economic insecurity allowing no safety zones (Horkheimer 1974: 140–1, 158). This adapted corporate individuality survives by an almost absolute mimicry of peer-groups within modern institutions, by 'selling oneself', and is reinforced by the celebrations of sameness in modern mass culture (ibid. 141–2, 154). On the other side of the property relation, the superorganisations in which the modern working class find themselves virtually reduce 'the individual to a mere cell of functional response' (ibid. 145). Indeed as their own labour organisations recapitulate the logic of business in the administered society, and become vehicles apportioning and managing labour power, they complete the reification of humankind (ibid. 148–9). The primary task of the masses thus is not, according to Horkheimer, the promotion of a rational social centralisation of planning in opposition to market anarchy but the resistance to monopolistic organisation by the encouragement of non-conforming critical thought and spontaneous individuality (ibid. 146–7).

A number of things should be noted about this account for our current purposes. First, the new empty subjectivity of the era of state capitalism is defined by the absence of those features that constitute the philosophical subject such as individuality and autonomy, and the capacity for independent thought and action. The history of the self is thus the history of the presence or absence of certain attributes of the subject characteristic of modern philosophy. It cannot be a history of the diverse modes of self-formation in ethical practices, power relations, and forms of rationality, that we shall discover in Foucault.

Second, the apparently contradictory potential of early, liberal capitalism is contrasted with the decline of the individual within the administered society of monopolistic organisation, with its totalised purposive-rationality. This simple and total typology underpins their would-be historical sociology of modernity. Like Weber, the critical theorists envisage *laissez-faire* capitalism to be a moment in which individuality appears in a pristine form in the modern world, even if in the alienated form of the pursuit of material self-interest, as a region freed from the hold of metaphysics and tradition. However, the immanent logic set in train is one in which the pursuit of self-interest 'leads to the totalitarian extinction of that very individuality which originally set this logic in motion' (Dews 1987: 154–5). The end result of this is the formation of the individual as a shell, an empty, adapted subjectivity responding to a totally planned social environment. Thus, the potential of early capitalism for the history of the self is only a chimera, a ruse that facilitates the development of a human being who reduces reason into an instrument of self-preservation. Indeed, in the *Dialectic*, it is often hard to tell which register the understanding of the self is being played in – that of the adapted subjectivity of administered capitalism, or that of the self that seeks to subjugate nature for its own self-preservation. For a philosophy of history, this problem of registers is meaningless, for the calculating, adaptive individuality of the totally administered society is already implied in the existential choice of the domination of nature by the self.

Beneath this sketch of an historical sociology of the subject is a definite, and naturalistic, philosophy of history. The force that underlies the human strivings leading to the emergence of capitalist social relations and unleashing powers of instrumental rationality with such terrible results is the drive for 'self-preservation'. History is the fateful dialectic of reason and domination, in which the type of calculating, purposive form of rationality required of the subject to ensure this self-preservation comes to necessitate a corresponding repression of internal nature to such an extent that the individual loses the self-mastery it had set out to achieve.

For all its undoubted insights, and its continuing usefulness as a reference point in the understanding of modern forms of knowledge and science, the dialectic of enlightenment expires in a philosophy of history. The naturalistic origins of reason in the drive for self-preservation find their inverted reflection in the absolute domination of both inner and outer nature by instrumental reason in the administered society. The critical possibilities of the ideals of the Enlightenment, lauded by the Critical Theory of the 1930s, are reduced to the progressively narrower compass of the Hegelian 'determinate negation', the unrelenting theory which seeks to turn the negative spirit of relentless progress to its own end (Horkheimer and Adorno 1972: 24, 42; Jay 1973: 266–7; Habermas 1987a: 128). The charisma of reason has found its own inversion in the curse of demonic instrumentalism. Totalised critique, having deprived itself of its own basis, veers perilously close to the aesthetic nihilism it hopes to combat, and towards an élitist and ultimately privatised conception of theory. We could say that such a theory underwrites a global, one-dimensional historical sociology of the self and rationality, rooted in a conception of domination and its forms. But it may be more appropriate to say that such theory, in so far as it remains mesmerised by a philosophical understanding of the subject, and the quasi-eschatological notion for 'recon-ciliation', forms a barrier to a sociology that seeks to grasp dispersion in history.

THE FRANKFURT SCHOOL AND FOUCAULT

In his preface to the English translation of Georges Canguilhem's *Le Normal et le Pathologique*, Foucault noted (1980d: 53–4) that the 'question of Enlightenment' took different trajectories in Anglo-Saxon countries, France, and Germany. Particularly telling here is the comparison he made between the history of the sciences in France, which has its lineage in the positivism of Comte, and the historical reflection on society in Germany, from the Hegelians to the Frankfurt School. In both this French history of the sciences and in German critical theory, he suggested, what is at issue is a reason, 'the autonomy of whose structures carries with it a history of dogmatism and despotism – a reason, consequently, which can only have an effect of emancipation on condition that it manages to liberate itself from itself' (Foucault 1980d: 54). The resonances Foucault found here are perhaps even stronger when his own work is considered. In an interview (Foucault 1983b: 200), he frankly admitted to having never heard the name of the Frankfurt School mentioned by his professors, and suggested that he would have avoided several stupid remarks and detours if he had been aware of the avenues opened up by the Frankfurt School.

I have already noted that the Frankfurt School theme of the dialectic of enlightenment contains a statement of what is indeed a fundamental problem for an historical sociology of rationality, viz. that of the linkage between dominant forms of reason and systems of domination. However, the Frankfurt School theorists are unable to advance beyond what is at best an Hegelian philosophical critique of reason toward an historical sociology of rationality. Indeed, there are several epistemological obstacles to the constitution of such a project that can be highlighted by placing the analyses of Horkheimer and Adorno alongside those of Foucault.

At first glance, the relation between reason and domination which is at the centre of the problematic of the Frankfurt School would appear to be close to the rubric under which Foucault conducted his genealogical studies of the 1970s, that of power–knowledge (*pouvoir–savoir*). Indeed, both oppositions appear, at least in such a general form, to be different ways of posing a fairly similar, if not the same, problem, and thus to warrant the claims of a common lineage made by Foucault at several points in the latter part of his career (e.g. 1980d; 1983b; 1986b). However, it is the differences between the two projects that are of primary concern here. These differences not only allow a demonstration of the limits of the intellectual filiation of these two modalities of thought and analysis, but also bring into focus some fundamental problems of the Frankfurt approach from any critical historical account, and particularly from the present concerns of an historical sociology of rationality.

One might open this contrast at an empirical level and examine *which* discourses are held to embody the form of rationality subject to the various analyses in terms of power–knowledge or reason–domination (cf. Gordon 1980: 233–7). In other words, it is possible to contrast the terrain of the problematisation of reason in Foucault and Horkheimer and Adorno. In the case of the latter, the initial terrain on which the critique of enlightenment is undertaken is clearly that of the revolutions in the mathematical and physical sciences of the seventeenth century. Thus the central figure at the beginning of the first chapter, 'The Concept of Enlightenment', is Francis Bacon and the 'scientific attitude' he both initiates and symbolises, one encapsulated in his project of a unified scientific method, *una scientia universalis*, and in Leibniz's *mathesis universalis* (Horkheimer and Adorno 1972: 7). The problem of reason for the Frankfurt theorists, then, is of the origins of what they conceive as modern 'positivism', the regime of formal logic and mathematics, and the consequent reduction of the world to order, number, and fact.

At its root, such a critique seems to rely on the implicit neo-Kantian division inherited from the German hermeneutic tradition via Weber of the separation of the natural and cultural sciences. However, unlike neo-Kantianism, this critique is not simply aimed at the illegitimate extension into the cultural sphere of the forms of explanation and methods characteristic of the natural sciences. This critique is aimed at the instrumental domination inscribed within the form, logic, and presuppositions of the natural sciences themselves. Further, under their general philosophy of history, the Frankfurt theorists identify the instrumental form of reason most clearly manifest in the natural sciences with the problem of Western reason *per se*. This identification is presupposed, as we have seen, by their key notions of subjection to nature, the drive for self-preservation, and enlightenment itself. The ramifications of this are many. On the one hand, the identity of Western reason and its instrumental form can neither be argued for nor analysed as a concrete historical process. It is simply presupposed by their philosophy of history. On the other, there cannot be a meaningful study of the history of the sciences. Having presupposed the identity of Western reason with instrumental mastery *tout court* it is not possible to pose questions of the operation of various sciences, of how these sciences, their theories, concepts, and instruments develop, and of their relation with one another and their institutional, social and political contexts. Indeed, it is only possible, within such a philosophy of history, to ascertain whether specific sciences follow the putative principles and procedures of positivism, and whether or not they seek to replicate a unitary scientific method. The weakness of the approach to rationality of *The Dialectic of Enlightenment* is that it cannot (and is indeed unwilling to) move from this philosophical critique of science to effective historical and sociological analyses of the rationality and practice of the particular sciences themselves. This is one of the key advantages of the French tradition of the philosophy and history of the science, and one inherited in Foucault's account of the human sciences.

Horkheimer and Adorno have thus radicalised the ontological distinction seeking to define the specificity of the cultural sciences and turned it into a total critique of scientific reason. The latter does not merely reject the illegitimate extension of natural scientific rationality but the very form of reason incarnate in the natural and physical sciences. The critique of the cultural or social sciences is, in this sense, a critique of a second order. These latter sciences are not the primary sites of the manifestation of the pathological form of reason of the modern West, but rather the results of the application of an already pathological reason to the human and cultural realm. It might be said that the cultural sciences are accomplices after the fact in the murder of critical reason rather than the perpetrators of the deed. But it should also be noted that there is a redoubled critique of positivism: for if the positivism of the natural sciences consists in the objectification of external nature, then the positivism of the cultural sciences results in a reification of inner nature, of subjectivity itself. Moreover, because the instrumental mastery of objective nature already presupposes the splitting of inner and outer worlds, then any advance in the inexorable direction of rationalisation and disenchantment is, for Horkheimer and Adorno, inevitably a process of reification. Rationalisation is, quite simply, the world-historical process of reification manifest in the development of Western civilisation.

There are of course severe limitations as to how such a philosophy of history could be used. Indeed, it would be extremely difficult to use Horkheimer and Adorno's critique in the service of an analysis of any concrete scientific discipline or a discursive formation claiming the status of science. There are a number of reasons for this *besides* the general problem of their philosophy of history. In the first place, the target of their critique is notoriously difficult to pin down. This target is sometimes condensed into the term 'positivism'. This term has, however, several variants, and, at each mention, is linked to a new plethora of ills. Consider only a few examples. There is: 'modern positivism', that writes off all that is irreducible to numbers, and ultimately to unity, as literature (Horkheimer and Adorno 1972: 7); 'modern positivist science' that confounds itself in the separation of 'concept and thing' already present in the Homeric epic (ibid. 16); and the 'neo-positivist version' in which science exhibits an aestheticism, a system of pure detached signs (ibid. 18). These examples suggest something of the polyvalent nature of positivism as a term of critique. It would seem that any of the following characteristics qualify as positivism: clarity in the use of concepts, the employment of mathematical tools or formal logic, order and precision, experimental methods, and so on.

There is, however, a second related and somewhat deeper reason that the dialectic of enlightenment cannot give rise to a form of analysis of different types of science and rationality, viz. the very generality of their notion of 'critique'. For the object of critique is not simply the illegitimate extension of any particular features of disciplines or sciences but any project that valorises order, logic, system, and empirical inquiry. Horkheimer and Adorno's dialectic of enlightenment begins with the 'positivist' scientific revolutions of the sciences in order to show that the form of reason putatively manifest there has deep roots within Western philosophic and Homeric narrative traditions. These Frankfurt theorists fetishize certain issues raised by particular intellectual movements in order to indict a totalised Western rationality as a progressively unfolding manifestation of the drive to the technological mastery of outer and inner nature.

The studies Foucault conducted in the 1960s and 1970s were of quite a different order. It is clear that, for whatever reason, these are critical historical studies of the first order, and the popularity of Foucault's thought in sociology and history is related to this capacity to undertake historical analysis that subverts or at least places in question the suppositions of grand theory and transhistorical schemas. There are other important features to note before this historical precocity can be made intelligible. First, they were focused on the transformations of knowledge that occurred at the end of the eighteenth century, rather than those of the scientific revolution of the sixteenth and seventeenth centuries. Secondly, what is at stake is not the physical and natural sciences but the *human sciences*, a term under which can be grouped discourses that lie on both sides of both the neo-Kantian divide and the threshold of scientificity. Thirdly, the central concern is not with reification, in the sense of the falsification or distortion of the human essence in its representation, but with what Foucault calls *'assujetissement'*. The latter is a term which covers how the individual is 'subjectified' in relation to forms of knowledge and discourse, 'subjected' in technologies of domination, and 'subjectifies' him or herself in relation to rules and techniques of ethical conduct. This triple fabrication of the subject is thus not simply an effect of domination but a complex result of practices and techniques of power, knowledge, and ethics.

The different dating is interesting to note but is not the essential point of contrast between these two modes of thought. The second and third points are, however, extremely important and worth developing. As I have suggested, Foucault's position, like that of the French school of the history of the sciences, is not founded on a natural-physical sciences/moral-cultural sciences split. Various practitioners of this school have focused their studies on physics and chemistry (Bachelard) or biology and medicine. Given Georges Canguilhem's concerns centred on the latter, it is not particularly novel for Foucault to concentrate on what he terms the *human* sciences. What should be noted about the latter term is that it brings together forms of knowledge that would fall on different sides of the neo-Kantian division: thus it includes psychiatry, medicine and biology, on the one hand, and criminology, economics, sociology, psychology, sexology, on the other. In fact what constitutes the unity of the discourses under analysis in Foucault's work is not a division between nature and culture, or the problem of the illegitimate extension of a form of knowledge, but the way in which these discourses presuppose the unity of humankind both as rational subject of knowledge and its object.

This concern for the constitution of 'Man' as the paradoxical subject and object of knowledge is, however, only one part of Foucault's concerns with modes of subjectification. For the Frankfurt thinkers the dialectic of enlightenment relies on a problematic that identifies rationalisation with reification. The positivist form of reason fulfilled by and grounded in the modern natural sciences is one which objectifies the world making it into an object of instrumental or technological mastery. In so far as this form of reason enters the social or cultural sciences, or the systems of administration of human beings, the critique is redoubled. For here it is not only the problematic objectification of the natural world and its forces, it is the falsification of the essence of human existence, and the treatment of social subjects and social relations as if they were things. The treatment of human beings and their capacities as instrumental objects falsifies their true nature. No matter how reserved Adorno may have been about 'identity thinking', there remains in the *Dialectic* a notion of the true subject and its reason which is falsified in the processes of reification and rationalisation.

By contrast, Foucault's concern with the human sciences and the systems of practices within which they are embedded does not presuppose any philosophical or metaphysical conception of the subject as a principle of explanation or locus of emancipation or reconciliation. What follows from Foucault's concerns are the various ways in which human beings are constituted as subjects. As suggested above, this occurs in particular forms of knowledge (the human sciences) and particular forms of power and systems of institu-tionalised practices (discipline, surveillance, systems of administration, con-finement, treatment, etc.), and particular ethical modes of conduct and techniques of the self. The philosophical conception of the subject no longer exercises an enchantment over the analysis: the form of the fabrication of the subject as implicated in the process of knowledge, power and domination, and self-formation, becomes as much a topic for historical analysis as those of the fabrication of objects. This is why this concept of *assujetissement* found in Foucault's work from *Discipline and Punish* (1977a) to *The Use of Pleasure* (1985) covers both the exterior process of self-shaping and self-development in relations to knowledge and power, and the internal processes by which the self acts on the self within various ethical practices. Foucault's central concerns here are the various ways by which individuals are made subject to others and anonymous systems of domination and subordination, at the same time as they come to develop various subjective capacities and forms of reflexive self-formation and self-awareness. The formation of reflexivity as an attribute of human conduct may be said to be one of Foucault's principal themes. What is at issue between Foucault and the Frankfurt School is less a philosophical divide between humanism and antihumanism, between the death and life of the subject, than the forms of thematisation of the problem of the subject. For the moment, it is enough to note that Foucault's thematisation makes possible a realm of critical historical inquiry into the various modes of the constitution of the subject (ethical, epistemological, political) that is simply not available within the dialectic of enlightenment.

The dialectic of enlightenment and Foucauldian critical history may be distinguished by their terrain, their form and conception of critique and hence of analysis, and their conception of the subject. They may also be considered to differ in their conception of reason itself. It is clear that the presence of a concept of totalised instrumental rationality as identical to the present outcome of the trajectory of the West constitutes the dialectic of enlighten-ment as a problematic that does not fulfil the minimum criterion for a critical history of rationality, viz. the allowance of the possibility of the dispersed plurality of forms of rationality. This is a primary and continuing distinction to be made between the indictments of Enlightenment rationality laid down by the Frankfurt theorists and the critical historical analyses of Foucault.

For the former, the problem of enlightenment is a global one of the relation between reason (*Vernuft*) and domination (*Herrschaft*) resulting in the mutual and total identification of knowledge and power under conditions of modernity conceived as a 'totally administered society'. This totalistic critique possesses little of the subtlety and openness of Foucault's understanding of power–knowledge relations in terms of the complex, strategic, and shifting relations between systems of power and the procedures and processes of the production of knowledge (see Chapter 8). For Horkheimer and Adorno, reason is a unitary entity, so that each instance or component of instrumental rationality merely expresses the same form. This cannot be said for Foucault. While it is possible to specify common elements within the diverse power–knowledge relations concerning the treatment of the insane, the sick, or the criminal, for example, there is no metahistorical a priori that guarantees that each of these systems of practices embodies a unitary reason.

The Frankfurt conception of reason is fundamentally Hegelian (Jay 1973: 60–1). Here reason (*Vernuft*) is distinguished from mere understanding (*Verstand*), the commonsense comprehension of the finite entities of the phenomenal world. Instead, reason is synthetic, penetrating to dialectical relations beneath appearances, to reach a knowledge of totality. Even formal, analytical, thought is retained in the dialectical sublation characteristic of reason. The critique of the modern form of Western reason, then, seeks to show how, within the process of rationalisation, knowledge and cognition becomes severed from the dialectical and synthetic character of reason, and objective reason gives way to a merely subjective, instrumentalised form. The triumph of Western reason reduces nature to logic, number, and form, so that it becomes manipulable. This means that reason becomes locked into the immediate, the given, concerned at its best with the 'spatio-temporal relations of the facts' (Horkheimer and Adorno 1972: 26). Thus the process of rationalisation does not allow the 'determinate negation' of the given realm of facts, their sublation 'as mediated conceptional moments which come to fulfilment only in the development of their social, historical, and human significance' (ibid. 26–7). This form of instrumental reason is thus both the result of a process of reification and itself reified. Subjective reason objectifies nature as an external realm of objects to be manipulated and controlled as it becomes a mere tool of the administrative and economic apparatus.

It is clear that this is a normative conception of reason, of what reason ought to be like, of why existing forms of knowledge and thought are deficient in relation to a particular ideal of reason. The notion of reason that emerges in Foucault's work is not a normative but a performative one. It questions reason in its use, not as a norm by which various historical forms of reason can be evaluated. For example, in an interview Foucault characterises the central issue of critical thought in the following way:

> *What* is this Reason that we use? What are its historical effects? What are its limits, and what are its dangers? How can we exist as rational beings, fortunately committed to practising a rationality that is unfortunately crisscrossed by intrinsic dangers? . . . if it is extremely dangerous to say that Reason is the enemy that should be eliminated, it is just as dangerous to say that any critical questioning of this rationality risks sending us into irrationality.
>
> (Foucault 1986h: 249)

To pose the question of rationality at the level of the implicit normalitivity of forms of knowledge and understanding is to do so at a too global level for

Foucault's critical history of rationality. This is no doubt why we see a consistent attempt to redefine the problem or the relation between rationality and domination at a far more modest and manageable level. If one takes Foucault's *Tanner Lectures* at Stanford (1988h), the problem is reposed at the level of political rationality, of the forms of rationality that are involved in the practices of governing. This question of political rationality is taken up in chapter 9 of the present volume. However, in the preamble to these lectures, Foucault sets us the basis of a performative analysis of systems of rational-isation. First, he rejects (Foucault 1988h: 59) the idea that Reason should be 'tried' because of the inappropriateness of criteria of guilt and innocence, of the opposition between reason and non-reason, and of the boredom of deciding between rationalism and irrationality. He then suggests that 'another way of investigating the links between rationalisation and power' contains three components. The first is the regional rather than global nature of the rationalisations analysed, i.e. ones grounded in a 'fundamental experience', such as madness, illness, death, crime, sexuality. The third is the need to displace the Enlightenment as the horizon of problematisation for more remote processes.

It is the second aspect of the relationship between rationalisation and power that is most germane here. Here Foucault notes the dangers inherent in the notion of rationalisation and then proposes a clear suggestion of the priority of a performative over a normative conception of rationality: 'The main problem when people try to rationalise something is not to investigate whether or not they conform to principles of rationality, but to discover which kind of rationality they are using' (Foucault 1988h: 59). Foucault's approach to the question of rationality is thus multiple, pragmatic, practical, and problem-oriented, rather than unitary, formal, theoretic, and general. This is no doubt why the Foucauldian project is one of 'a critical inquiry into the history of rationality', or, if you like, a critical inquiry into the history of forms of practical reason and not an analytical of truth in the sense he ascribed to Kant, of discovering the universal principles of the legitimate use of reason.

These key Frankfurt School thinkers sought to problematise contemporary forms of reason by reference to a Weberian notion of instrumental domin-ation. They indicate the space that could be occupied by an historical sociology that can correlate forms of domination, social divisions of labour, and forms of rationality. In this sense there is an ambition and potential analytical framework that could constitute the kind of transdisciplinary critical historical–sociological study envisaged here. However, in failing to break with a philosophical conception of the subject, by basing an analysis of domination on the inexorable path of instrumental rationality and the deformation of the subject, and by remaining within a Hegelian conception of reason, that possibility of a critical historical study of rationality was by-passed in favour of a philosophy of history. This is undoubtedly the reason Horkheimer and Adorno left history to the historians and pursued their own philosophical paths freed from the violence of historical time. Leaving history to the historians, however, is a dangerous option, not only because of what they might do with it, but because of what the critical theorists imagine that they do with it. It is to Michel Foucault's vast credit that he could pose a similar philosophical problem to one of the Frankfurt theorists against the horizon of a form of concrete historical analysis no longer mediated by the philosopher's imaginary concerning history or the historian's practice.

POSTSCRIPT: THE PROBLEM OF CRITIQUE

It may be that the term, 'critique', has nestled within the folds of critical thought for some time now without insufficient attention. Undoubtedly, one could fruitfully undertake a history of the term in German philosophy and social theory from at least Kant and Hegel, by way of the Young Hegelians and Marx, to the present day. This is not the appropriate place to undertake such a task. Nevertheless, I want to sketch some reasons why we might wish to be more cautious about the use of the term than is generally the case and to suggest that a critical history need neither be a 'critique', nor employ its tools and invoke its assumptions.

The term 'critique', at least as it has been accepted into sociology by way of critical theory, would appear to raise two sets of related problems. The first may be summed up in the triad 'critique–truth–emancipation'. Here, critique is conceived as a process of unmasking the truth, one penetrating the categories and surface forms of bourgeois thought to reveal fundamental relations and structures, as in Marx's critique of political economy. Yet this epistemological dimension of critique as a way to truth is linked to a normative dimension of critique as a way to emancipation. Consider the following text as an an example of this double role of critique:

> If Critical Theory can be said to have had a theory of truth, it appeared in its immanent critique of bourgeois society, which compared the pretensions of bourgeois ideology with the reality of its social conditions. Truth was not outside society, but contained in its own claims. Men had an emancipatory interest in actualising the ideology.
>
> (Jay 1973: 63)

Granted that Martin Jay is here referring to the early critical theory of the 1930s, these sentences highlight the way the 'good' and the 'true', normative and validity claims, are commonly mapped onto one another in the notion of critique. In this sense, critique casts suspicion on a doctrine not merely to show that it is false and to reclaim the rational 'core' or truth hidden within it. It also attributes that falsity to the immersion of truth claims in elements extraneous and even inimical to truth – forms of social domination, power relations, interests, etc. To unmask the falsity of 'bourgeois ideology' for critical theory, then, is not merely to separate untruths from truths but also to show how truth was distorted by class exploitation, particular class interests and so on. Further, because the truth revealed is one purified of these extraneous elements it must be linked to a notion of the good. In the case of critical theory, this 'good' is understood as a general, human, emancipation.

The problem of such a notion of critique is that it needs to limit the scepticism it has unleashed and assume that the doctrine of critique is immune from the suspicion cast over other doctrines. Thus critique seeks to ground itself in something which is beyond critique. As the case of *The Dialectic of Enlightenment* demonstrates, it is extremely difficult to do this. For this grounding of critique in a notion of emancipation is already prepared in the notion of critique itself. Thus such a ground is found in the rational elements of the doctrines and ideals of the post-Enlightenment 'bourgeois' society that is the very object of critique. Critique thus becomes narcissistic and circular: it accounts for its own grounds in what it discovers in its privileged object. Further, the emancipatory interest it reveals is discovered by way of a specific conception of the generalisable truth of humanity. Here, the radical impulse of critique expires in a dogmatism about the true nature of human beings and their universal potential derived from a doctrine that is of a particular time, place, and social order. As a form of eschatology, of a reflection on the ultimate meaning of human existence, this notion of critique may be appropriate. From the perspective of a concern with a critical history, this type of 'critique' is not, however, a critical process but a dogmatic one working from a priori principles of human being.

Now, the dilemma posed by *The Dialectic of Enlightenment* is precisely that of the limits of critique. If we accept that critique is a thoroughgoing skepticism then it must ultimately turn on itself. However, having done so, critique loses the grounds from which to launch itself at its objects. The notion of critique becomes so complete that it can give no account of how there comes to be a space from which to engage in critique. As such, it turns against itself and collapses into a complete relativism. The doctrine of critique cannot be protected from its own weapons.

Critique is condemned therefore to either a total critique cannibalising itself or a dogmatism that asserts the a priori truth of the grounds on which it rests. It is time to say enough to such nonsense and to note several things. First, there is no reason why the unmasking of an untruth reveals a truth, unless one accepts the proposition that every untruth conceals a truth. Why should not this unmasking simply reveal untruths all the way down? Secondly, the problems of critique arise when critique assumes the position of an analysis of the pathological character of society, of the long march of instrumental reason, and so on. Critique assumes a totalistic relation to its object even before it turns on itself. Thirdly, if critique assumes such a position in relation to its object, it is because it conceives of the end of critique in similarly totalistic terms, exemplified here in the notion of emancipation.

I am conscious that Foucault employed the term 'critique' to describe his own analytic practice. His use, however, transforms the sense of the term from that of the practice of a legislating subject passing judgement on a deficient reality to an analysis of the assumptions on which taken-for-granted practices rest (e.g. Foucault 1988i: 154). 'Critique' and 'criticism' are here used interchangeably to denote the exposure and contestation of assumptions rather than to express a general oppositional stance to the putatively pathological character of a social or cultural totality. Practising criticism is a 'matter of making facile gestures difficult' (Foucault 1988i: 155).

It is clear that the content of the term critique is here radically different from its conventional sociological and social theoretical uses. These uses carry with them quite a lot of excess theoretical baggage, as I have shown. It therefore may be time to drop both the term 'critique' and the perspective from which it derives. One of the strategies for doing this might be to develop a distinction between a notion of critique and one of *criticism*. Unlike the Frankfurt notion of critique, criticism implies no necessary unity of its object, no necessary end of the criticism, and no necessary and universal grounds from which criticism is undertaken. Criticism is thus not only present-relevant but forced to be reflexive about its perspective, its value positions, and the ends it seeks. If criticism is not a totalistic posture focused on a unitary conception of the existing social order, if its objects are always multiple, then there are always grounds from which to criticise. These grounds do not have to be universal but simply defensible from the perspecitve undertaken by criticism. It is true that criticism cannot guarantee its own value but by being explicit about its perspective criticism itself enters into the space of the contestation and evaluation of arguments and ideas.

Chapter 7

Habermas' modernist translations

The only Thought which Philosophy brings with it to the contemplation of History, is the simple conception of *Reason*; that Reason is the Sovereign of the World; that the history of the world, therefore, presents us with a rational process.

(Hegel 1956: 9)

Hegel inaugurated the discourse of modernity.

(Habermas 1987a: 51)

In previous chapters, I have sought to define the conditions for historical–sociological study as an effective history that resists the characteristic moves of the dialectical and synthetic philosophies of history. I have opposed the philosophers' History to the philosophic meditation on the practice of historians. I have sought to suggest ways in which the relations between subjectivity, rationality, and conduct, can be rearranged. I have opposed the rational subject to rationality as a condition of forms of subjectivity and conduct, the unitary process of rationalisation to the multiple rationalities inscribed within social practices, and a normative to a performative conception of reason. I have refused, in short, to understand historical practice in terms of either the epic of the subject or the destiny of the West and its universal reason.

As a consequence, the following conditions for an effective historical sociology have emerged. It must be able to undertake a non-reductive analysis of forms of selfhood and rationality, and to grasp the relation between kinds of rationality and social and institutional practices without recourse to universalistic a priori models. It should seek a clearing, freed from reductionism and anachronism, in which it is possible to make intelligible specific configurations or ensembles of socio-cultural practices and their conditions of emergence and existence. It must be able to arrange these configurations within serial and multiple trajectories without definite origin or necessary end. Where the synthetic philosophy of history would enclose us within the smooth arc of a transcendental-historical destiny, the task of an effective historical sociology is to undertake an organisation of historical knowledge without compromising the field of uncertainty and contingency.

Above all, we must refuse the 'blackmail of the Enlightenment', as well as the blackmail of reason and the blackmail of modernity. Today, however, it is precisely the Enlightenment and the 'project' of modernity to which it gives birth that is used to undermine the claims of an effective historical study. In this chapter, I propose to investigate the claims made for a 'project of modernity' by Jurgen Habermas and his consequent criticisms laid at Foucault's philosophical-historical practice. My general argument here is that, while these criticisms fall short of their target, they demonstrate a further condition for our task, the need to become aware of the limits of the discourse of modernity. If, today, modernity has become problematic, it is not because we have moved into a post-modernity. It is rather that the debates over these terms have long ceased to be the province of an effective history and entered the domain of the philosophers' History.

HABERMAS AND MODERNITY

Jürgen Habermas may at times in his career have been regarded as a social theorist or even a sociologist. During the 1980s, at least, his central concern – despite his own self-understanding[1] – has been that of the philosophy of history, if we take the criterion presented to us by Hegel in the statement quoted above. Habermas is centrally concerned with the course of reason throughout history and the potential for its realisation that is held to exist in what he calls modernity. The fact that this reason is intersubjective and 'dialogical', rather than subjective and monological, cannot save Habermas' theory of social evolution from the fate of the philosophies of history. The problematic of communicative rationality can no more fulfil the requirements of an effective history, and form the basis for a critical historical sociology, than can the teleologies of subjective reason.

Habermas (1987a: 1) draws upon Weber's conception of universal history and its identification of modernity with Western rationalism. He understands Weber as proposing that the twin processes of rationalisation and disenchantment led to the disintegration of religious and metaphysical world views and replaced them with three differentiated 'cultural spheres of value' instanced by the empirical sciences, the autonomous arts, and theories of morality and law. The substantive reason expressed in religion and metaphysics, Habermas notes (1985: 9), gives way to the differentiation of aspects of validity now placed within these value spheres. As is well known, these spheres and their areas of concern are: cognitive-instrumental rationality, concerned with problems of truth and knowledge; moral-practical rationality, encompassing normative rightness and justice; and aesthetic-expressive rationality, involving authenticity and beauty. These spheres develop 'learning processes' in accord with their own inner logics and give rise to areas of expertise and to distinct groups of experts. This rationalisation of value spheres eventually leads to a culture of experts whose control over these areas publicly threatens the ground of everyday communication and existence, the *Lebenswelt* or life-world. The problem of cultural modernity, then, is how to put these different value spheres into contact with one another, and back in touch with the context of communication found in everyday life, without reducing or collapsing them into one another or compromising their potential contribution to human emancipation.

This, however, is not the end of the problem of rationalisation for Habermas. For him, modernity contains an internal tension between the processes of societal rationalisation and cultural rationalisation (Habermas 1987a: 2), or even between social and cultural modernity (Habermas 1985). Again using Weber, Habermas argues that modernity is the generalisation of the structures of purposive rationality giving rise to functionally interdependent systems revolving around the capitalist market and the state bureaucracy. However, drawing on Durkheim and George Herbert Mead, he argues that it can also be characterised by the breakdown of traditional forms of life and occupation, self-reflection on traditions, abstract individuality, and the universalisation of norms and values. But modernity presents a paradox, or rather an 'incomplete project'. These types of individuals equipped with the capacity of reflexive critique and such norms are open to the enormous potential of a communication undistorted by ascribed differences and traditional forms of hierarchy and domination. Yet, by contrast, the imperatives of the economic and administrative systems evolving within societal rationalisation colonise and thus threaten the conditions of human existence in the lifeworld.

This contrast between system and lifeworld is at the heart of Habermas' diagnosis of the pathologies and potentials of modernity. The form of rationalisation diagnosed by Weber and adopted in the analysis of *The Dialectic of Enlightenment* is not a necessary part of Western rationalism, but the pathological colonisation of this lifeworld by system imperatives (Habermas 1987b: 303–12). Under such conditions, humans cannot realise the potential to communicate with each other because of the noise coming from the functional demands of these intrusive systems. This is a complex and interesting philosophy of history but not a vision which would allow an effective historical–sociological study. In so far as it adopts a suprahistorical perspective that turns history into the drama of a humankind caught between system and lifeworld, the last act of which always remains to be staged, it is a philosophy of history. In so far as it projects the processes of becoming a universal reason onto history, it is a thoroughly Hegelian one.

This particular becoming of reason is called the Enlightenment project, or project of modernity, a project entailing the development of the cultural spheres to enrich everyday life (Habermas 1985: 9). However, today the value spheres are almost completely autonomous and are divorced from what he calls the 'hemeneutics of everyday communication'. This gives rise to what Habermas sees as *false* attempts to overcome this differentiation by mere negation, such as surrealism, which sought to break the specific container of art by proclaiming the end of the distinction between art and life. Also included in such attempts are virtually all the major philosophical movements of the nineteenth and twentieth century that have sought to settle accounts with the Hegelian philosophy of history. By contrast, Habermas considers his own philosophy as one seeking to fulfil the promise of modernity contained in the Enlightenment. This is the *true* response to the situation of modernity. Habermas thus distinguishes between the false attempts to pronounce the end (in the sense of 'death') of philosophy and the true project of the realisation of the end (in the sense of goal or *telos*) of philosophy. Such a project seeks 'a differentiated relinking of modern culture within an everyday praxis that still depends on vital heritages', and to set limits to the system imperatives of economy and state by means of institutions developed out of the lifeworld (ibid. 13).

The relationship between cultural and societal modernisation is also at the centre of Habermas' classification of the anti-modernism of various intellectual and political figures and groups. The 'old conservatives' reject both societal modernisation and its cultural products, to withdraw to a premodernism (Habermas 1985: 14). The 'neo-conservatives', like Daniel Bell, approve wholeheartedly of societal modernisation while deploring the effects of the contents of cultural modernity. The 'young conservatives' draw upon the experience of decentred subjectivity to oppose the regime of instrumental reason as one of power *par excellence*, and so oppose societal modernisation. It is the final category in which Habermas lumps Foucault, as a figure between Georges Bataille and Jacques Derrida, at least in his programmatic speech of 1980 (ibid. 14).

If, then, this is Habermas' characterisation of modernity, then what of the discourse to which it is attached? Here, it is Hegel, reflecting upon the legacy and achievements of the critical philosophy of Kant, who inaugurates the 'philosophical discourse of modernity', and, for the first time, poses the problem of the self-consciousness and self-groundedness of modernity. Modernity, in a word, is self-identity.

For Habermas, the distinctiveness of the discourse of modernity is its self-consciousness of a new age which actively breaks with the past and for which the future has already begun. He cites the intellectual historian Reinhart Koselleck to the effect that around 1800 *nostrum aevum* (our age) became the *nova aetas* (the new age) (Habermas 1987a: 5). For Hegel, moreover, this new age is the modern age, and his present the glorious sunrise on this, the last stage of history. Hegel dated this age from around 1500, from the time of the discovery of New World, the Renaissance, and the Reformation. From such a viewpoint the synthetic philosophy of history of the Enlightenment was born. This notion of the new age lends the past a world-historical quality in which history becomes the progressive overcoming of problems and obstacles, and time a scarce resource. The key words of the end of the eighteenth and early nineteenth centuries all express the openly messianic nature of this philosophy of history: revolution, progress, crisis, emancipation. In Habermas' striking phrase modernity had to create 'its normativity out of itself' (1987a: 7).

This self-groundedness is central to Habermas' characterisation of modernity and its philosophical discourse. This is true especially of its relation to the past, which has to be continually reconstructed: 'A present that understands itself which the horizon of modern age ... has to recapitulate the break brought about with the past as a *continuous renewal*' (Habermas 1987a: 7). Habermas shows that this self-grounding of modernity is found in the understanding of avant-garde art and is present in Baudelaire's conception of art in which the actual and the eternal intersect (ibid. 8–9). If the aesthetic experience splits from the conventions of everyday life, it is only to effect better this self-grounding. He also draws upon Walter Benjamin's conception of *Jetzeit* (now time) as one shot through with messianic or completed time (ibid. 10–12). Benjamin rebels against the borrowed normativity implicit in the social evolutionary levelling off of history and its replacement by an homogeneous and empty time in evolutionism and historicism.

Habermas (1987a: 15–16) seeks to combine aspects of both Benjamin and Koselleck. On the one hand, the latter views modernity as a future-oriented present historically responsible to solve present problems for future generations. On the other, Benjamin allows us to point out the 'secret narcissism of effective-historical consciousness' which, because it breaks with the past, can only ever appropriate it for its own interests under the stress of this responsibility. Benjamin could be said to complete the self-grounding of the present by extending this responsibility to past eras and epochs. It is not only the future but also the past that can claim the 'weak messianic power of the present' (ibid. 14). By correcting present amnesias about past injustices, modernity can become the point of intersection of the past with its future and the present with its future and so becomes the communicative locus for all generations, dead, living, and yet to be born.

Like Foucault, the affirmation of presentness is certainly central to Habermas' thought. But, unlike Foucault, the present is conceived as an arena for reconciliation and identity, rather than problematisation and uncertainty. Moreover, the present it fitted out with the ready-made identity of modernity. As I have pointed out in chapter 3, the notion of the present as a unity of interdependent elements present to one another is itself problematic in that it is both a form of teleology and begs crucial questions such as 'which present?' and 'present for whom?' The thrust of Foucault's position would appear to abandon the notion of modernity as a period, age, epoch, type of society, and so on, and restricts it to a particular attitude for a specific cultural and intellectual grouping. For Habermas, by contrast, this present as modernity is both a form of time-consciousness, one which commences with a particular group but is necessarily universalising, and a period, in that it defines the result of the trajectory of rationalisation. If the present can potentially become the locus of a 'universal historical solidarity' it is only by first asserting one version of presentness over all possible and actual alternatives. The present can only be understood as modernity – to use Habermas' term – by the exclusion of those presents that are not modern, and by the subjugation of those presents and those forms of collective and individual experience that are neither self-grounding nor self-identical within modernity, including the experience of the facticity of language, of the body and death, and the discovery of the unconscious and desire. Habermas seems to be ignoring at least one more conventional sense of the word 'modern' in art and literature, which would suggest that the dissolution of certainties and identities, and a problematisation of perspective, lie at the base of modern experiences.

For Habermas, the fundamental problem of all modern philosophy is modernity's self-groundedness, a problem coming to a head only at the end of the eighteenth century with Hegel. Hegel, according to Habermas, was to obtain criteria from the principle of subjectivity which, while taken from the modern world, were fit for orienting oneself in itself (1987a: 20). If modernity is to be grasped as a self-grounding, self-reassuring age without unreflective appeal to ancient models and tradition for their own sake or their own interests, then it must establish a coherent self-identity out of its own divisions or 'diremptions' (ibid. 16). For Hegel the solution lies in subjectivity, the structure of self-relation, a unitary centre of rational consciousness and autonomous will transparent unto itself. The three events which establish subjectivity as the principle of modernity, the Enlightenment, the Reform-ation, and the French Revolution, enshrine the rule of individual insight over tradition, and of freedom of will over historical law and morality. Science, art, and morality, as well as religion, state, and society, become embodiments of the principle of subjectivity.

According to Habermas, Hegel finds that Kant's critical philosophy best describes both these 'diremptions', and the transcendental place of the principle of subjectivity in relation to these divided spheres of art, morality, and knowledge. He thus states that 'Hegel seeks the essence of the modern world gathered into its focal point' in Kant (Habermas 1987a: 18–19). However, even in Kant, Hegel found a one-sided problem of subjectivity. On the one hand, the bringing about of subjective freedom and autonomous reflection and action undermines the unifying power of religion. On the other, in undermining religion, modernity sunders the harmony of life by placing reason alongside religion and splitting faith from knowledge (ibid. 20).

If Hegel wished to diagnose the problem of modernity through its manifestation in Kantian critical philosophy, Habermas finds the very unresolved problems of modernity in Hegel's mature position, together with all post-Hegelian thought which has tried to free itself from Hegel's absol-utising solutions. For Habermas, the young Hegel sought to resolve the above dilemma by working through a conception of the reconciling power of reason which traces the authoritarian side of self-consciousness not to an 'overblown subjectivity that overextends its claims' but to an 'alienated subjectivity that has broken with common life' (1987a: 29). In so doing, Habermas continues, Hegel stood at the crossroads at which he could have chosen to attempt to re-establish the divided totality of ethical life not by the monological self-transparency of the knowing subject but by means of an intersubjectivity of mutual understanding.

At this point the philosophical discourse of modernity reached perhaps its most fundamental turning-point and took a direction from which it has yet to recover, at least according to Habermas' diagnosis of our current dilemmas (1987a: 29–31). The later Hegel rejected the route toward grounding the project of modernity in the conditions of intersubjectivity because he could not conceive the idea of an ethical totality outside the idealised form of definite historical communities such as primitive Christianity and the Greek polis. This is because modernity had attained self-consciousness without recourse to exemplary pasts, and because modern society encompassed the novel reality of 'civil society' uncovered by the political economists. Hegel thus fatefully abandons the possibility of intersubjectivity as a means of overcoming the diremptions of modernity, and embarks on the course of overcoming the problems of the philosophy of the subject with an overblown version of itself in his notion of the absolute. The absolute is neither subject nor object but is 'apprehended only as the mediating process of relation to self that produces it free from conditions' (ibid. 34). By its invocation, Hegel uses the principle of subjectivity to overcome a subject-centred reason.

If Hegel stood at the crossroads, and took the wrong path, all that has occurred since is a series of mistaken attempts to move away from Hegel. For Habermas (1987a: 53), we are all contemporaries of the Young Hegelians in so far as we seek to distance ourselves from Hegel and philosophy in general. The discourse of modernity continues in a variety of guises, none of which respect the privileges of academic philosophy. The intellectual appears on the margins of academic philosophy: as 'dismissed privadozents, journalists, literary men'; as 'political and social scientists' and enthnologists; and finally within physics, biology, psychology, and the historical sciences (ibid. 52). In the twentieth century, philosophy responded to this by pronouncing its own end in a variety of forms:

> No matter what name it appears under now – whether as fundamental ontology, as critique, as negative dialectics, deconstruction, or genealogy – these pseudonyms are by no means disguises under which the traditional form of philosophy lies hidden; the drapery of philosophical concepts more likely serves as the cloak for a scantily concealed end of philosophy.
>
> (Habermas 1987a: 53)

In short, it would seem that Habermas asks that we silence the legion voices of dissent and the rights of forms of positive knowledge to speak to their contemporary situation. If modernity presents us with difficult existential dilemmas for humanity that can only be resolved within modernity, the philosophical discourse of modernity remains an expression of such dilemmas rather than their resolution. Speaking in the name of communicative reason and a 'normative conception of modernity', Habermas issues the call for the fulfilment of modernity and a restoration of the rights of philosophy. For our present purposes, included in this call is the right of philosophy over history, the right of philosophy to issue the final interpretation of history. From the perspective of effective history, however, this history can only be the philosophers' imaginary History, the history of the realisation of a reason already awaiting release, of the discovery of an identity contained but hidden within the present.

Habermas diagnoses our problems as those of the Young Hegelians. But the path he chooses is precisely that of the latter or of at least one group of them. He is, on his own criteria, a left Hegelian philosopher of history and cultural critic: '*Left Hegelian* critique, turned toward the practical and aroused for revolution, aimed at mobilising the historically accumulated potential for reason (awaiting release) against its mutilation, against the one-sided rational-isation of the bourgeois world' (Habermas 1987a: 56). With the exception of revolutionary arousal, there is no better description of that which passes for theory in Habermas. Let us now turn to his criticism of one of the problematic dissidents of modernity, Michel Foucault.

HABERMAS' CRITIQUE OF FOUCAULT

What, then, is Habermas' developed position on Foucault? We have noted that he placed Foucault in the camp of the 'young conservatives' of the Weimar period, who adopt modernistic cultural attitudes only to justify an antimodernism, and who celebrate the experiences of decentred subjectivity as they claim emancipation from the instrumental imperatives of work and usefulness (Habermas 1985: 14). This is not a reserved charge for the German young conservatives, including Heidegger and Carl Schmitt, like Nietzsche, are understood by Habermas as politically suspect due to their influence on or complicity with Nazism.[2] This is a position which has been contested quite vigorously from quarters not entirely sympathetic to Foucault (Fraser 1985). We shall also note that Habermas' memorial address a few years later admits that he did not understand Foucault very well (Habermas 1989). We might thus expect that when Habermas devoted two full lectures to Foucault (Habermas 1987a), a quite different and more complete understanding would emerge. Let us turn to those lectures while keeping this earlier characterisation in mind.

Readers might justifiably conclude from the length of this critical engage-ment that Foucault is Habermas' 'preferred partner' from recent French thought (McCarthy 1987: xiv). From the point of view of the concerns of the present work around historical methodology and historiography, this engagement is extremely valuable because of the centrality of such issues to Habermas' critique. We can agree that Habermas' disagreements 'certainly do not amount to a blanket rejection' of Foucault's position (ibid. xv), although they could hardly be said to be products of a favourable reception. Indeed it might be argued that the very length of the engagement (some sixty pages in its English translation) suggests something of the value of the position to be engaged with.

It is not too much to argue that Habermas' critique boils down to the claim that Foucault undertakes a *total* critique of modernity. There are two aspects of this claim turning on different senses of the word 'total'. In the first, a total critique makes a general statement about the nature of modernity and the form of reason characteristic of it. In the second, a total critique threatens to undermine its own claims because it does not possess criteria of validity and a normative basis for critique. A third aspect of Habermas' critique, which can be taken less seriously, is a kind of 'guilt by association' charge, i.e. the identification of Foucault's positions with those of politically suspect thinkers. I shall outline and address each of these three charges in turn and then examine what Habermas considers the consequences of this 'total critique' for Foucault's methodological project of genealogy. This section is a critical exposition of Habermas' thought on Foucault; the final section formulates a more sustained response in terms of my concern to displace the philosophy of history as a precondition for an effective and critical historical–sociological study, and in terms of a reflection on intellectual ethics.

The first thing to notice about Habermas' critique is one must accept that Foucault (and all its other targets) can be understood as attempting to characterise modernity and can be located within – or at least in relation to – the philosophical discourse of modernity. Modernity is thought as the inescapable horizon of contemporary thought. In this sense, despite his claims to have escaped modernist narcissism, Habermas refuses to read thinkers as operating in any field other than the one he has outlined and defined the possible positions within. In the terms of recent sociology of science, Habermas is engaged in an act of 'translation'.[3] Foucault's enterprise is then interpreted as having a fairly simple relation to such figures as Enlightenment, modernity, and reason, that of condemnation. Where Foucault's genealogy sought to make intelligible various relations between forms of discourse, rationality, and the human sciences, and the power relations and institutional practices in which they are inscribed, Habermas undertakes a somewhat gross reduction of such issues (Habermas 1987a: 246) to that of 'the internal kinship between humanism and terror that endows his critique of modernity with its sharpness and mercilessness'. Habermas translates Foucault into the discourse of modernity in order to attribute to him a general position within it. The first aspect of the charge of total critique is thus an artefact of Habermas' own position.

This move also allows Habermas to position Foucault in relation to more familiar ground for critical theory, the ground mapped out in *The Dialectic of Enlightenment*. Habermas (1987a: 248–9) characterises genealogy as an anti-science which aims at a radical critique of reason, and argues that 'the entire weight of the problematic rests on the basic concept of power that lends the dimension of being a critique of modernity'. For Habermas, this concept of power is at once transcendental and historicist (1987a: 256–7). On the one hand, power is synonymous with what he calls a 'purely structuralistic activity', the operations or rules of discursive formation which bring order to the non-subjective, decentred, elements of discourse. On the other hand, the concept of power serves the purpose of empirical analysis of forms of discourse (ibid. 256). These two elements of Foucault's concept of power allow it to function as empirical analysis and total critique of reason (ibid. 256), as 'functionalist social science' and 'historiography of constitutive conditions of reason and truth' (ibid. 274). This reading thus permits Habermas to claim that Foucault's genealogy of the human sciences is not simply a method of critical analysis but rather based on the supposition that *in their very form* the human sciences are an amalgam of knowledge and power (ibid. 272).

In such statements, Habermas continues his act of translation: not only is Foucault positioned as a dogmatic critic of modernity but is now translated into the terms of critical theory and assigned a place in its retrospectively constructed trajectory. Thus Habermas cannot but read 'power–knowledge' relations in terms of the complete identity in form and content of reason and domination, i.e. the diagnosis found within *The Dialectic of Enlightenment*. I would suggest that there is a world of difference between 'knowledge is power' and 'forms of knowledge have specific and analysable rapport with particular power relations'. Having identified Foucault with the former position, that of this seminal text of critical theory, the next move allows Habermas to distinguish Foucault from critical theory. Indeed, Foucault's account of power–knowledge becomes translated into the terms of Horkheimer and Adorno's argument so that it might be made into a deficient version of it.

This is accomplished in a series of arguments to the effect that a truly critical impulse passes by the total critique. Foucault is now characterised as at first a stoic, concerned with a history of the 'crystalline' formations of discourse, and later a cynic, for whom 'the only thing that lasts is power, which appears with ever new masks in the change of anonymous processes of overpowering' (Habermas 1987a: 253). This cynicism is anathema to critical theory, because it lacks the latter's *emancipatory* character. In short, Foucault is charged with lacking a conception of human being and its potentials as a normative basis to mount his analyses of power–knowledge; i.e. he lacks the procedures of critical theory. There are several points to be made here.

First, it is worth recalling our earlier reflection on this notion of 'critique'. Within the terms of critical theory, 'critique' stands for that process by which the pathological processes of rationalisation can be judged from the perspective of universal values and in the name of 'emancipation'. It thus presupposes a conception of the universal potentials and emancipatory interests of human beings that are stifled or deformed by current forms of rationalisation. Because Foucault undertakes an analysis of different forms of rationalisation, and the differential relations between power and knowledge, no such general position external to processes of rationalisation need be taken. Such analysis allows us to make criticisms of, say, prison systems, welfare arrangements, forms of governance, practices of psychological counselling, from various standpoints (e.g. the concern with the maximisation of life chances, the optimisation of autonomy, the limitation of forms of domination), without undertaking anything as grandiose as a critique. A critical historical study does not have to take the form of a critique.

Secondly, it follows from this that a normative position does not have to be couched in terms of a universal conception of human being and human interests. It simply requires that there is a possibility that things might be otherwise than they are and grounds for deciding which state of affairs is preferable. These grounds themselves are in principle contestable. Thus while it might be argued that systems of governance are necessary components of advanced liberal states, there is no necessity as to the form this governance takes. Various modes of governance can be criticised from a variety of ethical, political, and technical perspectives, such as potential for individual or collective choice, degree of participation in decision-making, their cumbersome nature, and so on. One of the satisfying things about Foucault's analyses is that they do not feel the necessity to invoke strict, universal, normative standpoints and political visions from which forms of power might be judged. The radicality of his position – missed by critics such as Fraser (1989: 17–34) – is its capacity to multiply forms of criticism while abstaining from the sacred and hierarchical duty of the social critic to speak from the position of privileged access to a superior world or set of values. Increasingly, however, as I shall show, Foucault offers us conceptions of power and domination and their ethical implications that provides means of considering social practices and arrangements.

The third problem with the charge that Foucault is a deficient critical theorist is that in it the term 'power' is identified as the weapon of total critique, in much the same way that the term 'domination' functions in *The Dialectic of Enlightenment*. As I shall also show in the following chapters, Foucault does present us with the resources for a differentiated understanding of problems of power, governance, and domination in contemporary societies, especially in his fragments on what he called 'governmentality'. The point to note here is that it is possible to distinguish such concepts without invoking a general concept of emancipation, its implicit essentialism concerning human being and its normativity concerning human arrangements. Indeed, the concept of general human emancipation (as distinct from the notion of liberation or emancipation within the demands of such struggles as anticolonial or women's 'liberation movements') is only possible within the philosophies of history which seek to construct stories of the origin, fall, and salvation of human beings. In this sense, rather than a creation of the Enlightenment, it is quite possible that 'emancipation' is more closely linked to the secularisation of Christian eschatology.

The final point is to note that Habermas' position on Foucault remains continuous as to the charge of complicity with reactionary thought. For example, Habermas discovers (1987a: 254–6) in the concept of power many 'aporias' analogous to the theoretical moves made by Heidegger. They are both undialectical. He compares the Heideggerian destruction of metaphysics with a putative destruction of historiography in Foucault, and the overcoming of philosophy with what he describes as 'the surpassing' of historical science. The transformations of the rules of discursive formations in which truth is located are compared to the changing 'horizons of given world' of Heidegger. Finally, this leaves both thinkers in a similar paradox: while they assert that truth is formed under specific, historically changing conditions, they claim a 'paravalidity' which can explain the very course of these changing conditions, by referring back to the history of Being as a 'truth-occurrence' and source of mystical illumination, or by recourse to the transcendental concept of power.

The assumption of this final line of attack is an elementary but highly dubious one: that theoretical structures have necessary political consequences. If there is no necessary correspondence between theory and political position, then no condemnation by association can be issued. Further, what becomes important are the uses to which specific theories, their structures and contents are put. As for the more specific argument by analogy with Heidegger, the comparison does not allow for what is particular to Foucault's position. Rather than the epistemological problem of the validity of given propositions, Foucault is concerned with the problem of inscription of truth within the various practices of its social production, and its consequences for social life. In other words, Foucault examines truth and its historicity rather than truth and its procedures of validation. As I have argued in regard to Weber's proposed ontological foundations of the cultural sciences, Foucault is not seeking the grounds for a cultural, human, or social science. One condition for communication between positions, it might be added, is to take seriously the projects and argument of one's opponents.

Let us now turn to what Habermas views as the consequences for Foucault's genealogical and historical method. The general form of Habermas' argument is the familiar one of showing that what is rejected is in fact not effectively banished and returns in an unacknowledged form. Thus, for Habermas (1987a: 274), while genealogy is supposed to displace the tran-scendental and empirical 'doublet' of the subject, its concept of power actually reproduces the position of the subject in Kantian philosophy in reversed form. Foucault is said simply to reverse the dependency relation of power and truth. Such a move cannot break with the 'strategic conceptual constraints' of the philosophy of the subject, and in fact results in three substitutions by genealogy of the assumptions underlying the human sciences (ibid. 275): for a hermeneutics of meaning, an analytic of meaningless structures; for validity claims, the systems or regimes of power; and for value-judgements, the erudite and positivist historical explanations. But Foucault's genealogy cannot remain the 'fortunate positivism' it seeks to be: 'the radical historicist extinction of the subject ends up in an unholy subjectivism' (ibid. 276). Foucault's positivism becomes haunted by the remnants of the internal aspects of meaning, of truth, and of value, it had sought to overcome. The return of these components gives rise to three characterisations of Foucault's work: presentism, relativism, and cryptonormativism. I shall now examine each of these.

The issue of presentism was dealt with in chapter 2 in considerable detail. I want here only to add a further observation. It will be recalled that, for Habermas, the critique of hermeneutics leads Foucault from an objectivism to a genealogy ultimately linked to a narcissistic diagnosis of the present moment, i.e. a history of the present. Habermas rejects the legitimacy of the genealogical move in which criteria of relevance constructed from within the present could lead to an historical examination that addresses a historical field first by means of its own terms and without invoking the standards of present-day science as epistemological norms. The point to note is that the genealogical-archaeological approach of Foucault's 'history of the present' suggests paths combining the criteria of relevance of a critical history with an effective historical method freed from the burden of anachronism and narcissism. The alternative – that of Habermas – is to retreat into a philosophy of history in which both critical history and effective method are not problems. This is because a philosophy of history is always already satisfied that it knows the meaning and value of history as the progressive realisation of reason and truth. The alternative is between hard and patient historical labours and the fairy-stories of the project of modernity.

Turning to the issue of relativism, Habermas claims (1987a: 279) that genealogy is caught in the contradiction that it cannot account for the basis of its own superior claims. If the meaning of the validity claims of all discourses is to be found in their power effects, then genealogy is afflicted by the same condition as the human sciences it analyses. There is no way it can demonstrate the greater validity of its own claims. Habermas cites Foucault's attempts in his 1976 lectures at the *College de France*, which present the formation of genealogy in terms of a historic link between 'local memories' and 'disqualified knowledge', to argue that he fails to demonstrate why the validity claims of the counter-discourse or anti-science of genealogy have greater force than those of the discourse of power (Habermas 1987a: 281). The problem with this criticism is that it mistakes both the point of the particular discussion referred to and genealogy itself. As for the latter, genealogy is not a surrogate epistemology: it is another form of relationship to statements. If epistemology is concerned with the validity of statements, with statements as true knowledge, genealogy is concerned with the conditions and effects of particular regimes of truth. Habermas not only construes Foucault as a defective critical theorist. He attributes to him the task of critique, of unmasking the false within what passes for true knowledge. In regard to the account of the relation of genealogies to popular struggles, the point of this discussion would seem less to establish the truth of genealogical study than its position, and hence pertinence, within a field of contestation over truth. Again, it is Habermas who displays the narcissistic relation to his own present, and his own membership of a particular intellectual community.

This problem is even more evident in Habermas' final criticism (1987a: 282–6) of Foucault. Here, Habermas argues that Foucault cannot wholly succeed in banishing value-judgements from his genealogy. While genealogy is an engaged form of discourse, it constantly refuses to provide the basis of that engagement, and so cannot function as critique. Openly depriving himself of a normative basis in the experiences of aesthetic modernity, and thus distancing himself from his obvious forebears, Nietzsche and Bataille, Foucault is only left with an occasional flirtation with a vitalistic *Lebensphilosophie* which refers to the body and its pleasures. As we have already shown, it is indeed beside the point to suggest that genealogy cannot function as critique. It is not critique but rather a critical and effective form of history concerned with the analysis of the differential regimes of truth and their consequences. It refuses a universalist normative basis because it does not seek to function on the basis of the defence of universal values. It is concerned rather to analyse and reflect upon the effects of holding such values and their implications in practices. This does not mean that Foucault's position cannot be connected to various normative regimes – it is just that it is simply not pertinent to the task of genealogy as effective history, as a history that is capable of problematising that which we take to be true and universal. Foucault's concern for ethics, which would become more explicit in his later writings, is directed to ethical practice rather than moral values. This led him not to a search for universal moral values which guaranteed the rightness and truth of one's position but to a concern for the ethics of the intellectual, which I shall now examine.

THE ETHICS OF THE INTELLECTUAL

Habermas' extended critique of Foucault's historical method, then, has less to do with Foucault's position itself than with the philosophy of history characteristic of critical theory. Structuring Habermas' criticisms is a grid of interpretation depending on a specific understanding of Weber's conception of rationalisation and its reception within earlier critical theory, particularly *The Dialectic of Enlightenment*. Habermas' criticisms are driven by considerations such as the desire to elucidate the normative underpinnings for a critical theory that conceives its relation to statements in terms of a 'critique', i.e. the unmasking of certain statements as false in relation to a conception of

a true knowledge serving emancipatory interests. These normative foundations are themselves part of the task of Habermas' philosophy of history: to
discover within modern Western thought a new dialectic of Enlightenment
indicating the path to the emancipation of humankind through its communicative rationality. This is a particular perspective through which to
approach Foucault's work. The tasks of the histories of the present are very
different. They are certainly more modest in both their aims and their claims.
As I have argued throughout this study, the history of the present combines a
systematic and methodical attempt to make intelligible forms of organised
discursive and non-discursive practice in order to problematise contingent
features of the present revealed within contemporary fields of contestation.
These studies call to be judged not in terms of the degree to which they can
rectify the path of rationalisation in the quest of emancipatory goals, but to the
extent that they provide politically useful, novel, interesting, insightful,
historical analyses into mechanisms of power and domination, practices of self-
formation, and forms of rationality and discourse. The political content of
such analyses does not derive from a universal set of normative values or a
rationalist conception of the relation between theory and practice but from
genealogical analyses of what is necessary and what is contingent within a
particular present. Genealogies reveal what is possible and even desirable from
particular perspectives; they do not prescribe what is to be done. It is this
capacity to reshape the limits of the possible by means of historical problematisation of the present that is perhaps the reason why Foucault's works,
some thirty years after the appearance of *Madness and Civilisation* (Foucault
1965), are today perceived as subversive and threatening. This is something no
philosophical critic can take from these studies.

It follows from this observation that, at a minimum, Habermas' critique
becomes tied up in a reading which falls short of addressing *our* critical
historical–sociological concerns. For example, the charge that the concept of
power fulfils contradictory functions in Foucault's discourse is of issue in a
reading concerned to stand in judgement of Foucault's contribution to the
philosophical discourse of modernity. If, by contrast, we adopt a reading
which seeks to address the methodological sources of Foucault's historical
perspectives on such themes in the service of effective historical study, then we
would be more concerned to analyse how the concept of power led Foucault
to produce particular historical analyses, where it facilitated these analyses,
where it presented an obstacle, and where it is superseded by other concepts.

From our perspective of an historical sociology, the transcendental theory
of discursive constitution imputed to Foucault by Habermas is simply not
pertinent, and the issue of whether or not such a theory does exist in
Foucault's work becomes of value only for an academic history of ideas. The
concern to elucidate the usefulness of Foucault's histories for the reconstruction of the sociological appropriation of history directs attention away
from this putative metaphysics toward the analytical and empirical intel-

ligibility given to the historical relationship between regimes of practices and the formation of veridical discourses, particularly those of the human and social sciences. Rather than providing the epistemological and normative foundations for critique, Foucault's historical studies can assist in the establishment of a form of historical study reflexively examining its own position, norms and values, and immersion in historical struggles.

The issue of reflexivity brings us to the core of the problems with Habermas' general philosophy of history. The latter refuses to reflect upon its own particular conditions of existence as a form of 'critique'. Instead, it unproblematically assumes the stance of critique and reinterprets other tasks and projects as deficient attempts to engage in that task. Needless to say, such an unreflexive position is condemned to a narcissism which interprets what is said according to that which has already been said. Even here, the form of critique adopted by Habermas is a specific one that privileges the problem of the completion of a project of modernity by resetting the path of its philosophical discourse. This standpoint then gives rise to particular – and, in this sense, arbitrary – methods of evaluation and discrimination when reading texts, e.g. where the texts or their author stands in relation to the problem of modernity. In such a reading, it is simply not possible to have given up the problem of modernity altogether. This, however, is what precisely constitutes the novelty and imperative of Foucault's position, as we saw in Chapter 2. For Habermas, however, Foucault is bound to appear as a critic of modernity. Coupled with the earlier claim of the transcendental nature of the concept of power, Foucault becomes not simply a critic but a *total* critic of reason, modernity, the Enlightenment, the human sciences, or whatever. In other words, what might otherwise seem to be analyses of the specific ways in which forms of discourse that thematise their own objectives in terms of the production of truth are implicated in forms of power, becomes transmuted into a dogmatic anti- or post-modernism. Let us simply say that Foucault is at best understood as an analyst and critic of certain dimensions of advanced liberal societies – modern, if one must – societies, not modernity *per se*. The terms modernism, post-modernism, anti-modernism, denote a different intellectual terrain from the one on which Foucault's histories can be properly situated.

If it is the lack of reflexivity concerning the nature of his own project that infirms Habermas' capacity to read positions which are other to the terrain of critical theory, it is Foucault's keen sense of reflexivity that leads him to insist on the specification of the ethical role of the intellectual. I wish to conclude this chapter with an examination of Foucault's appreciation of the ethics of the intellectual.[4] To do so, I shall commence with the vexatious issue of humanism.

First, Foucault suggests that humanism is a singularly unsuitable basis on which the critical intellectual can make normative judgements. In an interview in the United States, he says:

What I am afraid of about humanism is that it presents a certain form of our ethics as a universal model for any kind of freedom. I think that there are more secrets, more possible freedoms, and more inventions in our future than we can imagine in humanism as it is dogmatically represented on every side of the political rainbow: the Left, the Center, the Right.

(Foucault 1988l: 15)

It is not the place here to survey the various usages of the term 'humanism'. Nevertheless, Foucault's usage is less general than Heidegger's treatment of humanism as the secret of the history of Western metaphysics with its technological orientation to natural and social worlds (Heidegger 1978). Following his identification of the relatively late eighteenth centuary emergence of 'Man' as the condition of possibility of the modern episteme (1970), Foucault would seem to mean by humanism that thought which discovers a human essence in the autonomous subject of Enlightenment rationalism. In this sense, the ethics of the intellectual is not a humanist ethics because to hold to such an ethics would be to place an unnecessary and paradoxical limitation on the autonomy such rationalism extols. Moveover, it is anathema to the process of invention which is crucial to the intellectuals' role. It takes one version of what it is to be human and constitutes that as the basis of intellectual and political invention. By contrast, for Foucault, ethics concerns the rule-governed practices of acting on the self rather than the application of a true knowledge of what it is to be human. We fully develop this idea in the final chapter. As it applies to the intellectual, however, it is a vigilance about the practice of intellectual freedom, about how that freedom is used, under what conditions and with what safeguards.

The second reason that humanism is singularly unsuited to the delineation of the ethical position of the intellectual is that to adopt it is to return to a way of conceiving the relationship between the subject and power, as we shall see in the next chapter. This humanism binds the intellectual into an all or nothing position in regard to forms of power and governance. It leaves the intellectual in the ethical position of endorsing or rejecting power relations as a result of the opposition it holds between the subject and power. This is characteristic of not only the philosophy of the subject but also that of intersubjectivity. This is quite clear in the forms of critical theory we have examined. Because power distorts the human essence or its existence undermines the conditions of the 'ideal speech situation' of communicative interaction, one is simply left to reject all power, and there are no grounds on which to distinguish between forms of power, governance, and domination. The forms of social theory built on humanism have coincided with the political marginalisation of the intellectual for a good reason – they leave the critical intellectual no option but to reject power on universal ethical grounds.

A third point follows from this and clarifies the intellectual's position in relation to power. If Foucault's intellectual ethics call for a more neutral than usual analysis and evaluation of forms of power, this is not so that the intellectual can join in the 'will to power' or the 'will to govern'. During the 1970s Foucault wedded genealogy to a politics of resistance, and an ethics which led him to write of the possibility of a 'non-fascist' life, and to find sustenance in the 'nomadism' of Gilles Deleuze and Felix Guattari (e.g. Foucault 1983a). In his preface to *Anti-Oedipus*, Foucault writes of the essential principles of this non-fascist life. The final one is put simply: 'Do not become enamoured of power' (ibid. xiv). The ethics of the intellectual are thus defined between two quite different imperatives: the need to be able to produce analyses of forms of power freed from the humanist reduction of political choice and the imperative to guard against the danger of a kind of libidinal attachment to power, the enjoyment of the exercise of power for its own sake.

A fourth aspect of this ethics is its principled refusal to adopt the form of practice characteristic of established critical and revolutionary traditions, on one hand, and the mantle of science, on the other (cf. Patton: 1984/5). This refusal was given by Foucault's analytic understanding of the position of the intellectual (as a 'specific intellectual') in relation to society, and particularly in relation to the prevailing politics of discourse (Foucault 1980h: 126–33). To adopt either or both of the above positions was for Foucault inimical to the task of analysing the way in which 'regimes of truth' operate within advanced societies, and the connection to other features of power. An analysis which sets out to discuss the principles of inclusion and exclusion within discourse, or to examine the politics of truth, could hardly appeal to the authority of science, with its hierachicising claims, and/or the authority of traditions and authorial references, again a key mode of ensuring the legitimacy of one's discourse. As such, Habermas' claims that Foucault's histories swing between positivism and perspectivism seem to miss the point of the archaeological and genealogical projects to define and analyse the specific operation of scientific and other intellectual norms in modern societies.

It should be noted that this ethics does not rule out a priori arguments for the scientific status of specific human sciences. It only demands that we take into account the specific politics of truth that is being played out within a particular region of knowledge. It could be argued, for example, that Foucault's historical studies themselves display many features which could in themselves be called 'scientific' (e.g. conceptual coherence, systematic procedures, evidential criteria, formalised methods and techniques, attempts to distinguish between statements of value and ones of fact, etc.) even though they refuse to adopt the mantle of science. One might argue that such a position was a feature of the specific politics of truth pertaining in France and Europe generally in the 1970s at the time of the contestation of the claims of structural and scientistic versions of Marxism. A similar conjuncture was present in sociology in Anglophonic countries in the 1970s when that discipline was engaged in breaking first with functionalism and positivism and, later, with Marxism. In a 'politics of truth' where the main dangers arise less from the status of scientific claims than from the rejection of all criteria of validation and a political threat to the continued institutional existence of sociology then the argument that sociology is a science assumes a quite different status. The key point is not whether one is for or against science, but to attain a degree of reflexivity about the effects of arguing that a particular discourse is or is not a science within a particular politics of truth.

Fifth, there is the concern to give renewed centrality and significance to various features of modern societies which appear to have reached a level of saturation regarding their intelligibility, and hence start falling below the threshold of visibility into a certain givenness or taken for grantedness. This would certainly be true, for example, of the questions of madness, of imprisonment, and of sexuality at the time Foucault devoted volumes to each. Genealogical analyses are conjunctural but, *pace* Habermas, it does not mean that they are contaminated by presentism. The will to knowledge of such a genealogy is first of all one seeking a rigorous and systematic understanding of aspects of the past, an intelligibility freed from anachronism and the claims of a totalistic and exhaustive historical reconstruction, and the presuppositions of the teleological philosophy of history. It is also, however, a form of history arising from specific engagement with the particular regimes of truth the specific intellectual is located within, regimes which almost invariably involve forms of social science and social theory.

Indeed, it may be argued that implicit in Foucault's reflexive intellectual ethics is the idea that the social and human sciences should not be protected from historical problematisation and analysis in terms of the social, political, and institutional practices to which they are linked. This intellectual ethos does not arise from a rejection of these sciences *tout court*, a desire to unmask these as pseudo-sciences, nor from a wish to reduce them to the context from which they arise. Rather, it arises from an historical analysis of the degree of rapport between such sciences and the art and practice of government in certain contemporary societies. This is why genealogy seeks to construct an intel-lectual place outside that of human sciences. Thus to grasp the intelligibility of notions of madness, mental illness and mental health, one cannot take the internal perspective of psychiatry, psychotherapy, and psychology. Rather, it is necessary to address such disciplines from the perspective of the conditions of existence of what they take to be their domains. A similar point could be made for the issue of poverty and disciplines of political economy, applied social investigation, and social policy. Genealogy openly seeks a space outside the presuppositions of the human and social sciences allowing it to contest assumptions concerning the inevitability, marginality, low theoretical status, and so on, of the formation of various governable object-domains. In short, genealogy is a reflexive method enabling us to go beyond the extant categories of the social sciences and make them a part of the object of analysis.

This is not, as Habermas suggests, a precipitous replacement of validity claims with power structures, that inevitably leads to a relativism which cannot sustain its own claims or account for its own foundations. Rather, it is an attempt to place the validity claims of discourses within the systems of truth embedded in current social practices and technologies of governance. This of itself is an interesting move which suspends rather than denies the truth claims of specific discourse in order to understand how discourses come to circulate and function as true. Because genealogy is peculiarly sensitive to the procedures and practices governing truth, and because of its explicit stance in countering the hierarchical effects of claims to scientificity, it seeks another intellectual practice which does not rely on appeals to truth, universality, class consciousness, and so on. The 'truth-effects' of genealogy are always limited, partial, incomplete, open to revision, and of local application. This does not mean, however, that they are somehow arbitrary, or narcissistically relative to the standpoint of the historian, as Habermas claims.

This, then, is not value-free sociology, and the genealogical position of a counter-science existing in the interstices of particular sciences cannot be equated with Weber's cultural science blending decisionism with positivism. Genealogy would form the basis of an effective historical sociology within a normative framework arising from a general concern with the functioning of knowledge and truth in contemporary society, and a desire to construct its analysis without anachronistic recourse to those categories and concepts which themselves are knowledge-effects of the constitution of domains of objects and terrains of governance. There is no need for a genealogical historiography to appeal to some 'cryptonormative' basis within a vitalistic *Lebensphilosophie*. It has long secured such a basis in its desire to disrupt and induce critical effects in the human and social sciences. Perhaps it is Habermas who falls into naturalism with his unconditioned realm of communication, the *Lebenswelt*.

Habermas' critique of Foucault is, in short, both too overblown and too unreflexive. This arises from the particular form of reading he adopts, admitting only philosophical questions of modernity as central, and judging all endeavours accordingly. It is thus Habermas himself in this case – and not the target of his critique – who advances a form of totalistic thought applying a type of reason which abolishes the possibility of a form of analysis with different aims and objectives. Power, far from being a transcendental concept, is, as we shall see, a perspectival concept which allowed a great deal of intelligibility of the human sciences during the middle-period of Foucault's thought, and which came to be replaced with far more circumspect and differentiated notions of government, biopower, pastoral power and so on. Habermas' contention concerning Foucault's linking of humanism and terror, his totalistic critique of modernity, and his view of societal modernisation as the indefinite expansion of the panopticon are similarly overblown. Little more needs to be said about such charges at the moment except that the highly differentiated and complex approach to practices and systems of knowledge and power present in the work of Foucault and others contrasts quite vividly with the historical vacuity of the type of general concepts found in German critical theory, based as they are around such jaded oppositions between *laissez-faire* and planned capitalism, etc.

The charge that Foucault merely inverts, and therefore does not escape the aporias of the philosophy of the subject in his analytic of power, has something more to it. It is worth considering in the course of the following discussion. I would suggest that there is a certain tendency, in Foucault's efforts to free himself from the structures of phenomenological discourse, to engage in theoretical moves which make power as unconditional in its effects as the subject of classical philosophy. However, as his work on governmentality and ethics demonstrates, it was Foucault himself and not his critics who produced domains of thought beyond the confines of such formulations.

Chapter 8

Thematics of state and power

Previous chapters have been oriented toward general methodological concerns of the statement of the conditions of an effective and critical form of historical study. They have also sought to define histories of the present against reflections on historical–sociological writing and in relation to various key thinkers. In so doing, they have tended to downplay the placement of such study within particular, substantive, domains. The final three chapters seek to balance this earlier emphasis by examining aspects of the critical histories offered by Foucault and their convergence and divergence with similar problems taken up within historical sociology. These chapters address issues arising in Foucault's work of historical forms of power and government, on the one hand, and his history of sexuality, ethics, and the self, on the other. These, it should be noted, are not unrelated dimensions of Foucault's later thought. Taken together, they retrospectively situate his archaeological and genealogical projects in a triple concern for government, ethics, and rationality.

The present chapter is also an exemplar of the thesis stated in Chapter 1: that both historical sociology and Foucault's histories of the present can be understood as responses to transhistorical schemas and grand teleologies. These responses may take the form of attempted operationalisation, modification, criticism, rejection, and so on, of global forms of theory. To this end, we compare aspects of the recent 'historical sociology of the state' with Foucault's thought on power. The first section of the chapter presents an overview of certain significant features of the historical sociology of the state. These include fundamental issues, characteristic themes, and methods. This chapter also draws out – not entirely randomly – several problems raised and charted by this historical sociology. The second section examines the trajectory of Foucault's thought on issues of power during the early 1970s. Here, I discuss several aspects of his 'microphysics of power' and comment on the limitations which would give rise to the problem of governmentality in Foucault's later lectures. I attempt to indicate the fundamental differences with the historical sociology of the state in method, perspective, and substantive analyses. Pervading both this and later chapters, too, is a concern to show how Foucault's thought on power and government makes possible a differentiated analysis of forms of power relations, and an analytic of resistance to power relations, contrary to certain claims of Habermas and others.[1] An excursus at the end of this chapter focuses on the objections raised by Anthony Giddens to Foucault's account of power, time, and space.

HISTORICAL SOCIOLOGY OF THE STATE

During the 1960s, and more particularly the 1970s, social scientists and political activists alike discovered what was termed the 'theory of the state' either as a regional domain of the characterisation of societies and social relations or as a necessary counterpart to a political practice. In one sense, at least, the project of a 'theory of the state' was hardly novel, having roots in Western political philosophy and questions of the legitimacy of existing or projected forms of political rule. Indeed, the emergence of post-feudal territorial and national states in Western Europe and modern political thought were coterminous and linked in that the latter often sought to provide the grounds for the acceptance of the authority of the former. What was perhaps novel about the 'theory of the state' of the 1970s was the degree to which this was a resolutely Marxist undertaking that, while recognising the absence of a theory of the state in Marx, nevertheless sought to accomplish that theory on the basis of Marxist principles and analyses. Much attention was devoted to the problem of the state's definition, the nature of state power, the form of relation between state power and classes, their fractions, and other social forces, the question of hegemony, and the functionality of the state in relation to the mode of production. The theory of the state was a formal undertaking attempting to establish the theoretical conditions for understanding and explaining the state. The debate over the structural versus instrumental nature of state power, the apparent conflict between the logic of capital and the strategic logic of class in determining the state's form and function, the problems of legitimation functions of the capitalist state, and above all, the attempt to account for the 'relative autonomy' of state power from class relations and material interests, were its dominant themes (Jessop 1990). To say that this 'theory of the state' literature remained at the level of the characterisation of the state as the institutional form of the maintenance of social order, is not to say that it was incapable of complexity and sophistication. This is particularly the case in the writings of Nicos Poulantzas (e.g. 1973), in which the state emerged as a social relation and a specific institutional ensemble, and state power as the strategic condensation of social forces.

At the same period, and with much less fanfare, there developed and continued an explicitly macrosociological undertaking which sought to address the state in its concrete historical forms and to explain the diversity of these forms (e.g. Eisenstadt 1963; Moore 1966; Anderson 1974; Tilly 1975; Poggi 1978; Skocpol 1979). This undertaking explicitly placed itself in the tradition of grand sociological theorising but, by reference to historical analysis, did not follow the path of the 'theory of the state' noted above. Here, the intellectual lineage is more pluralist and, while Marx is certainly still present, his legacy is more likely to be mediated through that of Weber, particularly the latter's formal concepts and typologies of the state and domination. In the USA, the work of Talcott Parsons also continued to be important in this arena.

This alternate literature might be called the 'historical sociology of the state' to emphasise its intellectual inheritance and its ambitions to analyse and explain historically specific forms of state and their formation and evolution. It could be characterised in the following ways (Abrams 1982: 146–89). First, its methods are loosely comparative, the objective being the use of different cases to isolate historical causes. Secondly, its concerns are macrosociological ones to establish and verify regularities in the formation and development of states and thus offer general explanations of salient features of the state. It thus situates itself in relation to the expected regularities of the modes of explanation of grand theory, whether Marxist (e.g. Anderson 1974) or structural functionalist (e.g. Eisenstadt 1963). As a result, it makes little effort to address microsociological concerns of the individual and the event and assumes the 'top-down perspective' of the state itself. Thirdly, it follows Weber in seeking to provide more sophisticated formal definitions of the state in terms of its territoriality, its claims over the monopoly of violence, its institutions, their range of functions, and so on (e.g. Mann 1988, Poggi 1990). Following from this, fourthly, this literature typically regards the state as a 'social fact', as a datum that, once adequately defined, can be explained in terms of its extrinsic relations to other social forces and factors. Finally, what emerges in the explanations sought and offered by this literature does not typically concern the state itself or the nature of state power but the development of the state in relation to the formation of capitalism, the processes of bureaucratisation and rationalisation, or the development of the institutional forms of liberal-democratic constitutionalism.

This historical sociology of the state seeks to activate research problems stemming from various forms of social theory even where it finds the existing theory seriously lacking. Thus, for example, Anderson's *Lineages of the Absolutist State* (1974) takes the problem of the form of state which appears at what Marxists would regard as a transitional stage between feudalism and capitalism. The character of this form of state, and its relation to the various modes of production and class power, is a hotly disputed one in Marxist theory. Indeed, the 'absolutist state' appears to disrupt neat schemas of historical development, and even to develop a greater than allowable autonomy from a dominant class, and thus to challenge the fundamental premises of Marxist theory. Anderson's response – that this state form is a 'redeployed and recharged apparatus of feudal domination' consequent upon the dissolution of serfdom and the rise of the urban bourgeoisie – is clearly a well constructed and complex attempt to save and even enhance a totalising theory. Strangely enough, the result is not so much a new understanding of the form of the absolutist state *per se* but that of the old question of the genesis of capitalism, or the Weberian problem of the historical preconditions for the formation of capitalism.

A similar relation to global theory is found in S. N. Eisenstadt's *The Political Systems of Empires* (1963) in which the language of functionalism is used to assess the persistence of a type of state he calls 'historical bureaucratic regimes' which covers but goes beyond Anderson's absolutist state. Here notions of tradition, structural differentiation and stability serve only as the backdrop to the characterisation of the strategic intent of such regimes. This is defined by a series of contradictions between, first, the project of state-making and empire building involving the support and cultivation of non-traditional groups, and, secondly, the persistence of value-commitments and economic, cultural, and political orientations toward the traditional social order. Both these texts present a similar form of explanation: they construct the state as a kind of structurally located social actor to whom a specific intentionality might be attributed with regard both to the balance of social forces and to the form of its own administrative apparatus. There is little reflection, however, on the development of the mechanisms of state administration, or the means of political calculation and strategy.

During the later 1970s and 1980s, the historical sociology of the state came to ask rather different questions, focusing more directly on the space occupied by the state itself. Here, explanations in terms of class are considered 'reductionist'. In the first instance, this takes the form of a recognition that such explanations involve an unnecessary and dogmatic restriction of the range of factors which can be given causal status. Thus we find a renewed emphasis on themes which had earlier been the province of conservative forms of thought, on the state as a centre of the use of violence, a theme which had reached the historical sociology of the state most obviously by way of Weber. Now an analysis of state formation in terms of domestic relations between classes at least must be complemented by the problem of international relations of war and diplomacy. The state as nation comes into view. So, too, does the role of the military in state formation, and the place of the nation in an international system of nations. One of the first comparative studies with both internal, class relations and external, international relations in mind is Theda Skocpol's *States and Social Revolutions* (1979). She draws upon the work of not only Weber but also Otto Hintze's model of the determinants of the organisation of state by the 'structure of social classes' and 'the external ordering of states' (ibid. 30). By combining these two sets of factors, the historical sociology of the state is able to carve out a niche in which the state élite has a degree of autonomous power from contending forces and interests, and is able to play off the demands of dominant classes against war factions and other states. In a more general sense, the role of the military, war, and diplomacy in shaping the internal structure of the nation is explored and given due weight in a range of analyses (e.g. Poggi 1978; Mann 1986; Giddens 1985). One might suggest that the reintroduction of external relations of states in this literature is more an additional complexity, and not, of itself, a radical departure from conventional analyses.

Nevertheless, by opening up this problem of the autonomous space of state power, a more profound questioning of issues of power, domination and rule would begin. Of particular concern here is the problem of how rule works, of how one group is able to command and secure obedience of others, and of how this meshes with the complex administrative tasks required of and undertaken by contemporary states. What are problematised here are the actual state practices themselves and the division which they presuppose between the neutral, technical aspects of administration and their political dimensions. In a general sense, the actual activity and space occupied by the state comes to be problematised and thought through in this literature of the state in the 1980s.

I shall restrict the following discussion to drawing out three problems posed by different thinkers which may serve as a preliminary to an exploration of Foucault's contribution on power and governmentality. They are Michael Mann's notion of the infrastructural power of the state, Anthony Giddens' idea of particular locales as 'power containers', and Corrigan and Sayer's conception of the role of the state in what they call 'moral regulation'. These notion are attempts to interrogate: first, the technical-administrative dimension of state power; second, the operation of administrative power in time and space; and, third, the relation between macrosociological concerns of state formation and microsociological concerns of individuality, identity, and subjectivity. It is worth noting that at least two of these contributions are undertaken at least partially in explicit response to Foucault's deliberations.

I want first to draw upon, but not summarise, an essay by Michael Mann with a title which is worth quoting for our purposes, 'The autonomous power of the state: its origins, mechanisms and results' (1988: 1–32). As the title suggests, Mann is concerned to define the space in which the state might be said to have autonomous power and is thus very much concerned with the issues of reductionism canvassed above in relation to the theory and historical sociology of the state. Mann finds this space in what he calls the 'territorial centralisation' of the state, the fact that only the authoritative power of state, of all forms of social power, is centralised within and delimited by a specific territory (ibid. 16). I shall leave aside the question as to whether this notion is indeed the innovation that Mann claims it to be, except to note that this feature of the modern state has been stressed by virtually all commentators since at least Weber's seminal definition (1968, 1: 64).

More important are the consequences of the claim that territorial centralisation forms a potentially independent basis of power mobilisation necessary to social development (Mann 1988: 18). For it follows that it is necessary to account for state power in terms of the very mechanisms of state rule themselves rather than simply reducing it to extrinsic factors of class and nation. This insight leads Mann to offer the valuable distinction between the despotic power of the state, the 'range of actions which the élite is empowered to undertake without routine, institutionalised negotiation with civil society groups', and the infrastructural power of the state, the 'capacity of the state to actually penetrate civil society and to implement logistically political decisions throughout the realm' (ibid. 5). The former is occasional, episodic, subject to no general development, and exemplified by Mann in the capacity of the despot (whether monarch, god-king, or dictator) to shout 'off with his head' and to have this command obeyed. In contrast, infrastructural power operates continuously, has been subject to a general process of historical augmentation, and seeks to penetrate all of 'civil society'. Where it is possible to hide from despotic power, it is not easy to escape infrastructural power. The latter includes a range of state capacities that influence and structure the day to day lives of its population including taxation, information collection, enforcement of laws, and the provision of jobs and subsistence. The ideal type of the modern, 'bureaucratic state', of which constitutional democracy is an example, is one in which despotic power is low and infrastructural power high (ibid. 7–8). Perhaps the key word in describing this latter form of power and its augmentation for Mann is 'logistics'. He describes the following 'logistical techniques' as being crucial to the development of infrastructural power: a centrally co-ordinated division of labour of the state's activities; literacy, and all that enables regarding the transmission of messages and the codification of legal responsibilities; coinage, weights and measures; and communications and transport (ibid. 10).

For Mann, state power thus does not derive from techniques of power peculiar to the state itself. It is evident that the above techniques have no necessary site of social invention, and are taken up by the state in response to particular historical needs and demands and with particular objectives. One thinks here of the example of social insurance techniques as they are applied to the financial security of workers, which were first applied by working-class mutual assistance societies at the end of the eighteenth century and only much later made a principle of social welfare in Bismark's reforms. On the other hand, the state cannot keep control over its own logistical techniques, as the example of the invention of 'statistics' as a science of the state in the seventeenth and eighteenth centuries suggests. These techniques of power are thus subject to a 'diffusion' from the organisation that invented and first used them, both from and toward the state (ibid. 11).

As we shall see, Mann's analysis is consonant with certain themes appearing in Foucault's analysis of techniques of power and government. One point should be noted, however. The primacy of territory in Mann's analysis stops it short of examining the political nature of these 'logistical techniques'. Mann argues, quite rightly, that territorial centralisation promotes the infrastructural techniques of power. He is quite mistaken to imagine, however, that politics simply concerns the processes of territorial centralisation and not the techniques of power themselves. As I shall argue in relation to Foucault, these techniques of power are themselves political in that they are inscribed within forms of political rationality. Although polyvalent, and capable of being put to different ends, the techniques of power are not intelligible outside the particular forms of rationality and relations of power and strategy within which they are employed. Moreover, the 'techniques of power' are not merely 'means for acquiring power' but the very material form of power itself.

A parallel, if more complex awareness, of the infrastructural nature of power in contemporary states is found in Giddens' book-length treatment of the nation-state (1985). Unlike Mann, this contains an explicit acknowledgement of the contribution of Foucault on matters of power, surveillance, and particularly disciplinary power, and something of a critique of it. The elements of Foucault's work that Giddens picks up are mainly those of one text, *Discipline and Punish* (1977a). This focus on one text presents limitations on the latter's understanding of Foucault's work. Nevertheless, the contribution of Giddens to the understanding of the mechanisms of state power is not inconsiderable. Before reviewing his notion of a 'power container', I want to mention several aspects of Giddens' work on this area which advance our knowledge of the state.

Above all, Giddens moves some way in rejecting the language of political philosophy as a way of understanding the operation of the nation-state. In an important sense, he 'brackets out' the notion of sovereignty and popular representation as too implicated in the intrinsic development of the state to form an analytical or descriptive language (Giddens 1985: 20). He also importantly rejects the notion of civil society as that which is 'outside of the state', arguing that there is in principle nothing which is outside the scope and reach of the modern administrative state in the same way that there is in 'traditional states' (ibid. 21–2). Secondly, and in keeping with the rejection of the language of political philosophy, Giddens is keen to bring questions of what he calls 'administrative power' to the forefront of his analysis. One could view this as a parallel move to the one undertaken by Mann. Here Giddens adds a strong sense of the complex and detailed way in which this administrative power operates (e.g. 1985: 172–97), particularly emphasising its temporal and spatial aspects, and the centrality of practices of communication, transportation, information-gathering, surveillance, discipline, and supervision.

Much of what Giddens has to say about administrative power can be illustrated through his notion of specific locales as 'power containers'. Power containers are 'circumscribed arenas for the generation of administrative power' (Giddens 1985: 13). They are places where material and administrative resources can be concentrated and combined so that they might both be used and multiplied for various ends. Offices, factories, schools and universities, hospitals, and prisons, can be regarded as power containers in this sense, but so too can manors, castles, and cities, in traditional states, and, above all, the modern nation-state itself. Giddens argues that the level of concentration of power depends on several factors affecting the 'authoritative resources' (i.e. those which effect the domination over human beings) of these institutions: the possibilities of surveillance, including both the means of the accumulation, storage, retrieval, and use of coded information, and the direct supervision of individuals; the possibilities of the assemblage of human beings in large numbers not directly involved in material production; the facilitation of the scope and intensity of sanctions by the development of military power; and the creation of conditions of the formation of ideology, such as the architectural representation of power in state and religious edifices (ibid. 14–17).

'Power containers' in Giddens' sense do more than provide the infrastructure of state power. They generate power by the concentration and combination of the administrative mastery of both the material world and human beings ('allocative' and 'authoritative' resources in Giddens' terms). The nation-state can thus be regarded as a power container in which the 'administrative purview corresponds exactly to its territorial delimitation' (Giddens 1985: 172). The generation of power within these containers, for Giddens, crucially depends on the timing and spacing of activities. For instance, the very nature of social organisation depends on its capacity to 'bracket time-space' and to monitor processes of system reproduction and articulate its own 'history' (Giddens 1987: 153). This implies means of self-monitoring of activities within the organisation. In contemporary forms of administration, for Giddens, we witness an intensification of the processes of surveillance and recording of activities, the collation and retrieval of information, the establishment of specifically designed locales, and the co-ordination of the timing and spacing of activities within locales with those at other locales. The administrative power of the nation-state depends on means for increasing the scope of 'time-space distantiation', its capacity to stretch its rule across time and space, such as developments in rapid transportation, the electronic communication media, and information technologies. Giddens (1985: 172–81) treats the timetable, the railway, the origin of the universal day and world standard times in 1884, the telegraph, the postal services, the telephone, records, files, reports, routine data collection, and the collection of official statistics, as means for acting upon, ordering, manipulating, and shrinking time and space, and as such crucial to the capacity for the generation of administrative power in the modern nation-state.

I have said enough, I hope, to suggest some of the issues which arise when the infrastructural or administrative power of the state itself is brought into focus. We shall see how Foucault's reflection on the art of government approaches similar issues from a quite different perspective, and with different results. There is, however, one component of governmental activities downplayed in much of historical sociology and theories of the state – with the exception of the later Poulantzas (1978: 63–75) who explicitly incorporated

Foucauldian themes – that of individuality and practices and process of individualisation. This is a massive oversight if we accept that central to the means of governance and administration of the state and other authorities in the contemporary West is the objective of promoting, shaping, and regulating the conduct of individuals and groups.

One recent historical sociology of the state has begun to address this question. Corrigan and Sayer's historical sociology of English state formation, *The Great Arch* (1985), may be taken as an influential and instructive exemplar of the problems involved here. This book is resolutely not comparative. It is not seeking to verify a causal thesis about the formation of the state. Rather it is trying to introduce considerations of culture into the processes of the development of one particular state, the English state. In this it is remarkably successful, but one must also note that the limitations of the book derive from what amounts to a culturalist understanding of many of the features of state activities and power it examines. Its principal thesis, echoed in its subtitle, is that English state formation is cultural revolution. I take this to mean that the narrative of the state cannot be divorced from the regulation and even constitution of particular cultural forms, and that the state itself is constructed within such forms. At the heart of such a problematic are the *meanings* created by and attributed to the state and the material and historical forces – of class, gender, race, religion, and so on – that give rise to such meanings. However novel and interesting such an analysis promises to be, there are problems with posing it at the level of 'culture'.

A crucial part of this cultural transformation, and at the heart of the way these authors consider the effects of the state, is what they term 'moral regulation'. They argue that 'moral regulation is coextensive with state formation' (Corrigan and Sayer 1985: 4). Indeed, if one were to try to give their thesis a theoretical form, it is that state formation effects cultural transformation through the mechanism of moral regulation. In keeping with the general approach, the notion of moral regulation is given a culturalist rendition. Moral regulation is above all a project of normalisation and naturalisation of the premises of a specific social order. It concerns the *meaning* of state activities for the constitution and regulation of social identities and subjectivities (ibid. 2). This moral regulation takes place by giving universal expression to what are in fact different experiences and identities. It legitimises forms of individual and collective identity as it denies the legitimacy of different, and alternative forms of identity, and the realities of inequality of class, gender, race, ethnicity, age, location, occupation and so on.

Corrigan and Sayer inflect what would be a quite straightforward Marxist account of the representation of individuality within 'bourgeois' state forms with two manoeuvres. The first is borrowed from a reading of Foucault's writings on governmentality and the second from Durkheim's conception of the state. First, they argue that moral regulation has a 'totalising' and 'individualising' aspect (Corrigan and Sayer 1985: 4–5). It is totalising in that it represents 'people' as members of an illusory and imaginary political community in notions of nationality and citizenship. It is individualising in that it represents people within various categories of identity, such as taxpayers, jurors, parents, consumers, voters, and so on. The crucial terms in their account of how these identities are represented and how they have determinate effects are the 'routines' and 'rituals' of state. The 'routines' embody these forms of identity, treating people as if they fall within such categories. The 'rituals' of state, on the other hand, broadcast these identities, particularly the totalising ones, in a grandiloquent form and so naturalise and normalise them as a part of national identity. There are problems with this notion of representation and its mechanisms I shall return to in a moment. Simply note now that the effectivity of state formation on moral regulation is restricted to the ways in which identities are constructed in various forms of *representation* and the consequent meaning 'people' (a highly naturalistic term if ever there was one) attach to their activities, lives, careers, and relationships.

The second inflection within their Marxism comes from its marriage with Durkheimian thought on the nature of the state as an organ of social thought and moral discipline, at first a parasite on the *conscience collective*, which it then comes to regulate (Corrigan and Sayer 1985: 6–10). The dual sense of the word *conscience* as conscience and consciousness, as normative and cognitive, comes into play in the analysis. Collective representations are both forms of description of social identities and relations and in this sense constitute them, and also prescriptions of the legitimate forms of existence possible. The state becomes a focus of such representation. It takes on an active role in the regulation of those collective representations which prescribe the limits of what is permitted as they describe forms of identity. Combining Durkheim with Marx, the authors conclude that the state project concerns the construction of aspiration and the internalisation of bourgeois norms as constitutive of personalities (ibid. 194–5). As a result, capitalism, for example, is not simply an economy but a 'set of social forms of life' regulated by the state (ibid. 188). *The Great Arch* is a highly interesting attempt to introduce questions of individuality, identity, and subjectivity into problems of the state and its consequences for social life. However, there are several weaknesses that follow from the way it constructs its account of 'moral regulation' which also become pertinent further in our account of Foucault's contribution on governmentality.

The first is the theoretical effect of a culturalist reading of the effectivity of the state. The way in which these authors think the problem of moral regulation is in terms of processes of *meaning*. In light of the emphasis on the 'infrastructural' or 'administrative' powers of the state this approach seems odd, particularly when the account of infrastructural powers is extended, after Foucault (as we shall show later), toward the question of political subjectification. This position ignores the Foucauldian insight that forms of subjectivity are linked to such powers through disciplinary and governmental practices aimed at the training and utilisation of bodies and their capacities. A reversion to a form of cultural or ideological analysis thus seems slightly misplaced. To try to think of the question of moral regulation in terms of representation and meaning is to ignore or at least underplay the various ways in which governmental practices operate both singly and in concert to promote the direction of conduct and capacities of actors, whether as clients, claimants, citizens, or subjects, and the degree to which this direction has come to be dependent on the construction of what one might wish to call life-choices. 'Representation' becomes efficacious because it is linked to attempts to promote and transform aspects of the conduct of life (in Weber's sense of *Lebensführung*) of various groups and individuals, often by means of the implantation of forms of self-relation by the marshalling of bodily capacities. To think of moral regulation in terms of the (mis)attribution of meaning to experience is to foreclose the analysis of language and representation and the relation between forms of governmental discourse, political rationality, and administrative practices. This theme is developed over the next two chapters.

If there is a tendency to overemphasise the symbolic dimension of the state in this study, there is also a tendency to overemphasise the unity of the state, domination, and its consequences. Corrigan's earlier understanding of the fragility of the construction of individual identity (1990) needs to be complemented by a greater sense of the fragmentary character of state formation and the difficulty (and, in a sense, fruitlessness) of seeking to locate a division between 'the state' and its outside.[2] This can be instanced by the development of non-profit community and social services which are funded at least partially by the state but run by citizen associations, and by the neoliberal use of corporations, and families, to achieve governmental objectives (e.g. the provision of welfare, the establishment of prisons, job-centres etc.). It can also be instanced by the introduction of management and efficiency norms derived from private corporations into state organisation and employment.

Unifying domination within the state does not allow sufficiently for dispersion of the strategies enunciated within various sectors of the state (say between the national Treasury and a Women's Unit of a regional Department of Health) and the possibility that moral regulatory strategies could be similarly dispersed and dissonant (e.g. between the forms of sexuality sanctioned within the military and within anti-discrimination legislation). The oft-used caveat implied by the word 'contradiction' cannot do justice to this dispersion of both strategies and effects, and within and between specific strategies, programmes, policies, and their consequences. Moreover, if policies, practices, effects and their consequences possess no necessary overall unity of function, then there would be reason to examine the activities and consequences of other agencies and authorities in this regard. Not only are there other agencies involved in practices of governance of the conduct of individuals that exist in various relations (legal, regulatory, fiscal, etc.) to sectors of the state, but there are also other practices and techniques which centre on the self and its construction. These run the gamut from ones promoted by 'psy' disciplines, social work and medicine, education, established religion, forms of sport and 'physical culture', to the plethora of practices associated with cults of self-liberation and self-improvement (from martial arts to sexual realisation) and 'how-to' programmes in work, business, money, and love. Indeed it may be that, by bringing these 'techniques of the self' into focus in relation to a consideration of governmental power and administrative practices, we are lead to a problematisation of the notion of the state *per se*, i.e. as a unitary entity concerned with the production or reproduction of a particular social order based on particular forms of subjectivity, i.e. as an (if not *the*) agent of 'social control'.

Finally, with regard to *The Great Arch*, it might be observed that amid all the emphasis on moral regulation and the production of individualities, the nub of the problem of modern citizenship is not addressed: how can government conceive its task as acting on behalf of citizens as self-governing individuals (within self-governing communities) when governmental practices are bound up with the production of such individuals. Surprisingly little attention is paid to the self-governing individual in not only Corrigan and Sayer but much of the recent literature on the historical sociology of the state. Such an oversight imperils analyses of forms of liberalism and, more pertinently, neoliberalism.

The above discussion has been partially tendentious in that it has been concerned to draw out some leading themes within the historical sociology of the state that Foucault addressed under one of two rubrics of 'the microphysics of power' and 'governmentality'. The rest of this chapter concentrates on the first of these, while the latter is discussed in the following chapter. We shall refer back to the themes of the historical sociology of the state in the course of the following discussion.

POWER: THE ANTI-LEVIATHAN

To chart the trajectory of the different aspects of Foucault's thought which are pertinent to 'matters of state', it is helpful to take note of the two main rubrics or headings under which such matters appear in his work from 1970 to 1984, the 'microphysics of power' and 'governmentality'. The analyses grouped together under these headings are rather different, but broadly consistent, approaches toward the problems of power, domination, governance and state. Both of them foreground the means of the exercise of power and rule, and the formation of the self within practices of government. In this sense they are consonant with the problems of the recent historical sociology of the state. They also, however, offer a sustained reflection and analysis on political rationality, at best a secondary theme in historical sociology. As such they show little respect for conventional boundaries between the history of political thought and philosophy and the history and sociology of the state.

The rest of this chapter will explore the theme of power as it appears in Foucault's writings during the earlier years of the 1970s, and concentrates on the relations between his 'microphysics of power' and the juridical-political discourse on the state, the framework of power–knowledge, and problems of political individualisation. As we shall see in the next chapter, these researches tend to be subsumed under the new heading of governmentality in the years 1978–84. The later studies do not so much represent an acknowledgement of critical deficiencies but a recasting of the earlier themes within a more finely tuned field of reflection on the practice, rationality, and objects of government, and their forms of political 'totalisation'. In both sets of analyses, Foucault invokes the same style of analysis: rather than addressing the state as a theoretical problem, he approaches it through the perspective of the practices and rationalities that compose the means of rule and government. By changing the point of attack, I suggest, Foucault has opened up the analysis of the state in a way state-focused theory and analysis could not.

In a remark in a 1976 lecture that neatly, if negatively, sums up his thought on power to that date, Foucault said: 'We must eschew the model of Leviathan in the study of power. We must escape the limited field of juridical sovereignty and State institutions, and instead base our analysis of power on the study of the techniques and tactics of domination' (1980i: 102). The first dimension of his thought on power and state could legitimately be said to be the Anti-Leviathan. For it is above all the language of political philosophy – of sovereignty, legitimacy, of the state – from the time of Hobbes which Foucault rejects in order to analyse the exercise of power.

It is difficult to characterise the type of intellectual activity in which Foucault is engaged in the major texts and interviews of this time. Roughly, the space of these problems lies between the region of the history of knowledge and science and that of the problems of political philosophy. It is a history of science that would place the investigation of the practical relations and application of the human sciences, their political consequences if one likes, against the propositions of the theories of power and sovereignty. Having said that, however, we have not exhausted the problem addressed in these writings. For beyond these problems of power and knowledge lies a third concern in what might be called political ethics, the problem of the conditions of the formation of the good and virtuous citizen or, what often amounts to the same thing, the 'docile and useful' subject.

If one, then, was to try to sum up the import of these analyses of the early 1970s, it is this: that the citizen who from the point of view of law and juridical-political discourse is regarded as a self-governing individual, is produced through an ensemble of governmental practices as a subject with particular capacities and orientations.[3] In order to understand the conditions of political life in what could broadly be called the 'modern West', one must investigate the practices of the political formation of individuals, practices of what I have called 'political subjectification'. Those practices, moreover, are always accompanied by a degree of calculation and rationality that is both the condition of and conditioned by knowledges, disciplines, and theories of human beings. This, if you like, is Foucault's political problematic at this time, the interlinking of the practices and techniques of power with the production of knowledge and the ethical conduct of life of the individual.

This aspect of Foucault's thought can be traced from about the time of Foucault's inaugural address to the *College de France* in 1970 (1981a) and extends beyond but crucially includes *Discipline and Punish* (1977a). The first volume of the *History of Sexuality* (1979b), published in France in 1976, may be thought to be both a summation of this aspect and its characteristic themes, and a movement beyond them. It is also noteworthy that Foucault seeks to clarify and elaborate on his notion of power in a series of interviews around this time.

From 1970, Foucault signals that an archaeology emphasising discursive regularities will no longer be the principal focus of his study. His own work would now include what he would later call a genealogy of the 'will to knowledge' (*la volonté de savoir*), as both his first course at the *College* (1989b: 9–16) and the first volume on sexuality (1979b) would be called. That is to say, this refocused study would be concerned to make intelligible the human sciences in terms of practices concerned with the regulation of bodies, the government of conduct, and the formation of self. It is such practices that constituted the will to knowledge of the human sciences for they were inscribed within an affirmative power, ' . . . the power of constituting a domain of objects, in relation to which one can affirm or deny true or false propositions' (Foucault 1981a: 73). While the terrain of analysis would remain the same, the theoretical strategy would shift from a concern with the rules governing the production of discourses to the various practices, and the relations, strategies and technologies of power, in which forms of knowledge are embedded and to which they are linked. Earlier concerns about the production of true knowledge, far from being surpassed, are now included as one dimension of the new field. 'Regimes of truth', the forms of the organisation of statements in disciplines or sanctioned bodies of knowledge, described and analysed by archaeology, should now be understood in terms of their complex relations to 'regimes of practices', the forms of the organisation and institutionalisation of various practices. The articulation of these two spheres would be the province of genealogy.[4]

It is clear that Foucault does not merely seek to apply an existing theory or conception of power to the epistemological field he had earlier studied in terms of its rules of discursive formation. He wishes to rework the concept of power anew. We might distinguish three dimensions of this change of focus:

1 the inducement of a set of 'theoretical' displacements by means of criticisms of conventional conceptions of power grounded in the problem of the sovereignty of the state;

2   the establishment of a relation between this new focus on power with earlier concerns around the production of knowledge, the interface of which is summed up in the notion of *pouvoir–savoir*, power–knowledge; and

3   the contextualisation of the claims of the representative form of the constitutional state in relation to the techniques of power and their consequences for the formation of subjects.

Let us address each of these features in turn.

The microphysics of power

The theoretical displacement of conceptions of power operates at a general level and finds its point of attack in what Foucault calls the 'juridico-discursive' conception of power (1979b: 82), which is anchored in a 'juridicial-political' theory of sovereignty (1980i: 103). Thus, within this conception, power is construed in a context which poses the problem of political sovereignty. The type of questions asked concern the foundations or origins of political power, of how it attains its legitimacy, and of the type of institutions securing this legitimacy. It asks, then, 'who holds power?' and 'what is the legitimate basis of this power?'. Foucault (1979b: 92–7) suggests that such a framework makes a number of key, problematic assumptions. First, it approaches power in a global fashion as emanating from a central location in a unitary agency. Secondly, it grasps power as being possessed by a sovereign political agency or force such as the King, the state, the people, the ruling class, etc. Finally, because power is interpreted through a framework which privileges law and legality, it is characteristically assumed to be expressed as interdiction and exercised as repression (Minson 1985: 43).

The implications for Foucault's position of the state are fairly straightforward. In an interview in 1977 (Foucault 1980h: 122) he argues that to pose the question of power in terms of the state means to remain in this model of sovereignty and law, which grasps power as 'essentially repressive'. The state, Foucault insists, should be understood as 'superstructual' in relation to local power networks, and as a 'codification' of them. At a minimum, we could conclude that at this stage of Foucault's thought the study of the state itself is intellectually and politically vacuous unless it is founded on a broader analysis of power relations. Counterposed to this juridico-discursive conception of power is a project which he occasionally called a 'microphysics of power' (e.g. 1977a: 26–8) and later, in the *History of Sexuality* (1979b: 82–3), an 'analytics of power'. Such an approach examines power relations in terms contrary to those which Foucault holds to be characteristic of the theory of sovereignty. Power is to be analysed at multiple points of its exercise rather than in the global form of the state. Indeed, its actual exercise and the specific, heterogeneous forms it takes are to be given privilege over problems of its ultimate source or of its possession. Power is to be thought in its positive existence, and as productive of forces, relations, and identities, rather than as a manifest in interdiction and operating by repression and deduction. Above all, the locus of this microphysics concerns the relationship between the mechanisms of power and domination and the forces and capacities of human bodies.

The focus on micropowers dispersed within different locales throughout the social body is quite evidently a polemical attempt to displace the 'theory of the state' as it would have been conceived by Marxist theorists in France during the 1970s. However, as noted above, both the theories and historical sociology of the state have been recently far more attentive to the strategic and relational aspects of power, its mechanisms, and the 'individualising' and 'totalising' aspects of state power, partially in an attempt to incorporate Foucault's ideas. Perhaps such a polemical displacement is no longer required quite so urgently. However, in so far as the language of political philosophy still remains the dominant form of political analysis, and attention to the mechanisms and machinery of rule remains subordinated to questions of sovereignty, territory, and legitimacy, it is doubtless still true that 'in political thought and analysis, we still have not cut off the head of the king' (Foucault 1979b: 89; cf. 1980h: 121).

Having completed this act, nevertheless, the problem remains of how is it that this headless body often behaves *as if* it indeed had a head. To put this in more prosaic terms, how are a macro-social order, and macro-forms of domination, constructed out of the diversity of micropowers? This is a question which Foucault does endeavour to answer in his reflections on power and I want to examine briefly how he does so.

First, consider the use of the term 'superstructural' as it functions in this sentence: 'The State is superstructural in relation to a whole series of power networks' (Foucault 1980h: 122). There is undoubtedly an element of parody here on the Marxist infrastructure/superstructure dichotomy Foucault is seeking to displace. On the other hand, there is a sense in which the materiality of power comes to form an 'infrastructure' of the state for Foucault. At several points, he argues that the 'methods for administering the accumulation of men' and the processes of capital accumulation were mutually necessary and reciprocally conditioning elements (e.g. 1977a: 220–1; 1979b: 140–1). By making disciplinary and, later, 'bio-power' (the more general term for the 'power over life' used in *The History of Sexuality* 1979b: 140) into infra-structural powers, Foucault is suggesting two things. First, that such forms of power are necessary conditions for the capitalist organisation of production and, secondly, that relations of power and authority, working through disciplinary techniques, are 'infrastructural powers' – in Mann's sense – of the state. Indeed, it would be clearer in Foucault's case to speak of a 'state-effect' rather than the state itself for, unlike much historical sociology, the state does not have a kind of quasi-naturalistic historical existence but is something that is the result of a composition of more primary forces and relations.

These notions of super- and infra-structures remain metaphorical if rich in polemical ramifications and provocations. I do not think that they can be inscribed in analysis. In his later writings on governmentality, Foucault would come to a more satisfactory formulation. This view is confirmed by the fact that even at this phase there are limits to their use. Foucault readily jettisons them when they do not suit his purposes. In *Discipline and Punish* (1977a: 222–3), for instance, he entertains the suggestion that 'the disciplines constitute nothing more than an infra-law', only to reject the notion and argue that they should be regarded as a 'counter-law', in that they do not simply extend the forms defined by laws into the micro-level but actually undermine the limits of the law. In so far as the law, the juridicial system, and the state, appear to occupy the same plane within Foucault's analyses, this example suggests limits to the notion of discipline as playing an infrastructural role to the law and state.

The second way in which Foucault describes micro–macro relations in the state is in terms of 'codification'. He says that the 'State consists in the codification of a whole number of power relations which render its functioning possible' (Foucault 1980h: 122; cf. 1979b: 96). Now this term again keys into the identification of state with law, the juridical instance and juridicial discourse. Again 'codification' is a second-order phenomenon, presupposing a greater agency or power that organises and collects together the elements that will function as a code. Thus the state brings together, arranges, and fixes within that arrangement the micro-relations of power. Something similar is suggested in a host of other terms and images that seek to describe this relation: the immanent multiplicity of relations and techniques of power are 'colonised', 'utilised', 'displaced', 'extended', 'altered', 'reinforced', 'transformed', 'strengthened', 'reversed', and so on, in their relations with one another, and within more 'global phenomena' and 'more general powers' (e.g. 1980i: 99; 1979b: 92–3).

This framework still leaves open the question of how these more general powers are formed. This is where it is possible to introduce the key term, strategy, into this codification of local relations of power. Strategy is the condition of the assemblage of the diverse relations of power into a code. Foucault uses the term 'strategy' in two ways: first, to describe how the interconnection of the multiple, heteromorphous, dispersed powers come to delineate general conditions of domination organised into a 'more-or-less coherent and unitary strategic form'; secondly, to describe the global action upon these powers that seeks to turn them toward a unified, or even global objective (e.g. 1980f: 142). Bringing these uses together, one can say that, for Foucault, strategies at once emerge out of and become available on the basis of the micropowers but, once constituted, are in turn capable of acting upon the multiple relations to form them into a 'chain or system' (1979b: 92–3). It is on the basis of such strategies that the 'general design' of the state is given form, that 'social hegemonies' can operate.

This notion of strategy could be taken to exemplify one of Foucault's central propositions concerning power: that it is both intentional and non-subjective (1979b: 94), that is, that while these global strategies are irreducible to the wishes, interests, or wills, of a particular social group or individual, they nevertheless cohere around and display some minimal level of rationality and calculation. This discovery, and the assertion that this political rationality has definite historical forms that are open to historical investigation, connects Foucault's earlier thought on power to his later thought on government. It also distinguishes it from the historical sociology of the state that can only conceive the rationality of the state in terms of the interests of classes and other forces or as *imputed* to a specific state form by the analyst. As we shall see, one major thesis of Foucault's later work is that the practice of government is, indeed, an art, i.e. a practice which has as its condition of existence a certain level of practical rationality.

Power–knowledge

The problem of strategy thus brings us to the issue of rationality and to the general problem of the 'will to knowledge', or 'power–knowledge'. The notion of strategy presupposes that political action of various agencies rests upon some degree of calculation. This strategic rationality uses but does not take the form of explicit, calculated, rational *programmes* of government and action. It is not the rationality of the master-subject programming reality. Strategy is minimally, rather than maximally, rational. As Colin Gordon perceptively argues:

> strategy defines the minimum form of rationality of the exercise of power in general which consists in the mobile set of operations whereby a multiplicity of the heterogeneous elements (forces, resources, the features of a terrain, the disposition and relation of objects in space-time) are invested with a particular functionality relative to a dynamic and variable set of objectives.
>
> (Gordon 1980: 251)[5]

In short, strategy is the cynical, implicit, and promiscuous assemblage of heterogeneous elements. A part of the resources available to strategy are these programmes, the planful attempts to render the real amenable to government and administration, to render it governable and administrable. Strategy also presupposes assemblages of techniques, inventions, material and intellectual means of government, which might generically be called technologies of power and government. Yet, strategy is never identical to either the explicit political rationality of the programme or the governmental technologies, techniques, and practices on which this rationality depends. These are the conditions and means of strategy but not its medium. Forms of rationality and technologies of power (e.g. from practical know-how, technical knowledges, 'intellectual technologies', the human sciences, social and political theory) may be drawn upon by strategy but never wholly displace the strategic component of the exercise of powers. Programmes and technologies of power have to do with the formation of the real in a governable, programmable, form, while strategy consists in turning that real into an instrument for certain ends. A morphology of the 'will to govern' thus is not a simple totalisation of knowledge by power, as Habermas would have it, but the multiple and serial divisions, disjunctions, and non-correspondences, between various forms of scientific and non-scientific discourse, theories, programmes, techniques, practices, strategies, their intentions, their consequences, and effects. Far from a mapping of power onto knowledge, Foucault's thought on strategy suggests the irreducibility of the multiple forms of the 'will to knowledge' one to another and to the forms of the 'will to govern'.

Strategy, then, is still an oblique angle from which to approach the dimension of Foucault's rethinking of power concerned with power-knowledge. Let us deal with it more directly. This, of course, is not an epistemological issue in a conventional sense of the term. It is not concerned with distinguishing between true and false statements but with the way in which the distinction between true and false statements operates within certain practices. Different dimensions and aspects of this domain could be rendered in any number of ways that correspond to different phases in Foucault's work – the problem of 'discursive practices' (e.g. 1972), of the 'will to truth' or the 'will to knowledge' (1981a; 1989b: 9–16), of 'power-knowledge', of 'regimes of truth' (1980h), of 'regimes of practices' and 'veridical discourses' (1980d; 1981b) or even 'governmentality' (1979a). These terms of course are not synonyms. All formulate the same problem in slightly different terms, or from different aspects, or even pose different problems (e.g. the analysis of forms of rationality, subjectivity, and government) in similar ways. What all these formulations have in common, however, is the attempt to pose in a general form the question of how discourses organised and systematised by the task of stating the truth exist in relation to organised and institutionalised forms of practice, of how the production of knowledge occurs within discursive, institutional and social practices.

It is perhaps best to approach these themes through an illustration of its uses. A stunning example of how this general terrain can generate specific research agendas is given by definition of the intention of *Discipline and Punish*:

This book is intended as a correlative history of the modern soul and of a new power to judge; a genealogy of the present scientifico-legal complex from which the power to punish derives its bases, justifications and rules, from which it extends its effects and by which it masks its exhorbitant singularity.

(Foucault 1977a: 23)

Without summarising this famous text here, the above statement is a faithful rendition of at least one of its major themes. Although this text is often understood as a description of disciplinary power as the key to modernity, a more coherent understanding can be had by concentrating on the problem of power–knowledge and in particular the issues addressed in the introduction of the book.[6] Here we find a concern with new 'forms of the power to judge' and the transformation of modes of punitive practice on the one hand, and the development of new forms and bodies of knowledge of the criminal and the crime on the other.

The first chapter of this text is a brilliant example of the genealogical capacity for problematisation, for an effective and critical history that diagnoses both a crucial dimension of the present and upsets the reassuring stories of how it came to be. What is at issue is the incapacity of an internalist history of punishment and criminal justice to account for its own conditions of possibility. Such a history notes but cannot explain the transformation of penal practice except as an internal one of the reduction of the severity of the penalty, of 'less cruelty, less pain, more kindness, more respect, more "humanity"' (ibid. 16). For what is at stake is the narrative of the post-Enlightenment humanisation of punishment.

This text, then, can be read as a problematisation of this internalist, triumphalist history of the increasing humanisation of the penalty and its effects on the judgement and punishment of offences. Starting from this history Foucault notes not only the changing empirical forms of punitive practice presented as evidence by this triumphalist account, but introduces four modes of problematisation – ones which parallel the analysis of ethical practices in the later volumes of the history of sexuality, as we shall see in the final chapter. These are: the changing object of punishment or 'substance of which the punishable element is made' (1977a: 17), the changing work of judgement, penalty, and punishment (ibid. 18–9), the changing mode of subjectification (*mode d'assujettissement*) of the punished (ibid. 24), and, perhaps most importantly for the direction of his research, the *telos* of punishment and its place within a broader schema or mode of being of related practices and forms of knowledge (ibid. 25–8). If Foucault can be characterised as foregrounding practices, of how they operate, it is not because he wishes to reduce all study to attention to the empirical description of practice. It is because such practices cannot be understood without an understanding of the complex of power–knowledge in which they arise. The thesis of this book could then be understood thus: the transformation of penal practice, so often taken for an increase in humanity, can only be made intelligible through the transformation of the epistemological and juridical framework and context in which the penalty occurs.

Let us briefly discuss the four aspects of the transformation of power–knowledge that accounts for the transformation of the practice of punishment. First, then, there is the transformation of the substance of the punishable element. It is no longer simply the act, the offence, or the crime which is being judged and punished but all those 'shadows' lurking behind the act that will constitute the knowledge of the criminal, his delinquency, his biography, his upbringing, his mental health, his capacity for rehabilitation, and so on. Thus the object of the whole penal ritual – from investigation, sentencing, confinement, and rehabilitation to the last day of release on probation – is not only the crime but also the circumstances, instincts, passions, desires, effects of environment or heredity, of the criminal manifest in the crime. For Foucault, the object is not the punishment of the body but the treatment of the soul. Foucault quotes Mably's mid-eighteenth century comment: 'Punishment, if I may so put it, should strike the soul rather than the body' (Foucault 1977a: 16).

Secondly, there is a transformation of the work of the punitive ritual. It is not simply a work of gaining knowledge of the offence, the attribution of responsibility, and the passing of the sentence. It is rather a work of assessment, diagnosis, prognosis, normative judgement, and the attempted normalisation of the offender. The work of the penalty is not simply to punish in the narrow sense, or to effect a social retribution for the crime, but to supervise the individual, to neutralise the dangers he or she presents, to normalise him or her in the ultimate hope of altering his or her criminal tendencies. The 'symbolics of blood', and the spectacular of judgement and punishment characteristic of the 'sovereign power' of the absolutist regime, gives way to the continuous, hidden work of assessment, management and normalisation.

Thirdly, there occurs a transformation of the mode of subjectification implied by the practices of punishment. This concerns the relations between the individual, the penalty, and the crime. The penalty takes the form it does not in adequation to the crime, but in relation to the myriad features of the criminal made available by the individualising knowledges brought to bear upon him or her through experts of various sorts: of psychologists, counsellors, social workers, members of the prison service, educators, and so on. It is on the basis of the dispersal of the power to judge among such experts that certain disciplines can gain their purchase: criminology and criminal anthropology, criminal psychiatry, the sociology of deviance, and so on. The criminal is subjectified/subjected as one who has infracted societal norms of behaviour, as the delinquent, the deviant, as maladjusted, as one capable or incapable of normalisation.

Fourth, Foucault effects a massive displacement in the history of penal structures by introducing the transformation of the *telos* of punishment: how the penalty is incorporated in a pattern of activities and knowledges leading to a specific end, a specific mode of being or, as Weber would have put, conduct of life. This, then, is the point at which discipline and disciplinary power–knowledge proper can be introduced into the argument. For the transformation of the penalty cannot be understood in terms of an internal history of criminal justice. It must also be understood in relation to the emergence and proliferation of what Foucault calls a new 'political technology of the body', a new 'political anatomy', designed to operate on the body so that the subject will govern him or herself as a docile and useful individual. It is not that Foucault commences a history of the transformation of modes of punishment and is suddenly led into a massive detour by the more interesting field of disciplinary power and the normalising discourses associated with it (cf. Donnelly 1982). Rather, the latter form the configuration in which the transformation of modes of punishment can be made intelligible. This is not to say that the chapters of the book dealing with the disciplines cannot be read in isolation from the rest and used independently of a critical history of punishment. It is simply to say that the logic by which the pertinence of this material is introduced is extremely clear.

In all these ways a transformation of punitive practice is accompanied by a transformation of forms of knowledge. This knowledge redefines the substance to be punished. It can be located in the practices and procedures that constitute the continuous work of normalisation. These practices focus on new subjects to be known which come to form the objects of new sciences and disciplines. Finally, the practice of punishment comes to be colonised and resituated by the configuration of disciplinary practices and techniques and normalising discourses and forms of knowledge.

The lesson here is that one finds in Foucault less the thesis of the mutual superimposition of knowledge onto power than an operating method that can pick out the fine stitching of many different forms of knowledge within the threads of power relations and organised systems of practices. If one was to put this into a more general thesis it would be of the interconnection and irreducibility of knowledge to power and power to knowledge, of forms of knowledge to one another, of the practice of knowledge to other practices, of different types of practices to one another, of intention and ambition to consequences, and of consequences to effects. *Pace* Habermas, the problem of power–knowledge rests on the supposition of a field of dispersion rather than a unity of elements. This, of course, does not mean that we cannot construct a morphology of this field.

Political subjects and liberal democracy

The final aspect of Foucault's position on state and power during the early 1970s I want to examine here entails a consideration of the claims of liberal democracy in a style allied to the displacement of the juridico-political theory of the state. It is, however, both more submerged, and, in some ways, more significant. This dimension is again in evidence throughout *Discipline and Punish* and the interviews published after its release. A key to the status of what amounts to a problematisation of the liberal vision is Foucault's willingness to make reference to classic social-contract theory. For example, he says in an interview: 'I believe the great fantasy is the idea of a social body constituted by the universality of wills. Now the phenomenon of the social body is the effect not of a consensus but of the materiality of power operating on the very bodies of individuals' (Foucault 1980a: 55). Foucault's claim here juxtaposes a disciplinary politics of the body to the image of a Leviathan composed of a unity of wills – the politicised body to the body politic, if you like. A similar point is made at the very end of the chapter in *Discipline and Punish* entitled 'Docile bodies':

> Historians of ideas usually attribute the dream of a perfect society to the philosophers and jurists of the eighteenth century; but there was also a military dream of society; its fundamental reference was not to the state of nature, but to the meticulously subordinated cogs of a machine, not to the primal, social contact, but to permanent coercions, not to fundamental rights, but to indefinitely progressive forms of training, not to the general will but to automatic docility. While jurists or philosophers were seeking in the pact a primal model for the construction of the social body, the soldiers and with them the technicians of discipline were elaborating procedures for the individual and collective coercion of bodies.
>
> (Foucault 1977a: 169)

We should note that Foucault carefully frames his approach to the language of political philosophy in such a way that these juxtapositions are not to be regarded as competing explanations of the formation of the body politic. I would suggest his principal point is not that the 'dreams' of the liberal social contract are undermined by the presence of a military dream, or that rights are vitiated by practices of discipline. Rather, it is this: we are used to understanding our political present in terms of the progressive extension of the institutions and guarantees of constitutional government in the form of liberal democracy. That history, however, must also take into account the history of disciplinary techniques and practices. If we are to make intelligible the processes of formation of the liberal-democratic political community we must investigate those practices seeking to shape political subjects, their capacities and attributes, as much as those seeking to guarantee its rights and liberties.

There is a danger here of overloading one side of this political equation. In some passages in the same text we find what appears to amount to a quite explicit criticism of liberal democracy, one asserting that the real possibility for 'the representative regime' is the 'guarantee of submission of forces and bodies' provided by the disciplines (Foucault 1977a: 222). Foucault speaks here of the 'mask' of the formally egalitarian juridical framework and asserts that 'the real, corporeal disciplines constituted the foundation of the formal, juridical liberties'. Moreover, when Foucault speaks in this book of the rights guaranteed by the juridical system and proclaimed by liberal theorists, or of the 'democratisation of sovereignty', as he does in a 1976 lecture (1980i: 105), he does so in the language of dissimulation. The organisation of a legal system according to a theory of democratic sovereignty is said to 'conceal', 'mask', or 'disguise' the actual procedures of power. For Foucault, the juridical systems may have allowed sovereignty to be democratised, but this was only to disguise the fact that such democratisation 'was fundamentally determined by and grounded in mechanisms of disciplinary coercion' (ibid. 105). To put it bluntly, the rights of the citizen in liberal democracy simply mask the complex process by which that citizen has already been formed through disciplinary mechanisms the objective of which is her or his body.

There are three points that should be made here. The first is that such formulations are overburdened with a kind of polemical weight. That weight is partially the assertion of the centrality of the disciplines to our political present. It is also partially the engagement in the terrain occupied by Marxist models of critique. Foucault is seeking to contest and occupy a similar political ground to that of certain Marxist critiques of liberal-democracy. He thus repeats the quasi-Marxist argument that juridical equality and rights of liberal democracy are not substantive but merely formal. However, they now become a mask for the indefinite extension of disciplinary practices ensuring the docility and utility of the body. Perhaps, too, there is a sense in which these formulations are necessarily imprecise and reflect the fact that *Discipline and Punish* was written for a popular, rather than academic, audience.

In any case, I would suggest, secondly, these are not necessary features of a position which would reject the idea that anything is fundamental 'in the last instance'. One might say that the extension of disciplinary power was a condition for the formation of the subject of rights and freedom of liberal democracy. But one might also want to say that the free citizen is surely a condition for the spread of disciplinary techniques and normalising procedures. Foucault will later suggest (1982: 221) that 'power is only ever exercised over free subjects' and that 'freedom may well appear as a condition for the exercise of power'. For the moment, this statement might be read as arguing that forms of power such as discipline can only be applied to a subject capable of resisting or acting otherwise. It would make little sense to apply disciplinary techniques to an unfree subject, one subjugated by gross physical constraint and the threat of violence, such as a slave. Similarly, while discipline was born and first developed in feudal societies or absolutist empires, it either only applied to limited groups (monks, monarchical state bureaucracies) or remained subordinate to traditional forms of authority and conduct. One might wish to argue that the massive extension of discipline required the breaking-down of ascribed statuses and traditional allegiances and the generalisation of a 'society of individuals' (a term used by Norbert Elias 1991). Indeed it is the very points of the social body where ascriptive relations persist that are least amenable to the regime of disciplinarity, such as in the relations between husband and wife.

The third point is that there are limits to the sense of the term *assujetissement* at this stage of Foucault's work, one in which domination or subjection is effected though the formation of the subject, through 'subjectification'. If one accepts what I have just argued about the formation of an individual freed from physical or traditional constraints as a condition of the extension of discipline, then it follows that there are other forms of practice concerned with the formation of subjects. Foucault occasionally gives the impression here that the subject – the modern soul – is completely determined by these disciplinary relations of power. As we shall see, such a view neglects possible bases of resistance to disciplinary techniques in a host of other ways in which subjectivities are formed. These not only include popular practices and culture, traditional relations of authority and communal solidarities, but what Foucault will later call 'techniques of the self' and ethical practices. Discipline subjectifies, to be sure, but it is not the only force of subjectification. There are other powers of subjectification, and there are other forms of subjectification that are not primarily power relations. This is consistent with Foucault's most developed positions.

To sum up, while Foucault's position occasionally lapses into a parody of a kind of Marxist critique of liberal democracy around the formal/substantive couple, and a certain determinism with regard to the operation of disciplinary power, what is offered is a key problematisation of forms of political subjectification (Pasquino 1986). Such a problem concerns the relation between the self-governing subject of liberal-democratic rights and liberties, and the formation of the subject through a particular complex of power–knowledge. When one takes into account Foucault's later work, his position would seem to be that these forms of individualisation mutually presuppose each other.

This emphasis on political subjectification has been picked up by the historical sociology of the state. However, Foucault's position differs from this historical sociology in several ways. Firstly, it would reject the thesis of the identity of 'moral regulation' with 'state formation'. The practices of political subjectification are not necessarily located within the state but operate from multiple and heterogeneous locale. Such practices are of diverse origins. While they receive a fillip from their application within enclosed institutions, Giddens' power containers, they 'swarm' within the social body. To restrict attention to the way in which the state is involved in political subjectification is to ignore the way in which disciplinary practices come to colonise, compose, and transform the state itself.

Secondly, rather than subjectification entailing processes of meaning and representation, for Foucault it involves the formation of different types of relation with the self. Thus the forms of self-surveillance promoted by discipline, and exemplified in Bentham's Panopticon, do not work by attachment of (ideological) meaning to one's activity but by the inducement within the subject of 'a state of conscious and permanent visibility that assures the automatic functioning of power' (Foucault 1977a: 201). This is achieved through the organisation of power within definite forms of time-space. In

Bentham's case, the very design and architecture of the enclosure is constructed according to the principle of the visibility and unverifiability of power. Subjectification concerns the establishment of forms of relation of self with self through disciplinary practices and techniques of surveillance, and through the material organisation of conduct in time-space.

Finally, these forms of subjectification operating through particular techniques of power are specified within forms of normalising and scientific discourse. Foucault would seem to be emphasising the 'routines' rather than the 'rituals' of power as the key to subjectification. Indeed, his account of the transformation of punitive practice within a changing complex of power–knowledge is sketched against the background of the diminution of the significance of the ritual form of sovereignty. The more crucial point, however, is that these routines do not simply operate according to more or less arbitrary classifications and categories of individuals. Rather, they are the loci of the formation of definite types of rationality and knowledge in turn linked to governmental programmes operating as the means of strategy and calculation. The 'routines and rituals' of subjectification cannot be made intelligible apart from the forms of knowledge which are invested in them and on which their operation depends.

Foucault's work on power and the state of the 1970s poses many problems even as it provides new perspectives. This is more a testimony to the open-ended and undogmatic approach of the 'history of the present' than the result of fundamental deficiencies. His microphysics of power raises the problem of macrophysical forms of order and domination. His mainly tacit polemics with Marxism make us more sensitive to the problems of discipline, of domination of the body and bodily forces, the exercise and mechanisms of power, and the inscription of power within social relations. In short they open up a vista on what the historical sociology of the state will later call 'infrastructural' powers. Such polemics do not effectively displace the 'macrophysical' problem of the state and the law, of their forms and claims, in social and political analysis. The problem of law is especially important, for there is a tendency here to elide the distinction between sovereignty and discipline with one between law and the micropowers. In these formulations, it would seem that law is reduced, in an analogous move to Weber, to a legitimation function in 'modern' states. However, it must be said that Foucault foresaw such an impasse when he argued that 'law is neither the truth of power nor its alibi. It is an instrument of power which is at once complex and partial' (1980f: 140–1). A further issue is the way in questions of 'political totalisation', and its relation to forms of political subjectification, may be posed when considering the larger programmes and rationality of the state.

Another area that will be continually subject to problematisation concerns the self and the notion of *assujetissement*. To paraphrase Minson (1980: 13–4), Foucault's power–knowledge complexes appear as unconditional in their power to constitute subjects as the state, its agents, and the ruling class of certain Marxian analyses are in their capacity to act as subjects who constitute power relations. At various points, Foucault acknowledges this problem and alludes to what is outside the disciplinary mechanisms of power: the resistances, themselves nothing more than the underside of power; the 'plebeian' quality and aspect present at every locale in the social body (Foucault 1980f: 137–8) resisting the incursion of the micropowers; or the quasi-naturalism of the 'bodies and pleasures' (in 1979b: 159), and so on. Given Foucault's anti-naturalist and anti-essentialist orientation, he appears to be left with an account of the self and subjectivity as fully implicated, if not fully determined, by the mechanisms and techniques of power–knowledge. This is the case, however, only given two conditions: first, the absence of any account of alternative forms of self-formation and self-relation, and of practices which sustain those forms. Secondly, if the analysis is a totalising one, an attempt to make a global characterisation of society. As we shall see, neither of these two claims can be upheld in regard to Foucault's later work. In the first instance, the techniques of power and domination come to be complemented by 'techniques of self'. Both sets of techniques are in principle separable if historically interconnected and reciprocally conditioning. More-over in both Foucault's lectures on governmentality and his writings on ethical practices of the self a stronger and more meaningful sense of the way in which freedom is implicated within the field of power emerges.

Even if we remain in the sphere of power relations, there are strong indications that Foucault regards the status of the disciplinary society, not as a complete picture of a concrete social form but a particular governmental project. Foucault himself will distinguish between apparatuses of sovereignty, discipline, and security which are all present in contemporary forms of government and correspond to different projects toward the social body, whether a society of rights, (*Rechtsstaat*), a society of normalisation, or a society of security (Gordon 1991: 20; Foucault 1979a: 20–1; cf. Foucault 1980i: 107–8). The point here is that if we are to regard the nation-state as a product of global strategies which fix and assemble relations of power into particular chains, and if we further admit that what sociologists call 'society' is simply the nation-state (Giddens 1985: 172), then we might wish to start talking about the different 'society-effects' of these different strategies. To talk of a disciplinary society or 'the carceral' (Foucault 1977a) is hence nothing more than to discuss the ideal or objective of a certain form of programme and strategy. Similarly, the existence of one global strategy and one society-effect does not preclude and is in no way incompatible with other such strategies.

These, then, are the types of issues one can see in operation both in Foucault's work on government and his consideration of ethics in the later volumes of his history of sexuality (1985, 1986a). The problems of global strategies of power, political individualisation and totalisation, and freedom and resistance, prepare us for his thought on governmentality.

EXCURSUS: TIME, SPACE, AND POWER

In the preceding chapter, we noted Giddens' notion of 'power-containers' as specifically designed locales for the concentration of administrative power. Although recognising the contribution of Foucault on the constitution of such power-containers and more broadly on the relation between power and the timing and spacing of activities, Giddens seeks to develop criticisms of what he takes to be the features of Foucault's views on these matters. I want here briefly to outline and address these criticisms. In considering them, several points emerge which will be crucial to our understanding of the theme of governmentality.

Giddens' criticisms are readily summarised. He argues that Foucault identifies disciplinary power with specific organisations in two ways. Giddens argues (1984: 154) that Foucault first takes enclosed institutions such as prisons and asylums to be most representative of disciplinary power because they are the sites of maximal use. Rather, he suggests, the relations between time, space, and disciplinary power are more typically represented by the everyday *journey* to work and school that exemplifies the temporal and spatial differentiation characteristic of modern societies. Giddens argues (ibid. 155) that, secondly, Foucault fails to appreciate the degree to which the procedures of 'total institutions' differ from the features of day to day life, and the way in which the timing and spacing of activities within them violates private domains of the self taken for granted outside their walls. These two problems stem from a more general one, noted elsewhere by Giddens (1987: 157), that Foucault treats locales and the concentration of administrative power as coterminous. A version of this same argument appears in the claim by David Harvey (1989: 213–14) that Foucault's thought on time and space is weakened by his exclusive concentration on spaces of organised repression and that spaces can more easily be contested and liberated.

Giddens' other criticisms concern the nature of what is subjected to disciplinary power. On the one hand, he maintains that those subjected to disciplinary power are not agents in Foucault's account (Giddens 1984: 154). They are passive bodies, acted upon through the technologies of disciplinary power to produce docile and useful subjects. As such they present no resistance, reservation, or counter-force, to the constitutive work of discipline. On the other hand, these agents are 'faceless' in that they do not enter into negotiation with the managers or supervisors of disciplinary power. To characterise the relations between time, space, and power, according to Giddens, we must be able to distinguish between institutions such as the office, school, and factory, and 'total institutions' like prisons and asylums. Invoking Erving Goffman's notion and analysis of 'total institutions', Giddens argues that these institutions are distinguished precisely through their violation of everyday 'territories of the self' and the degree to which they seek to minimise the negotiated aspects of power, the 'dialectic of control' between the governors and governed in these institutions (Giddens 1987: 162).

These criticisms exemplify common misconceptions of the subject-matter of *Discipline and Punish* and a lack of acknowledgement of the place of that text in Foucault's wider thought on government. In brief, such criticisms seek to make of Foucault's concern with disciplinarity a general theory of administrative or institutional power in modern societies. I shall now examine Foucault's positions on these matters starting from the type of problems addressed by that text. I shall suggest, contrary to Giddens, that there is no general theory of institutional power in this or others of Foucault's work, nor is there a general account of the relation between time and space and government and power. There is, as we shall see, a coherent set of suggestions about how we might analyse the relations between power, time, and space.

Turning to *Discipline and Punish*, it is first necessary to stress with Foucault the *programmatic* nature of much of what is under examination (1981b: 9–10). This is to say that Foucault is not primarily interested in characterising the nature of a well-disciplined society or of how things typically operate in the institutions of such a society. The subject matter of this book is the range of plans, projects, initiatives, and policies that sought to develop and implement a regime of discipline in smaller and greater locales, for particular requirements, and targeting various individuals, groups, and micro- and macro-populations. This is clearly instanced in the Benthamite architectural machine for the surveillance of its enclosed population, the Panopticon. What interests Foucault in such a figure is not that it represents a Weberian 'ideal type' of the actual operation of power in particular institutions but that it belongs to a whole technology and rationality of discipline providing the means by which institutions could be reformed, conduct regulated, forms of life promoted, and time and space ordered. The fact that the Panopticon does not correspond to the reality of life in prison and workhouses of the nineteenth century does not make it any less worthy of our attention or any less a component of the means by which the governance of such spaces could be organised. This was one sense in which Foucault's work on discipline was to affect third-generation *Annales* historians. It would convince them that one would have to have a 'very impoverished notion of the real' to exclude all those theoreticians' schemas, utopias, technologies, and projects that comprise this programmatic dimension of government (Foucault 1981b: 10–11; cf. Burke 1990: 84). One should also add that, for Foucault, the programmes of discipline cannot be reduced to the level of the ideal (such as in a history of ideas) for they themselves are 'fragments of reality' which induce particular effects in the ways humans govern and conduct themselves according to notions of truth and falsity. A critique made in terms of the reality of modern administrative or disciplinary power fails to grasp the nature of Foucault's project: to examine the relations between institutional practices and the rationality seeking to organise, codify, and direct such practices. The programmatic and 'epistemological' dimensions of the power–knowledge configuration of disciplinarity have disappeared in such a critique.

The second point that could be made here is the basis on which Foucault groups together various institutions in *Discipline and Punish*. This follows from the point I have just made. Factories, schools, prisons, hospitals, and asylums are not grouped together because they exhibit the same general features as one another. They are not thus more or less instances of empirical divergence from the ideal type of a 'total institution'. Rather they are grouped together because they were formed, to a greater or lesser degree, through various configurations of a disciplinary regime, what Hirst and Woolley (1982: 189–94) call 'disciplinarity' and Deleuze (1988: 34–44) a 'diagram of power'. In other words, these are locales both of the attempted implementation of schemas of discipline and of the reflection on the attempt to direct the conduct of those within them by disciplinary means. The historical development of each of these institutions, however different in other ways, cannot be isolated from its relation to the history of discipline. This does not preclude differences in the extent, intensity, and duration of the regime of discipline in each of these institutions, of the way in which disciplinary instruments such as hierarchical observation and normalising judgement, or the examination, are used and combined. Nor does it preclude the articulation of discipline with a variety of other practices that entail the use of time-space and affect the form of institutions, e.g. ones of production, therapy, education, punishment, and so on. To take Giddens' example, the limitations on time spent in the paid workplace and the spatial separation from homelife and other activities should be understood not as features of a unified disciplinary society but as components of other conditions of formation of these institutions. In this sense, the journey to work is formed through other processes and practices – from those of industrial production and mass consumption, to changing urban and family forms, the struggles over the length of the working day, and so on. It would be extremely foolish to reduce all this complicated history of contingent components to the form of the disciplinary regime. Of course, the workplace, home and family life, and systems of transportation, may and often have become the site of programmes for the installation of a disciplinary use of time and space (e.g. in the design of workers' housing or mass transportation systems, the policing of roads, transport routes and public spaces and buildings, the domestic education and health-care of infants, etc.). As for the history of the factory, one could perhaps distinguish between the sociology of the conditions of industrial work under capitalism and the genealogy of the programmatic rationality that has sought to make the worker more efficient, reorganise her or his relation with the processes and instruments of work, co-ordinate his or her activities with those of other workers, and so on. It is the latter history and its effects that principally concerns Foucault.

Institutions, then, are not simply examples of a 'disciplinary' type. Different techniques of discipline will be used in different combination and to different ends in various enclosed institutions. The examination has clearly different forms, purposes, and significance, in a hospital ward, a schoolroom, and in a prison yard. The type of enclosure and its internal partitioning will similarly vary according to the use of the institution. The cellular partitions of the prison are unlikely to be replicated in an office layout. Some enclosed institutions are likely to give greater emphasis to hierarchical observation and surveillance than others. A monastery or seminary with a regime of the internal regulation of conduct will place less emphasis on surveillance than a prison or a detention camp for refugees. The timetable has different applications in hospitals, factories, and schools. In short, the character of the enclosed institution cannot be viewed as an exemplar of a 'disciplinary type'. Its spatial and temporal organisation, and its use of the instruments of discipline, will vary according to its functioning as a therapeutic space, an educational space, a punitive space, a productive space, and so on, and the way in which these diverse spaces are mapped onto one another.

This is not to say that the history of discipline is not a history of the appropriation of innovations undertaken in one arena by another in which they are put to different purposes. Although Foucault holds that the systematic concentration of techniques of discipline occurs in closed institutions, this does not stop those techniques being used in other contexts. The 'swarming of disciplinary techniques' covers their appropriations at other locales and enclosures and their irradiation out of enclosed institutions into other spaces of the social body. In this sense, these institutions are only nodes in a disciplinary network. For example, although the household is not regulated by means of disciplinary power, disciplinary techniques can be applied in the domestic sphere: in the arrangement of domestic architecture and the design of public housing, in the internal arrangement and partitioning into rooms of workers' houses, and in the education, feeding, and caring for children, and so on.

Two final aspects of the account of disciplinary power the above criticism seems to miss are related to Foucault's notion of power. First, disciplinary power is positive, productive, and enabling. There are two senses in which the claim that disciplinary power does not act on agents is misleading. It never acts on a passive force: the body that is the target of such power is already replete with forces and capacities (Patton 1992). In this sense, disciplinary power acts on the actions and capacities for action of its subjects. There is thus a sense in which the human bodies it operates on are already agents. Moreover, disciplinary techniques may form the condition of agency: not only the corporate agencies formed through the complex division of labour or the units of an army, but the individual agency created through capacities such as literacy or qualifications to act in a particular professional capacity. The possibility of resistance is already implied in the suggestion that disciplinary power could be viewed as a kind of *dressage*, a training of an already active body and its forces, so that they may be harnessed toward a system of command (Foucault 1977a: 166–7). Further, there is no reason to assume that the capacities constituted through disciplinary powers will be used by the same social groups or to the same unvarying ends.

Secondly, Foucault's account of practices of punishment and the disciplinary regime are crucially linked – as we have seen above – to epistemological concerns. The exercise of disciplinary and biopower are not possible without the development of specific forms of rationality and discourse taking the individual, body and soul, and the population, and its component parts, as objects of knowledge. This dimension of Foucault's account seems to escape those who would sociologise it.

In conclusion, I want to mention several ways in which Foucault's thought provides some direction on issues of time and space. It would seem that Foucault regards time and space as constitutive dimensions of relations of power and rule. 'Time [and, we could add, space – M.D.] penetrates the body and with it all the meticulous controls of power' (Foucault 1977a: 152). Training organises and co-ordinates bodily activities through time and space, e.g. the analytical breaking-down of activity and gesture, its co-ordination with instruments, and with other actors, occurs through serially ordered time sequences and use of physical space, as in the example of the soldier and his weapon or the worker subject to Taylorist principles.

Similarly, if nation-states are to be regarded as 'power-containers', it is because certain techniques, practices, and forms of knowledge (statistics, economics, the social and behavioural sciences) have developed allowing the government and administration of whole populations, and their constituent segments, on a regular and continuous basis through the territorial space of the nation. When Michael Mann talks of 'territorial centralisation' he presupposes the means by which centralised forms of national and regional government can operate. In other words, he presupposes the development of the biopolitical dimension of government, or what Foucault would later call 'governmentality'. For Foucault, territorial centralisation is a necessary but not sufficient condition for certain forms of government. He suggests that the more interesting question lies in the problem of how some bodies are able to act as centres, how they are able to constitute themselves as sites of administrative power, and how government is possible over large distances and on a continuous and regular basis. Government is a form of 'acting at a distance' as Rose and Miller (1992) persuasively argue. If anything, the means by which it is possible to govern over space and through time are almost inexhaustible: the regulation of national and international time, the collection, retrieval, storage, and transportation of information and data, the development of relatively predictable transport and communication systems, locales and techniques of specialised arenas of administration (of the economy, of education, of social welfare, etc.), and so on (see, also, Foucault 1986h). The government of populations in time and space allows the means of co-ordination of activities with those at other locales and with state and non-state forms of agency (local and regional government, international markets, corporations, families, welfare organisations, individuals).

To summarise Foucault's suggestions here. First, one could argue the general thesis that time and space, and their mutual enwrapping, are constitutive elements in practices of government and technologies of power. Secondly, and following from this, it is extremely fruitful to analyse how practices of power, rule, and government, organise and co-ordinate activities in time and space; by doing so, certain of the lineaments of power, however naturalised, neutralised, and reduced to the merely technical, are laid bare. Thirdly, the intelligibility of particular regimes or assemblages of practices (around sexuality or madness, for example) should be understood in terms of multiple and diverse temporalities and the superimposition of heteromorphous spaces. This final point could be made by invoking again the notion of genealogies as serial histories, and the suggestion that the historian's task is to construct multiple series with varying temporalities composed of regularities, ruptures, and transformations. These series and temporalities intersect to compose the always transient and difficult form of the present, a present for particular cultural groups, their forms of life-conduct and modes of self-relation, and constituted in their engagement with regimes of practices (over incarceration, welfare, etc.). One might suggest that a similar point could be made for notions of space. Diverse forms of spatialisation (e.g. governmental, architectural, disciplinary, functional, etc.) could be said to compose the actual spaces inhabited, used, abused, resisted and transformed, by social actors. The form of the modern school, hospital, or office, could not be reduced to any one form of spatialisation but should be understood in the complex mapping of the different forms onto another, and their articulation with diverse forms of the temporalisation of activities.

Chapter 9

Governmentality . . .

Foucault (1986f) was eventually to offer a characterisation of his own abiding concerns as more ethical than political. Nevertheless, the term that best summarises the multiple directions of his thought from the later 1970s appears to be a political one. That term is 'governmentality'.

A glance at how Foucault uses this term, however, immediately reveals the multiplicity of its domains. In a seminar in America, he defines it as 'the contact between the technologies of domination of others and those of the self' (Foucault 1988k: 19) and so captures its role at the fulcrum of his political and ethical problematics. Again, in an interview after the publication of the second and third volumes of *The History of Sexuality*, he suggests that governmentality implies the ethical relation of self to self, and that it concerns strategies for the direction of conduct of free individuals (1988c: 19–20). What makes Foucault's later studies so fascinating, I would suggest, is condensed in this notion of governmentality. It defines a novel thought-space across the domains of ethics and politics, of what might be called 'practices of the self' and 'practices of government', that weaves them together without a reduction of one to the other.

This term can act as the general heading of two related transmutations of Foucault's thought in these years. On the one hand, the microphysics of power becomes, in his lectures, a genealogy of governmentality, with its concerns for political rationality and technologies of government, the emergence of liberalism and the analysis of neoliberalism. On the other, his history of sexuality becomes a genealogy of the desiring subject, concerned with ethical practice, techniques of the self, and the aesthetics of existence.

Foucault establishes a common approach to these two domains. He prefers to analyse the forms of governmental and ethical *practice* over their legal and moral codification and formalisation. He elaborates a methodology applicable to the analysis of the government both of self and of others that brings into focus: the substance worked on by the respective techniques; the mode of subjectification; the self-forming activity; and the *telos* of the practice. He also rethinks the problems of truth and reason in relation to these two domains in addresses on historical forms of political rationality and on *parresia* or forms of virtuous truth-telling as a technique of the self in his last lectures (Flynn 1988).

One might like to view this dual transmutation of Foucault's work as an openness to the questions put to his earlier genealogies by critics. In the first place, he addresses the problem of how it is possible to analyse the macro-level of the state from within the methodological framework that had developed the microphysics of power. Secondly, he seeks to show how it is possible to conceive of the subject as a site of independent conduct without relapsing into a humanist framework, and to address questions of resistance to relations of power and domination, and problems of freedom and autonomy more generally. Finally, by pursuing the consequences of these two interdefined problem areas, Foucault is able to suggest the contours of a differentiated analysis of power and domination that poses ways of thinking about political norms without recourse to a foundation in a universal system of values.

In these two final chapters, which together make up an exposition of the different axes of this domain, I range widely over this vast material. In this chapter, I introduce the general field and concentrate on practices of government. In the next, I examine aspects of the ethical dimension of the practices of the self, some points of intersection of the genealogies of governmental and ethical practices, and compare Foucault's approach to the work on the self and politics with that of Norbert Elias. I also offer some concluding reflections on Foucault's thought on power, domination, government, and ethics.

PROLOGUE ON ETHICS AND GOVERNMENT

The first 'phase' – if one may be permitted this term – of Foucault's work on power extends until and includes the first volume of the *History of Sexuality* (1979b). But that slim volume also contains suggestions, particularly in a final chapter introducing the notion of a *biopolitics*, or a power over life operating at the level of whole populations, that Foucault feels the need to say rather more about the global strategies of the state. That chapter most clearly foreshadows the direction of Foucault's thought on matters of state in the years 1978–84. The rest of the volume, as an investigation of the 'will to know' about ourselves through the injunction to speak the truth of our sex, foreshadows the broader elaboration of the way in which individuals work upon themselves in relation to 'games of truth' and techniques of the self. This is undoubtedly a critical text for Foucault's later thought, not least for the apparent crisis its reception seems to have provoked (Eribon 1991: 274–7). It is certainly the only major text in which he addresses at length both the institutionalised micro-forms of work upon the self, particularly the practice of confession, and the global strategies of the government of the state.

It is clear, however, that both these directions go beyond the domain conceived as the microphysics of power. The problematic of government goes beyond that of the disciplinary society uncovered through the investigation of the transformation of penal practice and, in fact, replots that transformation within a series of other transformations: of right, sovereignty, and security. Beginning with his lectures in 1978 and 1979 (Foucault 1979a, 1989b: 99–120, Gordon 1991) – and encompassing his American lectures (Foucault 1988h, 1988g) – Foucault moves away from the local, particular, microphysical studies of power to a new macro-level analysis of what he calls 'govern-mentality', a term which could easily be read, in the language of Lucien Febvre, as a concern with the conditions of emergence of the 'mentality of government', as Gordon (1987: 297) has suggested. It could also be read in a series of concepts addressed to the 'will to know'. This form of the will to know, however, no longer simply seeks to link forms of knowledge and relations of power, but addresses the rationality implicated in the exercise of governance, that which Foucault refers to as governmental rationality (1979a) or political rationality (1988h). It is germane – in light of the possible totalising reading of the 'carceral' apparently authorised by the final part of *Discipline and Punish* (1977a) – that here the power of government attains pre-eminence over other forms such as not only sovereignty but also, rather intriguingly, discipline (1979a: 20).

However central, it is perhaps true to say that this side retained an uncertain status in Foucault's thought. On the one hand, he did not bring the fragments on government together into a fuller, more explicit work at the time of his death, and we are left with a number of quite distinct, but nevertheless lucid and coherent, formulations of this notion. On the other, the notion of government is pivotal because it suggests two crucial sets of continuities in Foucault's thought. First, there are the continuities between the microphysics of power (and the political technology of the body) and the concerns of the government of nations, populations, and societies. Secondly, there is a continuum established between both of these and the practice of ethics as a form of government of the self. The notion of government suggests, then, first a project for the analysis of the state no longer reliant on the earlier juxtaposition of micro- and macro-levels of power and the conceptual antimony of an analytic of micropowers and a theory of sovereignty. It also, however, suggests a relation between the government of the self by the self, of one's own existence, and broader modalities of government, including political government.

This triple domain of self-government, the government of others, and the government of the state, is captured by Foucault's concern to mobilise an earlier sense of 'government', in evidence in sixteenth century Christian pastorals, neo-Stoicism, pedagogy and advice to the prince. Here government encompasses the government of oneself, of souls and lives, of children and households, as well as the art of conducting affairs of state (Foucault 1979a: 5). Moreover, Foucault's general characterisation of government as *la conduite de la conduite*, or the conduct of conduct (Gordon 1987: 296), suggests that the term marks out a massive domain between the minutiae of individual self-examination, self-care, and self-reflection, and the techniques and rationalities concerned with the governance of the state. This phrase is certainly redolent of Weber's themes of the methodical conduct of life (the rational *Lebensführung*) characteristic of Protestant asceticism (Gordon 1987: 296; Hennis 1983, 1988; Weber 1985). Moreover, it also picks up on the double sense of the verb *conduire*, to conduct, which means both to lead and to behave, to conduct others and to conduct oneself (*se conduire*) in a certain way (Foucault 1982: 220–1). Foucault himself was to note the similarity of his concerns here with the theme of 'asceticism' in Weber on more than one occasion (Foucault 1988c: 2; 1988k: 17), but even a prominent scholar of Weber has suggested that Foucault achieved an original contribution outside the Weberian problematic (Turner 1992: 233–5).

I want to note several points before proceeding separately to each of these domains. First, the genealogies of government and the self not only effect a displacement within Foucault's thought, but also within conventional forms of ethical and political analysis. Thus Foucault juxtaposes an analysis of the practices of government to the theory of the state and remarks that he refrains from the latter as one might abstain from an indigestible meal (Gordon 1991: 4). He also juxtaposes ethical practices, or practices of the self, to moral codes, suggesting that the history of moral codes in the West reveals little about changing modalities of ethical self-relation and self-formation. In both cases, where philosophers and historians had focused on a unitary entity ripe for a general explanation, Foucault approaches the problem from the perspective of a multiplicity of practices as distinct events that can be arranged and followed in their lineages and series.

Secondly, there is a constant cross-referencing from one to the other. On the one hand, ethics as an action of 'self on self' is linked to the practice of government, the government of others as well as oneself. Similarly, the problem of government cannot be dissociated from a reflection on the relation of individuals to themselves, whether as self-governing citizens in Athenian and other versions of democracy, or in the reflection on limits to government that are coextensive with what we call liberalism. At base, and of utmost importance, the problem of resistance, and the right of the governed to protest the actions of government, is an ethical one. It is in this light we should read what might be called Foucault's 'declaration of the rights of the governed' in 1981 (Eribon 1991: 279).

Thirdly, the problem of both politics and ethics is one of the use and practice of freedom. Foucault suggests that 'liberty is the ontological condition of ethics. But ethics is the definite form assumed by liberty' (1988c: 4). That is to say, ethics is simply not possible without freedom and that as a practice it seeks to shape freedom. Power – or at least the forms of power constituting liberal practices of government – comes to operate on the conduct of the governed. It seeks a direction of conduct rather than a violent or gross form of corporeal domination. In this sense, the microphysics of power may have been overstated if it gave the impression of a determinism of power operating upon the body. Here, governmental power assumes a 'free subject', not an individual existing in an essential space of freedom, but one whose subjection is consistent with forms of choice. This theme is particularly germane to Foucault's discussion of liberalism and neoliberalism.

The themes of government and the ethical practices of the self are thus two separate yet intricately interwoven strands of an increasingly worked-out thought-space. It may be that practices of the self and practices of government mutually presuppose, without ever collapsing into, one another, even when they are superimposed in a particular manner, such as within institutional Christianity. It is in the entwinement of these two themes that the character of Foucault's thought seems both to resemble that of Norbert Elias and to be most methodologically distinct from it. Both are concerned with the relation between political forms and forms of self. In Elias' case, however, this is conceived in terms of the grounding of modern forms of personality in the emergence of central state authority and the internal pacification of states. However, it is in what each would claim for their account of the rapport between power relations and self-formation that most clearly distinguishes their projects. Elias undertakes a dispassionate analysis of long-term social processes (see 1987a: 3–41), and seeks to establish the principles of a sociological theory by means of an analysis of historical data. He offers us an englobing thesis of 'the civilising process' in which there is a fit between the formation of the self and the rationalisation of conduct and broader societal processes consequent upon the state monopolisation of violence and taxation (Elias 1978, 1982). He claims no direct philosophical, political, or ethical status or consequence for such a venture. Foucault is both more modest in his claims and bolder in the spheres of their application. The relation between practices of government and practices of the self is an open one: these are simply two relatively independent, but interdependent, domains. There is no general thesis of their relation, but an open space, one of dispersion rather than general theoretical connection, that can lend itself to historical investigation. On the other hand, as a genealogy, based on what Elias would have thought of as an unwarranted political 'involvement', Foucault offers polyvalent and cross-disciplinary domains of application. The results of his studies can sometimes appear pertinent to political practice (around the status of medical power, the practice of psychiatric confinement, the role of scientific knowledge, prisoners' struggles, movements of sexual revolution, etc.), political philosophy (liberalism and neoliberalism, legal and contract theory, and socialism), ethics (forms of self-stylisation and self-practice, the debate on the 'culture of narcissism', the rights of the governed), and the reflexivity of the social sciences. Elias' project is worth considering as a point of contrast that borders on the same domain and I shall hence return to it on several occasions in the course of the discussion in these final chapters.

PRACTICES OF GOVERNMENT

Foucault's thought on government is contiguous with his earlier thought on power in one central way: the analyses of power and government cannot be made simply in terms of the historical development of state institutions and the language of legitimacy, law, and sovereignty. Having problematised the use of such language in the conceptualisation and analysis of the exercise of micropowers, he now problematises its use to characterise the state and its powers. Indeed, Foucault attempts to cut the Gordian knot of the relation between micro- and macro-levels of power by applying the same type of perspective to the state that he had earlier applied to the micropowers – one which emphasises *practices* of government. The earlier focus on disciplinary practices – the panoply of the political technology of the body – is displaced, and somewhat subsumed, under a more general concern for governmental practices seeking the direction of conduct. Rather than a theory of the state, Foucault proposes to analyse the operation of governmental power, the techniques and practices by which it works, and the rationalities and strategies invested in it.

Foucault's thought on governmentality can be read as an attempt to displace the macro–micro division, or to at least give explicit recognition to the relative nature of this distinction. Questions of the 'how' of power and rule, its mechanisms, its techniques, its strategies, its objectives and effects, can be asked of the 'global' forms of power just as they can be asked of the micropowers. As such, the perspective and concepts of governmentality are shaped against an effective historical analysis of the emergence of forms of national government and administration, and its techniques, particularly from the time of the Absolutist regimes, the attendant development of a sphere of public *policy* in its 'cameralist', 'mercantilist', and liberal forms, and the emergence of forms of rational knowledge taking the direction of public policy as their objective – principally, political economy, political arithmetic, vital and social statistics, and the moral or social sciences and economics.

Foucault's concerns overlap with those of a conventional historical sociology of the state, of the kind found in Max Weber's *General Economic History* (1927: 338–51), for example. Yet whereas Weber identifies the development of certain forms of national state administration, policy, and law as among the crucial preconditions for the rise and expansion of capitalism, Foucault's problem is the one suggested by his earlier deliberations on power, that of how particular types of power relations enable the state to act as a centralised, unified, locale, and the implications of this for the conduct of life of the governed. This would seem to be a decisive question for an effective history of the state that wishes to dispel the obviousness of centralised and *étatisté* forms of rule. I want now to show how the principal features of political rule that come to compose the state are rendered intelligible by Foucault's approach to governmentality.

As a preliminary, it is perhaps worth noting that Foucault's thought on the state, even in these years, is not all of a piece, despite the fact that it retains an overall consistency. In the 1978 lecture, 'On Governmentality', Foucault concludes with some reflections on the state. In keeping with his earlier position, he suggests that the state does not have the importance which is usually attributed to it (Foucault 1979a: 20). He claims that it 'does not have this unity, this individuality, this rigorous functionality, nor to speak frankly, this importance; maybe, after all, the State is no more than a composite reality and a mythical abstraction whose importance is a lot more limited than many of us think'. This first exposition on government then leads to a repetition of the theme of the inflated import of the state which had been a *leitmotif* of his political thought in the 1970s.

Four years later, the ground seems to have shifted considerably away from this earlier suspicion of the state. Thus, he was now moved to write that 'the state's power (and that's one of the reasons for its strength) is both an individualising and totalising form of power' (Foucault 1982: 213). He also wrote: 'It is certain that in contemporary societies the state is not simply one of the forms or specific situations of the exercise of power – even if it is the most important – but that in a certain way all other forms of power relations must refer to it' (ibid. 224).

Why such a difference? Is it possible to be consistent and to hold that the state is not as important as we think it is and that all other forms of power must refer to it in liberal societies? Rather than taking these different formulations as instances of a change of position, I would suggest that together they pose a fundamental problem over the existence of the state which Foucault is seeking to resolve. This problem stems from his consistent anti-statism which not only takes a methodological and political form but increasingly an explicitly ethical one.

For the later Foucault, it is necessary not only 'to cut off the king's head' in political analysis and method, but also to make intelligible government as an ethical practice, to thematise the dangers of its rationality, and consider the rights of citizens in so far as they share the status of the governed. This anti-statism both affirms the central role of the state in organising the field of powers of advanced liberal states at the same time as it denies that this role is a constitutive or a necessary one. On the one hand, Foucault's injunction to avoid the 'excessive value' usually attributed to the state as the *monstre froid* which confronts us (1979a: 20; cf. 1988g: 161) would appear to go beyond a mere methodological precept and encompass a political stance.[1] On the other hand, it is necessary to show the historical process by which all other powers came to be subordinate to the national state from the seventeenth century in western Europe. It is this tension that characterises Foucault's problem-atisations. It leads to a problematic of government that asks how the state comes to act as a centre of other forms of government, what are the means which enable it to act in this way, how its locales are constructed by specific means of knowledge and mechanisms of power, and how it enrols local relations and networks of power in its strategies (cf. Rose and Miller 1992). The problematic of government is not so much a solution to the paradoxical nature of the state but a research agenda into the contingent trajectories by which the state assumes it present and changing form.

In Foucault's fragments on government, the methodological question of the exercise of power, and the political question of the critique of liberal democracy gives way to a somewhat larger, ethical problem around the patterns of governance of modern states. This ethical problem concerns the transformation of the state by various governmental practices making human life a domain of power and knowledge. Foucault's later work now shows that the earlier problems around the individualising of human beings within techniques of power are ultimately also a problem of the state, of the formation and use of human characteristics within particular governmental relations. In these formulations, problems of state and politics become, for Foucault, ethical problems if, as he noted in an interview (1986f: 377), ethics is regarded as a practice or *ethos*, a mode of being. These issues of the government of the state and its relation to the forms of life of the human population in the twentieth century are spelt out in his public lectures in the United States (1988g; 1988h). Let us now examine two dimensions of the exercise of rule identified by Foucault, first that of political rationality, and secondly, that of political invention or the art of government.

Political rationality

Consider this striking passage from Foucault's lecture at the University of Vermont in 1982:

> The co-existence in political structures of large destructive mechanisms and institutions oriented toward the care of individual life is something puzzling and needs some investigation. It is one of the central antimonies of our political reason which I'd like to consider. I don't mean that mass slaughters are the effect, the result, the logical consequence of our rationality, nor do I mean that the state has the obligation of taking care of individuals since it has the right to kill millions of people. Neither do I want to deny that mass slaughters or social care have their economic explanations or their emotional motivations. It is this rationality, and the death and life game which takes place in it, that I'd like to investigate from an historical point of view.
>
> (Foucault 1988g: 147–8)

This passage is difficult not least for the positions which Foucault elaborates in order to negate. It is a passage finally affirming very little except this: in order to understand political action, from elaborate processes of policy formation and political decision-making to the daily, cynical exercise of power, it is necessary to understand the historically given forms of political rationality.

This, however, is a thesis that requires some underlining. For what is clear is that, for Foucault, politics is never, even in the most immediate or brutal action of the exercise of domination and power, without some degree of 'thought'. This is the first part of his thesis on political rationality. The second part is that this 'thought', this political rationality, does not simply arise from the rulers consulting their 'interests', or their capacity for rational choice, but from historically developed and modified forms of rationality. Political rationality, in this sense, is anterior to political action and a condition of it.

This thesis does not merely lead to a particular technique of analysis of political rationality. It draws attention to its fragility and dangers, particularly where political rationality is regarded as ahistorical common sense. What the opposition between genocide and what we might call 'geno-weal' suggests is the seriousness with which Foucault had come to regard matters of state, and the ethical grounding of his analysis of political reason. In the above passage, Foucault suggests that the right of mass death does not follow from the power over life. In the earlier discussion of bio-politics he argues: 'If genocide is indeed the dream of modern powers, this is not because of a recent return of the ancient right to kill; it is because power is situated and exercised at the level of life, the species, the race, and the large-scale phenomena of population' (Foucault 1979b: 137). It would seem that power may in principle be dispersed in a vast array of micropowers, but its exercise in advanced societies presupposes agencies capable of governing, and slaughtering, whole populations. It is little wonder that Foucault seeks to investigate both our political inventiveness and the nature of our 'limited' form of liberal government from a perspective that he conceded might be understood as ethical, if the latter is regarded as a practice, and ethos as a mode of being (1986f: 376–7).

In his earlier public addresses, those delivered as the *Tanner Lectures on Human Values* at Stanford University in 1979, Foucault's problem is directed to political rationality at the end of the twentieth century, a problem he locates as midway between the problem of the state as political organisation and the problem of the mechanisms of power. He is concerned with 'the type of rationality implemented in the exercise of state power' (Foucault 1988h: 73). This is a form of rationality acutely manifested in the 'welfare-state problem', a problem of the 'tricky adjustment between political power wielded over human subjects and political power wielded over live individuals' (ibid. 1988h: 67).

What constitutes this political rationality and makes it so problematic? What, if you like, constitutes a genealogy of the elements that continue to cause the welfare state so many problems? Foucault presents a compelling understanding of a political rationality constituted very broadly between two quite different and mutually problematising trajectories. The first has its origins with the Greeks, in which the 'political problem is that of the relation between the one and the many in the framework of the city and its citizens' (1988h: 67). This is the problem of citizenship, or of what he dubs the city-citizen game. We have noted that Foucault had earlier posed the problem of citizenship as one of the effective undermining of civil and political rights by the generalisation of disciplinary techniques. There, however, he limited the definition of the state to that of the juridical sphere and the institutions of political sovereignty. In so doing, the active citizen, whose rights are guaranteed by law and exercised in representative democracy, was opposed to the 'docile subject' secured by the 'swarming' of disciplinary mechanisms.

Now, however, Foucault expands his conception of the state to show how its characteristic elements are constituted within multiple trajectories. Political rationality has diverse roots in a complex genealogy. In addition to the juridical-political problem of citizenship, and the disciplinary problems of utility and docility, the present forms of political rationality have roots in ancient Christian notions of pastorship, and in the twin political doctrines of the seventeenth and eighteenth centuries, *reason of state* and *police*. As Foucault glosses, this genealogy of the problem of the state is one which leads to a 'a strange game whose elements are life, death, truth, obedience, individuals, self-identity' (1988h: 77).

The first of the *Tanner Lectures* takes us on something of a genealogy of what Foucault calls *pastoral* power, and the image of the politician as shepherd through ancient Hebraic, Greek, and Christian thought. It is a form of power with Hebraic roots, one which is not entirely compatible with Greek political discourse in which the task of the politician is to ensure the unity of the citizens in the city, not care for the life of individuals (Foucault 1988h: 67). The image of the leader as shepherd reaches its full elaboration only in early Christian literature. The Christian version consists of the introduction of a complete accountability of the 'shepherd' for all the members of the pastorate, the 'flock', the notion of obedience and self-control as a virtue of personal submission, the formation of an individualising knowledge, and the practice of mortification and a renunciation of the self and the world by oneself (ibid. 68–70). Stated in general, historical form, Foucault suggests that it is in institutional Christianity that we are witnesses to the domestication and subordination of the ancient culture of the 'cultivation of the self' by a notion of pastorship, or the care of others, and the development of a dynamics of self-decipherment as self-renunciation.

The second *Tanner* lecture brings this genealogy of governmentality forward to examine the trajectory of political rationality during the classical period and beyond. Here Foucault first charts the emergence of a doctrine of 'reason of state', of a conception of government taking the strength of the state as its ultimate objective and marks a break with a concept of the art of government as directed by God's laws (1988h: 74–7). Reason of state regards government as an art, a *techne*, as a set of techniques conforming to rules, and thus exemplifies Foucault's abiding concern for techniques and technologies of governance and rule. Such an art is rational in so far as it regards the nature of what is governed as the state itself and not something given within divine law. It shifts attention away from Machiavelli's problem of the binding of the prince to the state and poses the problem of the existence and durability, within a contested domain, of the state itself. Lastly, reason of state entails that rational government is bound up with knowledge, a political arithmetic or statistics of the forces of the state.

The development of a reason of state is thus an early example of a secular reflection on the art of government. It is consequent upon two fundamental processes: first, the crisis of feudalism in the sixteenth century and the long devolution of authority away from the estates onto the territorial, administrative states of absolutism; secondly, the dynamics of Reformation and Counter-Reformation, that put into question notions of pastorship and salvation by what might be called the politics of the confessional. The former provides a context for a problematising of the political obligation of individuals freed from traditional dependencies, hierarchies, and loyalties; the latter, the problematisation of the government of the soul, of the individual. The art of secular government is thus raised in the context of a revival of neo-Stoicism, and Foucault can remark that never before nor since, has government been so associated with the government of the self and others, of rulers and ruled (Gordon 1991: 12). This theme is developed further in the next chapter.

Foucault then discusses the notion of *police* in seventeenth and eighteenth century literature, pointing out that the term, before its current narrowing, encompasses a complete form of administration, whose object is the individual – 'a live, active, productive man' (Foucault 1988h: 79) – and whose intervention is 'totalitarian' in so far as it attends to every aspect of people's lives which concerns happiness (ibid. 80–1). For Foucault, however, the notion of police is totalitarian in another sense that becomes clear in the German attempts to found a science of police, a *polizeiwissenschaft*, which specifies a new and particular object of the art of government, the 'population', understood as a multiplicity of living individuals (ibid. 82–3), or as a 'species body' as opposed to the individual body, as he puts it elsewhere (1979b: 139). There is now a quite large literature on police, so I shall note in passing only several salient features.[2] First, it wavers between a series of general definitions, emphasising the maintenance of the good order within a community, the happiness of the population, and the strength of a state, and seemingly endless lists of regulations of diverse and apparently heterogeneous minutiae concerning such things as behaviour, dress, relations between social ranks, public hygiene, markets, the poor, beggars, roads, squares, municipal matters, public decency and morals, and so on. Secondly, the science of police, or cameralism, like English mercantilism, coexists and is interdependent with a peculiar conception of economy, one still articulated around the ancient theme of the *oikos* or householding and stewardship conceptions of the economy. 'Oeconomy' is the governance or husbandry of the household (of servants, women, children, of domestic animals, etc.) and political oeconomy is the governance of the state as household, and through its constituent households, even as late as James Steuart's political oeconomy of 1767. Thirdly, even though its regulatory fervour and preliberal conception of oeconomy make it appear clumsy, *polizeiwissenschaft* is a definite form of political rationality seeking to align the strength of the state to the happiness of a new object, the population, by means of interventions upon the life and relations of the members of the population and the employment of new forms of knowledge (political oeconomy, statistics etc.) and rationality. Finally, if one was looking for a contemporary equivalent that translates the term in a slightly different way, the *polizeiwissenschaften* may be equivalent to what is today called, particularly in the USA, the 'policy sciences'. This indeed may be the first 'modern' framework for public policy.

It is these elements – of citizenship, pastoral power, reason of state, and police science – which form the genealogy and assemblage of political rationality and it is their mutual superimposition that is at the root of Foucault's diagnosis of the ethical dilemmas of the state: 'Our societies proved to be really demonic since they happened to combine those two games – the city-citizen game and the shepherd-flock game – in what we call the modern state' (Foucault 1988h: 71). Political rationality may be seen as trying to reconcile two diverse yet constitutive impulses, one embodied in the legal-political instance in which the city-game is played, and the other in the governmental-administrative instance in which the shepherd-flock game is played. As Gordon (1991: 12–13) has pointed out, there is a series of moral ambivalences over the latter recognised by the German police thinkers. The ruler is as likely to be a husbandman (*Wirt*, from which *Wirtschaft*, economy, is composed) as a shepherd (*Hirt*), governing and exploiting a herd as much as caring for the welfare of a flock. Von Justi is the most advanced of the police thinkers, according to Foucault (1988h: 82–3), because he understands the paradoxical interchange between the objective of increasing the state's strength and fostering the happiness of its population.

Political rationality is thus a problem of mutually constitutive, yet agonistic, instances within state practices: those of law, rights and obligations, participation, the citizen, and liberty, on the one hand, and those of order, security, welfare, the population and submission, on the other. This problem arises from the attempt to reconcile the diverse political images of the liberal political individual, who is both a self-responsible 'agent' (as sociologists would say) within a polity and a living, dependent creation whose nurture and exploitation is essential to the might of the state and the quality of life within it.

If one likes, the ethos or mode of being of political rationality is the correlation between two diverse forms of political individualisation and political totalisation in which human beings are regarded as both self-governing citizens *and* members of the flock who are governed, members of a self-governing political community *and* members of the governed population. Thus the integration of individuals in the social totality 'results from a

constant correlation between an increasing individualisation and the reinforce-
ment of this totality' and, in reference to the conflict of a *Rechstaat* and a
police state, 'it is impossible to reconcile law and order because when you try
to do so it is only in the form of an integration of law into the state's order'
(Foucault 1988g: 162). The state is in a kind of win-win position with regard
to political rationality and its instantiation in struggles: demands for the
enhancement of civil, political and social rights, to use T.H. Marshall's (1983)
celebrated phrase, are responded to by multiplying the governmental domains
and capacities of the state; and demands of the rights of individuals against the
state necessarily require the development of new forms of governmental
practice to secure, defend, protect, and foster those rights. At the end of the
Tanner Lectures, Foucault points out this perilous paradox that the state
thrives through demands both for liberties and rights and for order, provision
and welfare. It is thus that 'liberation can only come from attacking, not just
one of these two effects, but political rationality's very roots' (1988h: 85).

The ethical problem, then, is not so much the state, but the ways in which
the art of government, and the political rationality that invests it, have
constituted various forms of individual and collective being and experience,
various modes of political subjectification. In a 1977 round-table discussion
Foucault states: 'my problem is to see how men govern (themselves and
others) by the production of truth. . . My general theme isn't society but the
discourse of true and false, by which I mean the correlative formation of
domains and objects and the verifiable, falsifiable discourses that bear on
them: and it's not just their formation that interests me, but *the effects in the
real* to which the are linked' (1981b: 8–9; 14; emphasis added). We might
conclude that if Foucault's problem concerns how we are governed and
govern ourselves and others in relation to the production of truth – here, in
relation to political rationality – then the 'effects in the real' to which he refers
are none other than what we have become, what governance by truth has
'made of us'. Perhaps we can cite Paul Veyne (1982: 197), that 'truth is not the
highest of the knowledge values', and argue that, for Foucault, it is the effects
of the discourses of truth on the real, on the formation of what it is to be a
human being, a citizen, and a governed and governing subject, which reveals
his deepest ethical concerns.

This reading of Foucault's political thought, then, opens up interesting
parallels with the work of both Max Weber and Norbert Elias. Foucault's
thought on government and conduct is not dissimilar to that which Hennis
(1988) places as Weber's 'central question': the development of *Menschentum*
(humankind), if that term refers to the principle of variability of the attributes
of humanity, a 'characterology' of the mode of being human made possible by
certain forms of rational governance of self and others. Nor is it dissimilar to
Elias' notion that what is rationalised are 'the modes of conduct of certain
groups of people', and his view of rationalisation as 'an expression of the
direction in which the moulding of people in specific social figurations is

changed. ' (Elias 1982: 289). We may conclude that the rationalisation of the conduct of life emerges in a central theme in the work of these three thinkers: for Weber, as an internal systematisation of self and a methodical conduct of life in response to changing religious ethics; for Elias, as the development of an agency of self-constraint in response to the increasing density and complexity of networks of social interdependence; and for Foucault, as the multiple work of subjectification inscribed in the various ways in which humans are rendered governable and in which they govern themselves according to forms of rationality. If Weber draws attention to the 'effects in the real' of ethical rationalisations and Elias to the functional requisites of socio-political processes, then Foucault's contribution here may be to draw attention to the historical relations that subsist between the ethical rational-isations of life-conduct on the one hand and the political rationalisations of the state on the other.

Liberal arts or political invention

Any consideration of the government of populations and individuals, how-ever, cannot remain solely devoted to the study of political rationality. For, as Foucault's deliberations on reason of state illustrate, government is an applied art, one that no doubt works within the forms of truth produced according to political rationality. Political rationality is a condition of governmental practice, but as a practice, government relies on means irreducible to this rationality. Moreover, government is not the totalistic implementation of the programme derived from a rationality, but an operation that is more clearly thought in terms of tactics and strategies of power, of specific, conflictual, and changing aims, ideals, and objectives, and varying degrees of success and failure, with a range of consequences situated across the spectrum between the intentional and the unintentional. I have developed the idea of strategic rationality in the previous chapter. Here, I would prefer to make some brief mention of the 'technical' aspects of the art of government and then examine liberalism as a key dimension of political invention.

Political rationality may be defined as the relatively systematic, explicit, discursive, problematisation and codification of the art or practice of govern-ment, as a way of rendering the objects of government in a language that makes them governable. By contrast the techniques of government are all the means, mechanisms, and specific instruments which make possible forms of administration, power, and rule. The analysis of these techniques has been undertaken and developed in the work of Peter Miller and Nikolas Rose (Miller and Rose 1990, Rose and Miller 1992), and I shall not repeat their advances in this area here, except to note several points.

First, one might wish to distinguish between *techniques of government* (e.g. systems of accounting, methods of the organisation of work, forms of surveillance, methods of timing and spacing of activities in particular locales, etc.) and *technologies of government* (e.g. types of schooling and medical practice, systems of income support, forms of administration and 'corporate management', systems of intervention into various organisations, and bodies of expertise) that are assembled through particular governmental programmes. This may help distinguish between the necessary and contingent aspects of certain forms of administration, bureaucracy, and expertise. It may be able to show how technical aspects of government function within particular programmes, and the way the latter take over and utilise for their own purpose techniques that have been invented elsewhere and for quite different purposes. Above all, it may help us understand the polymorphous nature of governmental techniques and the perverse ways in which they come to be implanted in diverse technologies.

Secondly, one could also distinguish from among these technologies of government, *intellectual* technologies, such as the use of statistical tables, graphs, reports, and forms, and all other means of the eliciting, recording, memorisation, and transportation of information. The distinction between political rationality and technologies of government is thus not a mental–manual distinction. The latter includes the mechanisms by which specific aspects of governed reality are rendered both knowable and amenable to governing. Thus the broad distinction between rationality and technology may be one between the representation of and intervention into specific governmental domains, but this distinction is also present within the technologies themselves. Political rationality may generally codify and assemble particular technologies within various programmes but the technologies themselves are a condition for that rationality and have forms of rationality inscribed within them.

Thirdly, Foucault's approach is less a general theory of the state or even of governing itself than a strict analytical attention to the mechanisms of government and rule and their manifestations in diverse practices. One might wish to counterpoise a theory of the state to an analytic of governmental practices. Having noted that, it is necessary to reiterate in this context that these practices, no matter how strategic and oriented to the short-term, are never entirely free from a regime of political rationality. In this sense, political rationality is itself a means and resource of governing, a part of the armoury of how one is governed and governs. There is thus a circuit between the rationality and the practices of government: it is the necessary problematisation of the latter that gives rise to the political rationality that is itself one source of political inventiveness.

Finally, one can note this is not only a highly fruitful path for the investigation of the features of the state designated by Giddens as 'administrative power' and Mann as 'infrastructural power', but also a veritable morphology of the contemporary forms of the 'will to govern', one which can be mapped onto and aligned with the morphology of the 'will to know' represented by Foucault's work on the human sciences.

I shall now concentrate on Foucault's thought on the modern form of political invention we call 'liberalism' and contemporary issues of neoliberalism. The question that appears to be posed most crucially by Foucault's discussion of liberalism in his lectures of 1978 and 1979 (1979a; 1989b: 99–120; Gordon 1991) is the degree to which liberalism can be posed as a practice or mode of government rather than a distinctive philosophy or world-view. Liberalism is, of course, an extremely fecund political discourse and practice that partakes a multiplicity of forms. It is today possibly coextensive with the active forms of contemporary political culture in industrialised societies. Foucault's thesis would appear to be that this fecundity stems less from the explicit doctrines of liberalism than from the capacity for political invention within liberal societies.

As political philosophies, all versions of liberalism would seem to embrace two common principles: first, that of limited government, one capable of being interpreted widely but, at the least, posing the question of the ethical limits to governmental action; secondly, that of the liberty of the governed, of the need for government to operate through a tacit or explicit conception of freedom or choice. In this sense, liberalism would appear to require a form of political invention that is irreducible to the obsessional ordering of the minutiae of life-conduct common to cameralist *polizeiwissenschaft* and twentieth century state socialism.

Here, I shall draw out two disparate and somewhat conflicting dimensions of liberal practices of government Foucault attends to: first, the discovery of the economy as both a quasi-autonomous reality and register of governmental intervention, and, secondly, the kindred issues of law, security, and population.

In Foucault's lectures (1979a, Gordon 1991) and in the writings of others (Tribe 1978, Meuret 1981/2, 1988), we find the beginnings of the complex genealogy of the government of the economy. This genealogy maps a series of the forms of economic government from seventeenth century Europe. It concerns the crystallisation of a notion of the economy as a quasi-naturalistic, autonomous level of reality, out of the older forms of *oeconomy* that served both the science of police and mercantilist methods of government. Put very crudely, this genealogy maps the descent from a householding conception of oeconomy in which there is an adequation between oeconomy as the government of the household or family and political oeconomy as the government of the state. In such a conception, oeconomy is the art of stewardship of the things and people that comprises the state and operates through the commonwealth of patriarchalist households.[3] As Foucault puts it, the problem of oeconomy for the seventeenth century art of government is one of 'how to introduce the meticulous attention of the father towards his family, into the management of the state' (1979a: 10). The family was both model for the patriarchalist police state and an element in its constitution, a model of governance and the oeconomic means by which the sovereign governed. By contrast, the liberal economy becomes a specific reality that places, at a minimum, constraints upon political governance by means of an arena of naturalistically conceived laws, including those of capital, population and subsistence, that it would be foolish for the state to ignore. In such a framework, the liberal family becomes less a model and means of government, and more a site formed and reformed through multiple state and non-state interventions (Donzelot 1979).

As Foucault points out, political economy is a peculiar discovery in this sense. It is a 'lateral science', a scientific form of discourse necessary to but incapable of producing an art of government, one which cannot provide a deductive programme of government (Gordon 1991: 16). Nor can it provide the administrative means of government of the population or of any specific sector, as I have sought to show in respect of the administration of poverty (Dean 1991a, 1992b). At best, political economy provides a mode of rendering the real knowable as a distinctive economy and a set of protocols concerning the form and substance of state activity. Moreover, it establishes a set of objectives and ethical ideals which animate a liberal mode of government that will, through a series of displacements, begin to draw the contours of a distinctive form of life for the propertyless populations.

'Laissez-faire', in this sense, as Karl Polanyi (1944) long ago realised, does not mean the absence of state or other forms of governmental intervention. For Foucault, it enjoins us 'not to impede the course of things, but to ensure the play of natural and necessary modes of regulation, to make regulations which permit natural regulation to operate' (quoted in Gordon 1991: 17). It is in this regard that Bentham could propose plans not only for Panopticon workhouses but also a national system of charitable administration, run by a National Charity Company, and, later, an Indigence Relief Ministry, that was consistent with the protocols of the liberal economy (Dean 1991a: 173–92). To put this another way, for Foucault, *homo oeconomicus* exists at the juncture of two liberal rationalities: in the first, it is an 'abstract, ideal, purely economic point' that populates the reality and density of civil society; in the second, civil society is the 'concrete ensemble' within which it needs to be situated to be made governable (Foucault, quoted in Gordon 1991: 23). In one, *homo oeconomicus* is the motor of the self-regulating economy; in the other, it is an element in the economy of government formed within the calculations of politicians, magistrates, and civil servants.

To paraphrase Foucault's summary of his course (1989b: 113), liberalism is neither a never realised utopia nor a dream at war with a reality in which it seeks to inscribe itself. It is a polymorphous and permanent instrument of critique: of previous forms of monarchical government, of potential despotisms and their abuses, and of contemporary forms it seeks to reform, rationalise, and exhaustively review. If liberalism deploys and seeks to ground itself in the rule of law, it is neither because civil society is a Lockean contractual order nor because of its special rapport with law, but because law, articulated through the 'truly representative' parliamentary system, provides general forms of intervention that disqualify particular measures. Further, the participation of the governed in the elaboration of the law constitutes the most effective system of a governmental economy (ibid. 115). In such passages, Foucault appears to suggest a view of law within the liberal form of governmentality that is not reducible to the problem of the legitimation of political sovereignty but is itself a specific and partial instrument or technique of government. It is worth noting that such a position suggests a break with a pervasive sociological view of law in terms of its legitimation functions, as well as with Foucault's account of the juridical instance detailed in the previous chapter.

A discussion of Foucault's reflection on liberalism as an art of government would be incomplete without a discussion of *security*. For him, liberalism does not derive simply from an alignment of forms of juridical reflection with economic analyses, nor from the superimposition of the contractual subject of rights with the economic subject of interests, as a Marxian analysis of the juridical and ideological conditions of capitalism would suggest (cf. Foucault 1989b: 109–20). The 'threshold of emergence' of liberalism, for Foucault, is a problem of 'the incompatibility between the non-totalisable multiplicity which characterises subjects of interest, and the totalising unity of the juridical sovereign' (quoted by Gordon 1991: 22). Liberalism seeks to avert both the reduction of political sovereignty to a function of political economy, and an abandonment of the market as a domain of governance altogether. This is why liberalism contains within its own problematisation an economy of governance, an incitation to the formation of a distinctive kind of governmentality, and a series of governmental actions and interventions. This is also why Foucault would place so much emphasis on the multiple uses of liberalism in late eighteenth and early nineteeth century English political philosophy and the evolution and ambiguities of Bentham and the Benthamites (1989b: 114). The liberal problem of security, reformulated by Bentham, is continuous with the problem of the 'holding out' or continuity of the state addressed by reason of state and police science, but is applied to a rather different domain. As Gordon puts it (1991: 20), 'liberalism discards the police conception of order as a visible grid of communication; it affirms instead the necessarily opaque, dense autonomous processes of population. It remains, at the same time, preoccupied with the vulnerability of these same processes, the need to enframe them in "mechanisms of security"'.

The closest one could come to a comprehensive position on the mechanisms of power in liberal governmentality for Foucault would be to say that they are fashioned through a complex and irreducible ensemble of elements that comprise the rationality and techniques of security, sovereignty, law, and, it is hardly necessary to add, discipline. This, one must point out, is very far from a totalistic reduction of political modernity and rationality to a specific form of power.

No overview of aspects of Foucault's thought on liberal government can be complete without mention of his discussion of two forms of neoliberalism in his 1979 lectures (1989b: 116–18), that of the post-war German liberal thought around the review *Ordo*, and the Chicago School, especially the work of human capital theorist and 1992 Nobel Prize winner for economics, Gary Becker. Again, I shall paraphrase some of what Foucault has to say in his summary. The *ordoliberalen* and Chicago School presented him with two case-studies in the critique of the excess of government and a return to Benjamin Franklin's technology of 'frugal government' (ibid. 117). The former seek the implementation of the regime of a competitive market in the historical context of the postwar Federal Republic and protest that such a regime has never been tried due to a 'socialism of the State' (*socialisme d'Etat*) instanced not only by Nazism and the war regime but also the economic intervention and planning of the mobilisation of 1914–18. The *ordoliberal* critique opens three different political fronts: soviet socialism, national socialism, and Keynesian techniques. It represents itself as combating any form of economic government that systematically ignores the market processes that can ensure stable price formation (ibid. 118). In the place of such forms of government, the German liberals argue for an institutionalist, rather than naturalistic, conception of the market as a game of competitive freedom (Gordon 1991: 41–2). The market economy is thus organised, but not planned, within an institutional and juridical officialdom which would offer legal guarantees and limits and ensure that the market did not produce social dislocations. One of the *ordoliberalen*, Alexander von Rustow, envisages this to imply the shaping of all dimensions of individual life, a 'vital policy', according to the ethos of an enterprise.

Foucault characterises the American neoliberalism of the Chicago School as also opposed to 'too much' government, exemplified by the New Deal, war planning, and the postwar macroeconomic and social programmes (1989b: 118–19). Their critique, like the German neoliberals, traces the dangerous and inexorable path from economic intervention, excessive public sector growth, maladministration and bureaucracy, toward a sclerosis of governmental processes. However, where the German version sought to support and amend the market by social provision for unemployment, health, and housing, American neoliberalism seeks to extend market rationality to domains that are not exclusively or primarily economic such as the family and children, and delinquency and crime. The shift is from *homo oeconomicus* as the subject of an activity beyond government to one of the 'manipulable man' of behaviourism, 'perpetually responsive to modifications in his environment' (Gordon 1991: 43–4).

One could argue here that this type of thought raises the ethical problem of contemporary liberalism in a very acute fashion. On the one hand, a severe restriction on the forms of political government of the state; on the other, a multiplication of the domains of government, or of the domains which might enable the achievement of certain political objectives. In its efforts to criticise the state and specify its limits, American neoliberalism creates the possibility of a potentially unlimited form of non-state intervention as a mode of government, one which is more pervasive for its subtlety and lack of visible institutional definition. It is in this sense that a thinker like Becker, for example, can provide an account of the 'entrepreneurial self' in his analysis of human capital as a qualitative relation of the worker to him or herself, and to his or her genetic and bodily endowment and environmentally acquired aptitudes and skills. Yet, if such a relation to self is the result of a manipulation of the environment of the individual so that the presumed features of the market comes to pervade every dimension of it, then it is difficult to grasp what makes this form of existence preferable to one directly shaped by the state. A totalistic determination of life-conduct by the embedding of market requisites in all life-spheres is just as much a possible danger here as the totalitarianism of the state.

This is, of course, where neoliberalism condenses all the tendencies of liberalism to distinguish it from despotic and statist forms of rule by invoking the single term, choice, a term that helps economics sidestep every determination of human existence revealed by the social sciences. To broaden this discussion, one might want to note that Foucault's suggestion that governmentality acts upon free subjects can be read in two quite contrary ways. Liberal practices of government might act on *free* subjects, i.e. those that exercise some type of choice. It equally might act on free *subjects*, those whose subjection operates through the exercise of choice. This double sense of a power over free subjects sums up the paradoxical quality of neoliberalism quite nicely. Neoliberalism is a peculiar art of political invention that at once problematises the state by an invocation of choice as it multiplies the domains of life restructured according to the norms of a market.

A final point can be made about the frugal technology of government of neoliberalism, focusing on the withdrawal of the state, and the implantation of this enterprise culture. For Foucault, the cultivation of the entrepreneurial self is as much a matter of ethics as it is of politics and, in this sense, the rise of neoliberalism cannot be separated from the independent revival of a culture of the self and self-improvement. The themes of liberalism and governmentality, in Foucault's latter years, cannot then be dissociated from his reflection on ethical practices of the self. The different dimensions of his work on ancient ethics and on government, then, force into focus the problematisation of the self and its political consequences that is common both to forms of neoliberal discourse and the 'Californian' cult of self-improvement. It is at this point that it is germane to turn from the entwinement of ethics and politics in contemporary political invention to introduce features of Foucault's thought on ethics as a practice of the self.[4]

Chapter 10

. . . and practices of the self

At this point, we can make some general observations about Foucault's approach to the analysis of the three broad domains that traverse his historical writings: rationality, government, and ethics. His approach to these three domains is anything but conventional, and maintains an awareness of their divergences and dislocations as much as their overlaps and interweaving. If you like, the lucidity Foucault achieves in his latter interviews – I am thinking especially of Foucault 1986d, 1986f, 1988c – would appear to stem from a three-dimensional grid of intelligibility that follows a path of permanent mutation.

In the first instance, these three dimensions are approached as multiplicities, not as unities. This is the case for rationality, as we noted in relation to Weber. It is the case for relations of power and government, as we noted in relation to the analysis of the state. It is, we should now note, equally true for his genealogy of ethics, which refuses to grant privilege to the task of the history of moral codes. If one wanted to characterise the lucidity Foucault achieved in relation to these three domains, one might say that they do not become intelligible until the unifying and totalising themes of the guarantee of truth, of the theory of the state, and of the quest for a universalist moral code are suspended in favour of an analytic of practices of truth, power, and the self.

Secondly, then, Foucault's approach to and utilisation of these three domains comprehends them as systems of practices. Thus, for a theory of truth, he substitutes an analysis of forms of rationality, the rules, procedures, and methods, by which truth is produced in a more or less orderly fashion, what he would call 'regimes of truth' or, later, 'games of truth'. For a theory of power and state, he substitutes rationalised systems of practices, organised ways of doing things, and the tactics, strategies, techniques and technologies of government. In a similar fashion, Foucault methodologically distinguishes between a history of moral codes and a history of forms of ethical practice. Indeed, ethics, like rationality or government, becomes intelligible only as a domain of practice, one concerned with the exercise of freedom in the formation of the self (Foucault 1988c: 4). In brief, one could say that Foucault came to complement a focus on 'games of truth' in the production of knowledge, and 'technologies of government' in the exercise of power, with a concern for the 'techniques of self' as a key to the exercise of freedom.

The techniques or technologies of the self (see Foucault 1988k) are independent of, and interwoven with, both the games of truth and the techniques of government. This brings us to the third common element in Foucault's approach to the three domains: its rejection of the founding or constitutive subject of philosophical humanism. Foucault's reflections and analysis of ethics are continuous with his earlier studies of truth and rationality, and power and government, in several ways in regard to the subject. Above all the subject is never given to itself, but formed, organised, shaped, and indeed dislocated within diverse modalities of practice. Moreover, it is not treated as a substance but as a form that is never self-identical and that always exists in a state of some dissociation. Nevertheless, these later analyses are to some extent discontinuous in that they establish a new harmony in what might be called the 'Foucauldian triangle' of truth, power, and the self. Now the self is not merely a derivative of power–knowledge relations or shaped within epistemological-political modes of subjectification. By opening up more fully this domain of ethics, Foucault can allow that the subject is not simply a space outlined from the exterior by a discursive practice nor purely an effect of a complex and subtle political technology aimed at the individual body and the population. This subject is now also formed in relation to practices of freedom and techniques of the self, by the historically specific complement of procedures, means, and instruments by which the self can act on itself.

Finally, Foucault came to understand his work in terms of what he called 'problematisations' and 'practices', viz. the analysis of different ways in which being is necessarily given to thought and the practices that give form to thought (1985: 11–13). Discursive practices problematise domains of objects (e.g. life, language, labour) within the production of knowledge; governmental practices problematise certain objects of knowledge (madness, poverty, illness, crime, delinquency) in so far as they are implicated in the exercise of power; and ethical practices problematise the formation of the self in certain knowledges as a practice of freedom.

In this sense, just as one might wish to understand liberalism as a permanent problematisation of the limits of government, and governmentality more generally as a problematisation of how to govern, one could understand the discourse and apparatuses of sexuality as a permanent problematisation of oneself and sex, and ethics as an elaboration that begins with the problematisation of conduct. For example, as Foucault points out, the large Greek literature on 'loving boys' does not simply stand in evidence of the existence of this practice in these times (1986d: 344–5). Rather it shows that loving boys was a problem in a way relations with women were not. Moreover, the problematisation was an ethico-political one involving the status of the boy as one who was supposed to become a free citizen being subject to and passive before the pleasure of another. More generally, the overall project substitutes the 'history of ethical problematisations based on practices of the self, for a history of morality based, hypothetically, on interdictions' (Foucault 1985: 13).

One can find in Foucault's writings on governmentality and ethics less a grand thesis linking the socio-cultural evolution of the self to the development of the state (such as that proposed by Elias) than the locating of ethics as the government of self on the same plane as the government of others and the government of the state. To illustrate this point, and to demonstrate how Foucault proposes to study ethical problematisations, I wish now to turn to his discussion of the features of the relation to the self called into question by practices of the self.

In chapter 8, I suggested that the genealogy of punitive practices in *Discipline and Punish* invoked four dimensions in order to make intelligible the transformation of the forms of punishment: the punishable substance, the mode of subjectification of the punished, the punitive work or self-forming activity, and the telos or mode of being in which the penalty is incorporated. In 'modern' systems of punishment these correspond to the 'soul' of the individual who commits the crime, to the individualising knowledges specifying his or her subjectivity within the network of delinquency or criminality, to the work of practices of normalisation, and to the docile and useful subject produced through disciplinary practices aimed at the body. This analysis was partially tendentious since here I would like to draw a direct comparison with Foucault's study of ethical practices. In the introduction to *The Use of Pleasures* (1985: 25–9, cf. 1986d: 351–9), Foucault proposes to apply the same analytical method to the genealogy of the desiring subject. It would appear that this method is equally fruitful whether in relation to the government of self or the government of others. The genealogy of the docile subject in the earlier text displaces a history of punishment as a history of moral values invoking the theme of the human-isation of the penalty. Now, the genealogy of the desiring subject displaces the history of moral codes as the intensification of interdictions from Greece to the Graeco-Roman period and the rise of early Christianity. A history of moral prescriptions 'actually only shows the poverty and monotony of interdictions' (Foucault 1985: 250) and, indeed, returns to the same themes of the dangerous, if not evil, domain of sexual pleasure and desire, the obligation to practice monogamous fidelity, and the exclusion of partners of the same sex (ibid. 251). For Foucault, the post-Renaissance debate on the relation of late ancient ethics to Christianity attests to the paltry and confusing results of a comparison that proceeds by means of the 'code elements' of ethics and their severity from the standpoint of the loftiness and pursuit of Christian ethics (1986a: 236–7). If a history of truth must avoid its colonisation by an epistemology, and a history of government is irreducible to a theory of the development of the state, a history of ethics cannot be a history of moral codes and behaviours. As Foucault put it:

the history of a morality has to take into account the different realities that are covered by the term. A history of 'moral behaviours' would study the extent to which actions of certain individuals or groups are consistent with rules and values that are prescribed for them by various agencies . . . a history of 'codes' would analyse the different systems of rules and values that are operative in a given society or group . . . a history of the way in which individuals are urged to constitute themselves as subjects of moral conduct would be concerned with the models proposed for setting up and developing relationships with the self, for self-reflection, self-knowledge, self-examination, for the decipherment of the self by oneself, for the transformations that one seeks to accomplish with oneself as object.

(Foucault 1985: 29)

The first two options are versions of a history of interdictions, of the extent to which action accords with them, or the way they are embodied in moral codes. The third, however, like Foucault's writings on governmentality, emphasises the way in which the self is formed as a subject of conduct, as one whose governmental or ethical subjection still leaves him or her free to give shape to his or her existence. Foucault's notion of the 'free subject', it should be pointed out, emphasises both sides of the term: on the one hand, being free is a qualifier of a relation of subjection of self to others, or self to itself; on the other, freedom cannot be determined in advance. Freedom is the indefinable ontological condition of both ethics and government. In any case, it is this last project, with its stress on the interwoven strands of the history of ethics and ascetics that Foucault proposes to undertake, and which he understands in terms of the forms of moral subjectification inscribed within practices of the self.

A genealogy of the 'desiring subject', of the forms of self-relation and self-governance, comprises the following four elements that arrange similar events in serial fashion. It first examines the determination of the ethical substance (*substance éthique*), the substance worked upon by techniques of the self (Foucault 1985: 26–7). Greek and Graeco-Roman ethics is concerned with the 'use of pleasures' (*aphrodisia*), observing their dangers and seeking their moderation, while Christian ethics will work on the flesh as a locus of impurity and sinful desires, of concupiscence, an 'ethical substance based on finitude, the fall, and evil' (Foucault 1986a: 239). One might complete this series by noting that in the contemporary government of the self, modern ethics still acts upon desire but this time in the form of sexuality.

Secondly, each form of ethical relation to self is characterised by a distinctive mode of subjectification (*mode d'assujettissement*), and concerns the kind of ethical subjects created (Foucault 1985: 27). Some examples are: the Greek self-formation in relation to an 'aesthetics of existence', an attempt to fashion a beautiful, noble, and memorable life (Foucault 1985); the Stoic and Kantian versions of creating selves as universal, rational beings, in relation to universal rules (Foucault 1986d: 356–7, 372); and the Christian method of creating selves in submission to a general law that is also the will of a personal god (Foucault 1986a: 239). In the contemporary world, self-formation is often undertaken in relation to various forms of psychological and psychoanalytic techniques and knowledge (Foucault 1986d: 362).

Thirdly, one needs to examine the ethical work (*travail éthique*) or the form of asceticism (*forme d'ascèse*), the self-forming activity, its methods, techniques and instruments (1985: 27; 1986d: 354–7). This is where, in a strict sense, the techniques of the self come into focus. This self-forming activity relies on a series of techniques or 'technologies of the self' discussed by Foucault (1988k): dialogue, listening, meditation, training of memory, examination of conscience and self-examination, diary and notebook keeping, letter-writing, and the mortification rituals taken up by Christianity including confession, penance, and fasting. Foucault charts the transformation of the *techne* in antiquity in relation to the three austerity themes of health and the body in dietics, wife and household in oeconomics, and boys in erotics. In the Hellenistic period, there is an increased anxiety and attention to the relations between the sexual act and the body, an increased valorisation of the marital bond as a universal form of mutuality, and a growing sense that loving boys is problematic 'as a sign of an imperfection that is specific to sexual activity' (Foucault 1986a: 238). While Christianity will take over these 'austerity themes' of late antiquity of the dangers of the sexual act, the need for monogamy, and the prohibition of relations between males as unnatural, it will replace the multifarious techniques of the 'care of the self' that bloomed during this period with ones of 'a decipherment of the soul and a purificatory hermeneutics of the desires' (ibid. 239). Self-decipherment and an hermeneutics of the self have remained a staple of contemporary liberation movements. This emphasis on forms of asceticism again brings Foucault close to Max Weber's sociology of religion, although the latter's typology of forms of asceticism is undertaken in relation to the rationalisation of religious codes.

Finally, Foucault seeks to address the *telos* of the relation to self, the mode of being in which the ethical practice is inserted and which forms its goal or end (1985: 27–8). We have shown how an analytic of practices of punishment came to reveal the *telos* of punishment in the disciplinary society and the political technology of the body. The telos of various ethical practices changes widely: for the Greeks, the mastery and governance of oneself by means of a moderation of the use of pleasure (1985: 37); for later antiquity, the self-control over a universal and rational being in relation to itself and to other such beings (1986a: 238–9); for Christianity, the form of a salvation requiring self-renunciation (ibid. 239); and for the contemporary movement of sexual and personal liberation, the goal of ethical self-fulfilment taking the form of an emancipation of the self. Thus human beings may act on themselves or others in such a way that grounds the 'good life' in not only a disciplinary society, a society of good police, or in citizenship and its rights and liberties, but also in a society of moderation, of universal reason, of the purity of saints, or of self-actualisation. Needless to say, none of these possibilities presents a global account of any particular societies or sets of social relations, and all are presupposed by various strategies, agencies, and practices in advanced liberal states.

In a formal sense, then, this is similar to the mode of analysis of what Foucault had earlier called 'regimes of practices' (1981b), i.e. organised systems of practices rationalised according to particular forms of knowledge. In this way, the introduction to *The Use of Pleasures* is more explicit than that of *Discipline and Punish*. To summarise, an analytic of practices can thus be worked out along four dimensions (Foucault 1985: 37): that of an ontology, of what we seek to govern in ourselves or others by means of this practice; that of a deontology, of what we seek to produce in ourselves and others when governing this element; that of an ascetics, how we govern this element, with what techniques and means; and that of teleology, of the aim of these practices, of the kind of world we hope to achieve by them, of the kind of beings we aspire to be.

Why antiquity?

The question of why Foucault would undertake this journey into classical Greece and Rome is an extremely open one and I do not seek to provide a glib answer here.[1] I want to suggest ways in which this question might be approached and ways of using this work. At the same time, I should like to keep in mind what we have learnt throughout the present work on Foucault's historical method and in the previous chapter on the theme of governmentality. In this way, it might be possible to repose that larger question as something more manageable and ask, first, whether this is still a history of the present.

In an interview in 1984, Foucault (1988d) responded in the affirmative. The genealogical 'question posed in the present' is that of 'an ethics as a form to be given to one's behaviour and life' (ibid. 262–3). On the one hand, he suggests, it arises from the lifting of moral codes and interdictions previously thought indispensable to capitalist societies. On the other, in response to a question concerning his role in relation to liberation movements, Foucault acknowledges that this genealogy is conducted in the presence of movements of sexual liberation but not on behalf of them (ibid. 263). Indeed, the core of the present-relevance of these latter volumes may be a certain diagnosis of contemporary life, how to construct oneself ethically in the face of the failing assurance provided by moral codes, generalisable norms, or universal values.

If we take Foucault's indications here, this genealogy of ethical practices is present-related but not in a utilitarian sense of speaking on behalf of, or placing oneself at the disposal of particular movements. In what ways could it prove amenable to the contemporary ethical situation? Above all, perhaps, it offers us the means and the possibility to undertake a comparison of the contemporary search for liberation. Thus the analytic of ethical practices provides a kind of serial history of different ways in which it has been possible for humans to constitute themselves as ethical subjects. This serial history provides several dimensions for comparison: of the four aspects of the analytic of ethical practice, of the relation between moral codes and practices of the self, and the different formulae for the problematisation of sexual behaviour in the relation between acts, pleasure, and desire (1986d: 359).[2] It is thus a resource that allows one to 'think otherwise' about questions of ethics and morality, of the self, and of liberation. I would not want to go so far as to suggest that Foucault was advocating a return to antiquity. I would say, rather, that his thought offers a strong sense of the historical relativity of both Enlightenment moral universalism and current liberation ethics, and the possibilities inherent within certain long-term aspects of European culture.

The history of sexuality remains a history of the present – a resource and a point of comparison – for those who seek to problematise contemporary relations to the self, the means and notions of self-decipherment and self-fulfilment, and the way in which sexuality has been historically and socially constructed as the path to liberation. But it also has a place within Foucault's intellectual trajectory, a further turning back on itself of his own thought, a 'folding', to use the term favoured by Deleuze (1988). In the interview just mentioned, Foucault suggested that it was the task of the intellectual 'to make oneself permanently capable of detaching oneself from oneself' (1988d: 263). In *The Use of Pleasure*, he speaks of philosophical activity as consisting in 'the endeavour to know how and to what extent it might be possible to think differently, instead of legitimating what is already known' (Foucault 1985: 9). Earlier in the same passage he writes of a kind of curiosity in which it is not a question of assimilating what is proper to oneself but the curiosity which 'enables one to get free of oneself' (ibid. 8). In this sense, writing became for Foucault a kind of ascesis, a technique of the self, in which writing a book is 'in a way, to abolish the previous one' (1988d: 263).

This theme of writing and thought as a kind of critical activity on oneself seems to have preoccupied Foucault for several years. Perhaps one might argue that this is a part of a further specification of the history of the present we requested in relation to Kant. At the end of 1978 Foucault was to describe his writings as an 'experience book' rather than a 'demonstration book' or 'truth book' (1991b: 25–42). Here we find Foucault seeking to thematise the relation between his books and his involvements and personal experiences. Again there is the emphasis on not confirming experience and ways of being but on changing them. Such a book 'is read as an experience that changes us, that prevents us from always being the same, or from having the same kind of relationship with things and with others that we had before reading it' (ibid. 41).

This late turn to personal experience to give texture to his books might seem at odds with his earlier anti-biographical pronouncements, and to require some elaboration to prevent a lapse into the naturalism of phenomenological categories of experience.[3] However, for current purposes, it is perhaps more fruitful to ask how the later sexuality volumes helped free Foucault from himself, and how his freeing from himself connects with a particular relation to the present. The answers here appear to revolve around the notion of the self.

In his earlier writings, including the first volume of the sexuality series, Foucault had trenchantly opposed the residues of psychologism and naturalism he felt were not overcome by the phenomenological attempts at bracketing out the contents of consciousness. In this way, his writings seem to oppose any conception of consciousness, even simply as intentionality, as the consciousness of things. Instead the subject is purely historical: it is formed within, first, forms of discourse and knowledge, especially medicine, the 'psy' disciplines, and the human sciences, and secondly, within forms of power relations, especially those that traverse the body. This could be interpreted as a kind of determinism, and lies at the base of all the claims that Foucault could not provide any grounding for his conception of resistance, or demonstrate the existence of any counterforce to power–knowledge.[4] This may be so, except that it would be necessary to note that these historical relations concern the harnessing of physical and psychological capacities to provide kinds of agency which in turn can be used in ways that cannot be read off the programmes that promote them. To become the subject of one's own desire through speaking the truth of one's sexuality may be a part of a transformation of the field of power–knowledge relations, and risk being encoded within the matrix of sexological discourse. Yet it also provides the means of contesting and even rejecting forms of identity and life presupposed and prescribed by institutional religion or patriarchalist practices.

In any case, as Foucault's position becomes more elaborated in the final volumes on sexuality and elsewhere, it becomes impossible to make this accusation. For, while the earlier writings may have given the impression of a kind of denial of interiority of the subject, there is now an explicit theorisation of this 'inside'. As we have noted, the self is still historically constituted through domains of practice but these now include a domain marked out by the great culture of a 'care of the self' that reaches its full flowering in the Hellenistic world. It is hard to decide whether *The Care of the Self* (Foucault 1986a) is central or marginal to the continued project of a history of sexuality or its transmutation into a genealogy of the desiring subject by way of a history of ethical practices of the self. On the one hand, we have Foucault's comments in 1983 that he intended this volume to be separate from the sexuality series (1986d: 342). On the other, one cannot escape the sense that the real novelty of the rethinking of the history of sexuality comes about with the uncovering of the techniques of the self in the Imperial period. Indeed, it is the problem of sexual austerity that leads Foucault toward the 'golden age' (1986a: 45) of the cultivation of the self in the Hellenistic and Roman world.

There is an 'added emphasis on sexuality austerity in moral reflection', Foucault tells us (ibid. 41), but this takes the form less of a tightening of moral interdictions than 'an intensification of the relation to oneself by which one constituted oneself as the subject of one's acts'. Thus this theme of the care of oneself seems to become coextensive with the entire field of reflection on ethics and the art of living in which the imperial Roman epoch can be seen as the 'summit of a curve' (ibid. 45). Perhaps one could say that, if the telos of modern forms of punishment could be found in the docile subject produced through the techniques of a disciplinary society, then the telos of modern practices and discourses of sexuality could be sought in the great culture of the self that reached a pinnacle in late antiquity and the techniques that it spawned. The Graeco-Roman cultivation of the self is present-relevant because it is exemplary of a more general trajectory to which we are linked today and which, through its explicit form and distance, allows us to make the taken-for-granted come over the horizon of visibility. If we ask, argues Deleuze (1988: 107), why Foucault suddenly introduces this long time-scale it is because 'in moral matters we are still weighed down with old beliefs which we no longer even believe, and we continue to produce ourselves as a subject on the basis of old modes which do not correspond to our problems'.

Moreover, it may be possible to hear a faint resonance throughout these writings between what Foucault called the 'crisis of subjectivation' of late antiquity and the problem of the self in our own times. In two beautifully worked-out small chapters of The Care of the Self (1986a: 72–95), Foucault charts how changes in matrimonial practice and in the political game came to call into question the close connection between classical self-mastery and the governance of others in the household and in the city. The integration of the cities in a more extensive and complex field of imperial power relations, and the transformations that made 'marriage more general as a practice, more public as an institution, more private as a mode of existence' (ibid. 77), and led to revaluation of the conjugal bond as one of some reciprocity, form the conditions for the culture of the self. This cultivation of the self formed an 'original response' conditioned by, but irreducible to, these social conditions. Rather than a growth of public constraints and prohibitions or an individualistic withdrawal into private life, Foucault finds a 'crisis of subjectivation', a crisis in the way in which 'the individual could form himself as the ethical subject of his actions, and efforts to find in devotion to self that which could enable him to submit to rules and give a purpose to his existence' (ibid.95). Whether or not we should be so grandiose to describe the present in terms of a 'crisis of subjectivation', we know that the problematics of the self has constituted a fertile ground for recent cultural criticism from the Frankfurt School to Richard Sennett (1977) and Christopher Lasch (1979).

Is this, then, still a history of sexuality? Here I offer only a brief sketch. Certainly, at the level of empirical inquiry there is still quite a lot about sex in these volumes! But, at the level of the conception of the project, there is a

deeper continuity. In the first volume Foucault's object is neither a history of
sexual behaviours or an intellectual history of sexual mentalities but the
conditions of what makes possible various forms of knowledge of sexuality
and allows sexuality to be a domain of normalisation and intervention. These
conditions are found in the apparatus or, perhaps better, *assemblage* of
practices and discourse (*scientia sexualis*) which constitutes sexuality as an
object of knowledge, a domain of governmentality, and a particular form of
self-relation.[5] Such an analysis, however, reveals sexuality as a social and
historical artefact of medical, psychological, and legal discourses, and linked
to the emergence of a biopolitics. But if the categories of sexuality, desire, and
liberation, properly only belong to our epoch, then it is possible to consider
where sexual practices are problematised within other regimes of practice. In
a sense the broadest telos of our discourses on sexuality concerns the kind of
ethical work we perform on ourselves and what we can hope from that work.
The telos of sexuality concerns the modes of problematisation of the relation
to oneself, the *rapport à soi*. An investigation of the historical forms of this
rapport à soi then provides an account of the conditions of what we
retrospectively recognise as sexual practice but without the lineaments of an
assemblage of sexuality. In the broadest sense, then, the history of ethical
practices of the self is a condition of what we understand by sexuality. But in
Foucault no privilege is given to the conditioned or its conditions: the
discovery of such conditions opens up a new quest for intelligibility of
practices of the self that, at first merely a part of an exploration of the
conditions of sexual problematisation, now take centre stage and become
what has to be made intelligible.

Foucault shows us a method of detaching ourselves from ourselves while
preserving and rethinking earlier questions and problematisation – there is no
point at which the quest for intelligibility ceases. This, then, is what constitutes the fundamental openness of Foucault's method and thought.

Elias and Foucault

I want now to compare the theme of the government of the self in Foucault
with the work of Norbert Elias. The work of both is idiosyncratic enough to
deny access to an easy comparison. Such a comparison is not facilitated by the
fact of what one might call a 'non-contradictory difference' between their two
projects, their methodological orientations and aims and, although this cannot
be explored here, the intellectual contexts in which their projects were
initiated, Weimar sociology, and the post-phenomenological French thought
of the '60s. My argument here is that despite differences in project, language,
and aim, there is a broad consistency between the problem of the self as it is
posed in their work. One way of encapsulating these differences may be to
contrast the genealogy of the ethical subject with that of the civilised subject,
the history of ethics with the history of manners, and ethical practices with

civilising practices. However, if Foucault enjoins us to regard ethics as a set of practices of the operation of the self on the self, then, after Elias, the prescriptions we call 'manners' must be understood as a component of the transformation and rationalisation of modes of conduct under the pressure of particular social relations. From the perspective of Elias, the ancient treatises on health and daily regimen, householding, and erotics – and indeed all the practices of 'the aesthetics of existence' – constitute a version of what it is to be civilised. Without underplaying the vast differences in conceptual frameworks, the position of each thus would be capable of being reinterpreted and appropriated from the vantage-point of the other.

We know that the Foucauldian grid is less a theoretical edifice than an analytical space populated by the dispersion and entwinement of discursive, governmental and ethical practices. Elias, on the other hand, is concerned to identify 'process universals' in relation to a theory of long-term social development conceived in terms of functional differentiation and integration. Foucault engages in a 'present-relevant' philosophical history that is interpretatively open and capable of multiple application; Elias undertakes a detached, 'value-neutral' contribution to positive historical–sociological knowledge. Even given these differences, both writers are united by a common mistrust of the invasion of historical knowledge by metaphysics and are concerned to limit the effects of involvements in the present in historical analysis while acknowledging them as a condition of historical studies (as was shown in Chapter 2).

The methodological differences are reflected in the way in which the two thinkers conceive the broad domain in which they are working. Foucault, as we have seen, came in his last writings to identify a broad problem area at the intersection of practices of government and practices of the self. This remains, nevertheless, an arena of problematisation rather than of theorisation. What he offers us is not a general theory of the relation of these domains of practices but rather a set of methodological suggestions and historical analyses of the relation of these practices to each other and to regimes and practices of truth. Elias, by contrast, is concerned to provide a general theory of the developmental relation between social formation and self-formation, social structure and psychic structure. This overlaps Foucault's critical histories, however, in so far as it is elaborated through empirical historical analysis. If genealogy is 'gray, meticulous, and patiently documentary' (Foucault 1977b: 139), then the Elias of *The Civilising Process* (1978, 1982) and *The Court Society* (1983) surely qualifies as a genealogist *par excellence*.

The first volume of the former (1978) has a dual status as patient documentation of the genealogy of manners and emergent sociological theory. Although it appears to be a very specific and detailed analysis of the development of the literature on manners and its prescriptions concerning a variety of behaviours (table manners, nose-blowing, spitting, excretory functions, aggression, relations between the sexes), it almost covertly announces a much larger problem, that of the relation between the individual, his or her conduct, and social structure. 'These poems and treatises', Elias tells us (1978: 84), 'are themselves direct instruments of "conditioning" or "fashioning", of the adaptation of the individuals to those modes of behaviour which the structure and situation of his society make necessary'. He thus uncovers through this literature the 'civilising process', a process that is a universal of social development by which the individual learns a social pattern of self-restraint (Elias 1987a: 230–231).

It would be out of sympathy with Elias' approach to concentrate solely on a theoretical framework abstracted from historical analysis. I shall thus try to do some justice to that analysis by rudimentary exposition. His entire sociology is distinguished from the 'static typologies and static concepts' of structural functionalism by employing an empirical analysis and a focus on the 'intrinsic dynamics of human societies' (Elias 1987b: 226). Thus what Elias offers is no less than a historical–sociological account of the 'sociogenesis' of the modern personality type and characteristic forms of conduct in the West in terms of the 'social evolution' made possible by the emergence of stabilised central state authority and the 'monopolisation of violence'. At the hub of the empirical civilising process in the West is to be found a particular social formation, or 'figuration', as Elias prefers, the 'court society'. The court society refers to a specific type of social and political organisation, like and distinguishable from feudal society and capitalist society. It also refers – and this is where Elias' empirical analysis is principally situated – to the specific 'high society', organised around the royal court and noble 'houses', that epitomises European absolutism generally and achieves a kind of typicality in the French court at the time of Louis XIV.

These three volumes may be read as a genealogy of the relation between manners and forms of self crystallised within the trajectory of this court society, and as an effective history that 'places within a process of development everything considered immortal in man' (Foucault 1977b: 153). They are also genealogical in another important sense: they propose no necessary beginning or end to this 'civilising process'. There is no stage of barbarism to which civilisation is opposed, no origin from which a civilising tendency evolves (Elias 1978: 62). There are other civilising processes in other places and at other times, and, presumably, other concurrent ones in Europe from the Middle Ages. Moreover, this genealogy does not adopt the standpoint of a particular evaluation. It rejects the usual triumphalism that condemns terms like 'civilised' and 'uncivilised' to evaluative positions within the path of social evolution (Elias 1978: 59).

This sociology also shares with genealogy the displacement of the position of the constituent subject. As Elias notes (1982: 289–90), the courtly aristocracy, itself the result of a long process of the pacification of feudal lords which he calls the 'courtization of warriors', is not the 'originator' of the rationalisation of modes of conduct and 'moulding of people' in this period of the absolutist monarchies in Europe. Changes of this kind arise not from one class but 'in conjunction with the tensions between different functional groups in a social field and between the competing people within them' (ibid. 289). In this sense court society is a specific 'figuration', a web of reciprocal relations, interdependencies, and power networks and struggles, between and among groups and individuals, that deserves attention as a particularly intensive site of the self-regulation of conduct.

The trajectory of court society has two nodal episodes: the constitution of the great feudal courts in twelfth century and the monarchical court societies of the seventeenth century. As Elias puts it:

> On the one hand, a loosely integrated secular upper class of warriors, with its symbol, the castle on the autarkic estate; on the other, the more tightly integrated secular upper class of courtiers assembled at the absolutist court, the central organ of the kingdom; these are in a sense the two poles of the field of observation which has been isolated from the far longer and broader movement in order to gain initial access to the sociogenesis of civilizing change.
>
> (Elias 1983: 90)

In the former, *courtoisie*, or 'curtesye', describes a first, and very rudimentary, movement of the tempering of the rule of the knightly sword and the regulation of affects that earlier 'have rather free and unfettered play in all the terrors and joys of life' (ibid.72). It is instanced by the activities of the newly-formed large courts, and in the products of the *minnesanger* and troubadours. Here, particularly around the figure of the lady at court, there is expressed a new sense of delicacy contrary to the prevailing brutal relations between the sexes, and a move in the direction of stricter drive-control (ibid.66–90). In the midst of a warrior society that is neither policed nor polite, the great feudal courts become relatively pacified spaces, where passions are moderated and sublimated, although the sword still hangs threateningly over the scene.

In the latter figuration mentioned in this quote, *courtoisie* has come to be displaced by *civilité*, a term that describes the entire range of bodily comportment and human conduct within the 'chief situations of social and convivial life' (Elias 1978: 58). This displacement corresponds to a new figuration, in which war lords have become pacific members of a court élite, and in which the balance of tensions between various fractions of the nobility and other élite groups and the absolutist rule of the sovereign mutually condition each other. Elias shows how the tensions between the *noblesse d'épée* (the older aristocracy), and the *noblesse de robe* (the aristocracy of office holders), in the first instance, and between these groups and the clergy, the new financiers and urban bourgeoisie, in the second, provided the framework for the construction of an absolutist structure in which the king could be both weaker than all other groups and stronger than any particular group. It is at the courts of the king and the highest aristocracy that the new intensified form of self-discipline took place in the status competition among the various groups for favours and title, in the power contests and intrigue among courtiers, and in the increased dependence of rulers and subordinates. Moreover, because the monopolisation of the means of violence implies the pacification of the society (a society of good police, in *that* sense), it is a condition for the extension of chains of economic transactions in time and space, the functioning of complex markets and an entire monetary system (Elias 1982: 163). The individual comes to be located at complex overlapping and lengthy chains of time–space relations requiring an internal differentiation of the psyche and intensification of 'the balance between drives and affects and drive- and affect-control' (Elias 1982: 284).

In more general terms, with the emergence of a more highly differentiated social structure, intricate interdependencies, social networks of increasing density, and increasing opportunities for upward and downward social mobility, the apparatus of individual self-control becomes more differentiated, more sensitive to its human environment, and more stable (Elias 1982: 234–5). Moreover, it is only with the monopolisation of physical force and emergence of societies of good police that individuals can become attuned, from infancy, to a highly regulated and differentiated pattern of self-restraint, which will become second nature (ibid. 235). The banishment of physical violence from large social and territorial spaces is not, however, an unmitigated movement toward the diminution of conflict: conflict, rather, becomes a feature of intra-individual psychic constitution, between the 'rational' controlling centre and the emotions, and between mind and body and superego and id. Further, it is sublimated rather than banished from the power relations between groups, and persists, even in an intensified form, in the wars between states.

Elias is concerned, then, with the way in which general social processes, manifest in specific figurations of power and dependency relations, and evidenced by particular conscious attempts at the moulding of conduct, lead to a transformation of the economy of drives of human beings in the direction of greater control of passions and emotions, monitoring of behaviours, and reflexivity concerning relations of self with others. He is concerned neither to endorse this process nor ignore its personal or global costs. His aim is, simply, to establish it as fact. The term civilisation is liberated from the evaluative form of historical narrative in which it is encased.

There are clear similarities between the relational conception of power in Elias and Foucault, and the importance accorded various practices within the penumbra of the centralised monarchical states of Europe in the constitution of both later modes of government and forms of self-relation. However, one must also highlight the specificity of Elias' general framework as one that situates his account of the transformation of conduct within a general theory of social development. Here the theme of the 'government of the self' is absorbed within an account of the sociogenesis of modern personality types.

While there is nothing illegitimate about that move, it forecloses the possibility of a more direct form of analysis that focuses on strategic, reflective attempts to shape, direct and promote conduct from early modern police science to contemporary neoliberalism (cf. Rose 1990: 220–1).

Elias' thought offers a form of closure in so far as it seeks to reinscribe the genealogical elements of its history of manners and state forms within a general theory of social and psychic development. This is eradicably distinct from the open analytic approach of Michel Foucault who, as such, does not qualify as a sociological theorist. To demonstrate something of the fruitfulness of the analytic domain traversed by Foucault's thought, I shall conclude with some examples of possible research agendas into the links between practices of government, practices of the self, and practices of truth.

PRACTICES OF GOVERNMENT AND PRACTICES OF THE SELF

I shall now conclude by exploring the way in which the Foucauldian theme of governmentality as the articulation of the government of self, others, and the state, can be used to generate historical problems. I underline the status of this section as a thought-experiment and do not pretend to offer a definitive version of the relation between practices of government and practices of the self, if such a thing was at all possible.

Recall that the genealogies of ethical and governmental practices, like that of the critical history of rationality, can be understood in the language of series. In this chapter we have investigated the results of Foucault's serial morphology of the history of ethical practices and ethical problematisation; in the last chapter, we offered a somewhat less formal, more fragmentary, account of the genealogy of governmental practices. In both cases, however, it is possible to derive a history of techniques and practices of government, or of the self, from the entangled lines of diverse trajectories of events, discourses, and practices. The genealogies of these practices of self and government then may be said to link these trajectories into independent series which, in turn, can be 'cross-tabulated' to form meta-series. Governmentality is a name for the meta-series linking the serial histories of the practices of the self with those of the practices of government.

The thought-experiment, then, consists in asking whether it is possible to derive interesting, or novel, historical questions from such a cross-referencing of these different serial histories. Instead of attempting a systematisation that becomes possible on the basis of drawing up the table of these meta-series, I simply offer some examples of the kind of problematisation I believe Foucault's later thought suggests. In so doing, I wish to recommend several areas for further research.

First, one could pose what is in fact a question of the *longue durée*, that of the historical linkages between the care of the self that reaches a pinnacle in Graeco-Roman culture with the pastoral care Foucault has identified as a persistent theme in the trajectory of the development of government (e.g. Foucault 1988h; 1982). Crucial to such a problem would be the specific historical question of how early Christianity came to take over, colonise, plunder, and use the techniques and themes of the care of the self. This would require a long genealogy of the encoding of the care of the self within the typical themes of the Christian pastoral isolated by Foucault – themes of obedience, personal submission, and salvation. While Foucault counterpoises the 'shepherd-flock' game of the Hebraic-Christian pastoral and the 'city-citizen' game descended from Athenian democracy, it might also be fruitful to investigate how forms of Christianity sought to domesticate the care of the self within the framework of its transformed Hebraic practices and notions of caring for the flock. There are fragments of this genealogy (e.g. Foucault's discussion of Cassian [1988b]), there is the unpublished book on early Christianity, *The Confessions of the Flesh* (*Les Aveux de la Chair*), but the historical question of the degree to which Christianity can be made intelligible through its links to the care of the self has yet to be taken up.

This may help contribute further to the clarification of the genealogy of the welfare-state. Foucault suggests (1988g, 1988h) that the latter is bound to the difficult relationship between pastoral and citizenship elements, and between individualising and totalising elements that construct human beings as both self-governing individuals within a self-governing political community and clients to be administered, governed, and normalised with respect to govern-mental objectives. However, this may be pushed a little further. The very practice and notion of 'care' is made problematic by the co-presence of elements derived from the care of the self, as an exercise of freedom seeking to establish an independent relation of the self to itself, with elements pre-supposing a subjection to agencies concerned with the provision, security, and happiness of populations and individuals. The 'shepherd-flock' game exists in some dissociation from not only the 'city-citizen' game, but also from the 'self-self' game it seeks to subsume. It is this latter problem that is manifest in all the recent welfare discourses on the need for an 'active society' to replace the welfare-state, and the redefinition of the social problem in terms of an emergent underclass characterised by chronic welfare dependency.[6] A further observation in this regard is the need for a rethinking of the central role of the monastery in this genealogy. This 'power-container' is understood by both Weber and Foucault to have been at the beginnings of discipline and the political technology of the body. It may be that its extraordinary inventiveness in this regard, and its importance in the formation of the 'West', can be attributed to the superimposition of techniques of pastoral care upon tech-niques of the self such as meditation, mortificatory rituals, fasting, prayer, silence, self-examination, and so on.

Secondly, another specific set of problems devolve from Foucault's observ-ation of the rough coincidence of the Reformation with an independent reflection on the state, with *raison d'état* or reason of state (e.g. 1979a; 1988h).

Here one could make use of the work of both Elias and Weber from within a genealogical framework. It would be possible to make intelligible the complex processes that led to the interdependent development of a secular reflection on the state and a new culture of the self. Thus it might be hypothesised that the breakdown of feudal relations and codes and their attendant modes of subjectification based around ascription, personal loyalty and dependency, was a condition for both the emergence of notions of an individual responsible for his or her own salvation and answerable to God through the mediation of conscience and a secular reflection on the government of the state in political philosophy, reason of state, and police. Here, one might follow the work of Gerhard Oestreich (1982) and investigate the elective affinity between the revival of ethical practices of the self in the Neostoicism associated with the writings of Justus Lipsius, and a rational art of government of the state. Neostoicism emerges as a secular ethic of command and obedience giving rise to an active form of life-conduct characterised by a prudential ethic of 'constancy' in which ruler and ruled share the same basic virtues. A minor, but nevertheless interesting, English example would be Calamy's instructions to MPs of 1641 that they first must reform their families before reforming the family of God (Corrigan and Sayer 1985: 81). This link between the government of the state and the government of the household and personal life may lead us to reconsider the whole question of sixteenth and seventeenth century patriarchalism as a form of political discourse and practice (Schochet 1975; Pateman 1988). As I have noted elsewhere, 'pre-liberal' modes of governance establish a kind of equivalence between the conduct of personal life and the conduct of the state when they make of the household both a model and a means of patriarchalist governance (Dean 1991a, 1992b). In more general terms, one does not have to have recourse to a global theory of personal and political development to witness the conscious, reflective attempt to align new modes of individualisation with new forms of governance. Such alignments were, indeed, necessary conditions for the emergence of forms of liberal discourse and practice.

Thirdly, a more contemporary form of this kind of critical historical study of political rationality may take up the relation between the recent flowering of a culture of the self, of self-improvement, self-fulfilment, personal development, and sexual liberation, and the rise of neoliberalism, with its notions of the 'entrepreneurial self' and the 'enterprise culture'. I have remarked about this coincidence in the previous chapter and want simply to note that, for those of us in liberal states in the last twenty years, Foucault's thought on the government of the self and the government of the state has an evident present-relevance.

In the realm of political philosophy and normative theory, for example, one wonders whether Foucault's genealogy might not offer the resources for a 'liberal criticism of liberalism' as they do a rational critique of rationalism.

Such a criticism might begin as an ethical one but one, in contradistinction to that of the Frankfurt School, no longer based on universal norms. Rather we could take Foucault's suggestion that his reflection on politics is ultimately an ethical one, and view politics as a set of ethical practices or practices of the self. Thus one could take the point that liberalism seeks to establish limits to government and inquire whether, having broken with the identification of government with the state, it might not be possible to establish limits to governmental practices when they operate not simply through the state, but through philanthropy, banks, corporations, families, etc., and even through Bernard Mandeville's 'public virtues and private vices'. In a world replete with extraordinarily subtle programmes and technologies of the regulation of conduct through 'psy' disciplines and medicine, administrative systems, information networks, and the enterprise culture itself, it is surely possible to ask whether or not economic liberalism, notions of human capital, social security systems designed to produce an active population, etc., transgress the same limits liberalism itself abhors in what it understands as forms of despotism.

These three problem-areas, then, hardly respect the intellectual division between politics and ethics, let alone that between philosophy and history and sociology. However they are ones that can be posed with a high degree of cognitive control on the basis of Foucault's exploration of the governmental entwinement of techniques of the self and techniques of government.

I want to conclude this cycle of three chapters exploring Foucault's substantive themes of power, state, discipline, governmentality, and practices of the self, by mentioning one, much more general problem that these studies raise. I claim no originality for this thesis, which can be found in quite different form in Giddens' recent work on self-identity under conditions of modernity (Giddens 1991), but which has received perhaps a more fruitful treatment in the important books of Nikolas Rose (1984, 1990). This theme, stated most baldly, concerns the rapport between reflexivity and government. It brings us back into contact with genealogy as a history of truth, and with the truth–knowledge–rationality corner of the Foucauldian triangle.

This theme can be given the form of a thesis: that historical forms of the relation of self to self, that is, the development of reflexivity (the capacity for the monitoring of thought and conduct and the self-regulation of behaviours) can only be fully understood in relation to the development and transformation of modes of government (with diverse agencies, domains, objectives, and ideals); that the means of translation of the objectives of government into forms of the promotion of life-conduct has become increasingly dependent upon specific forms of knowledge and expertise. Here the 'psy' disciplines, medicine, education, welfare, and the economic and social sciences, become the crucial relayers of a political culture in the promotion of forms of the cultivation of the self and the development of the self-relation. If the self is conceived as a spiralling ribbon which folds over and over itself defining a space of interior being without essential substance, then in contemporary political culture, this ribbon of the self is composed of the different cloths, weaves, colours, and patterns, of the various programmes of government, techniques of the self, and work of the human sciences.

This thesis brings us to the end of what I hope to introduce in the present volume. It is germane, however, to note that the division in critical thought today is no longer between humanist and antihumanist, if it ever was. Rather, the crucial distinction to be drawn is between those who understand the subject as a locus of reason that forms itself in relation to moral codes and universal prescriptions, laws, and values, and those who seek to understand how it is formed, and forms itself, within techniques and practices of power, self, and knowledge, or ethical, governmental, and rational practices.

Among the latter, I would place first and foremost Michel Foucault.

Conclusion

Permit me, if you will, to bring together some thoughts that have puzzled me while writing this book and to say something about its writing as a part of my own present and my own biography. Let this serve as a brief concluding summary.

There are two puzzles in Foucault's thought that remind me of the work of Escher I mentioned in the introduction to this book. Or perhaps they are only versions of the same one. It seems to me, in any case, that it is to Foucault's enduring credit that he persisted in the full recognition of these puzzles without ever trying to present us with a ready-made solution. The first is that of relation between philosophy and history. There were many times when Foucault declined the label, philosopher, and preferred to cite the work of historians, especially in regard to methods and perspectives. However, at what would turn out to be the end of his life, he came to understand himself as a philosopher rather than an historian. This is a striking change of specification of self and I wish to reflect upon it in the context of my own argument that a critical and effective history is only possible when one suspends the effects of a certain type of the philosophy of history. The second puzzle concerns the very notion of a history of truth and of what kind of historical knowledge is possible of divisions between truth and falsity.

In 1978, Foucault told Duccio Trombadori (Foucault 1991b: 30–1) that he did not consider himself a philosopher, that the authors he drew upon were not philosophers in the strict sense, not concerned with constructing systems but 'of having direct, personal experiences'. He spoke then of an 'experience-book' that prevents us from remaining the same and from having the same type of relation with things and others we had before reading or writing it. Many years before (in 1967–68), he had spoken of the 'curious sacralisation' of history (Foucault 1989a: 12), and, in response to Sartrean criticism that he had murdered history, that he had wanted to kill not history but the 'philosophical myth of History' (ibid. 41). At the very end, however, he seems to have made his peace with his intellectual activity as a kind of philosophical one. In the introduction to *The Use of Pleasure* (Foucault 1985: 8–9), he pays his respect to Paul Veyne, his friend and historical sociologist of antiquity, as one who 'knows the true historian's search for truth' and the labyrinth it leads one to enter. He also, however, describes his as 'studies of "history"', but 'not the work of an historian'. He prefers instead to designate them as a 'philosophical exercise' that aims 'to learn to what extent the effort to think one's own history can free thought from what it silently thinks, and so enable it to think differently'. Are we to regard this as a fundamental recanting, a stepping back into the philosophical fold, an admission that it was not history that was important all along? How do such statements tally with the work on Nietzsche's second *Untimely Meditation* we examined in the first chapter? What are the consequences for the thesis I have entertained here on the philosophy of history?

Without trying to resolve that which I do not believe Foucault himself sought to resolve, I would venture that it matters little whether we regard him as a philosophical historian or an historical philosopher. His domain was the history of thought, of 'the history of the systems of thought', as he named his chair. As an admirer of the effective work of historians, he sculptured an intellectual practice that was opposed to the Hegelian and phenomenological approaches to History, to the dialectical and synthetic philosophies of history of the nineteenth and twentieth centuries. But his domain was not that of the *Annales* histories he drew upon. It was not the *longue durée* of civilisations, or that of the social and economic histories that were the postwar fashion in Britain and France. His domain was that of the history of thought, given that 'thought' here is not identified with ideas, ideologies, forms of consciousness. Offering a displacement within the history of the sciences (after Bachelard, and especially Georges Canguilhem), Foucault undertook a history of thought as a history of the conditions of representations, knowledge, and ideas, conditions he found first in the rules of discourse, then in the relations of power, and, finally, in the relation to self. He wrote of thought as historical fact, as positivity, as having its own irreducibility, its own specific reality and singularity, its own weight and density. His domain was the history of thought as critical activity, as problematisation.

A critical history of thought, then. But this still does not help us understand Foucault's puzzle. How could the history of thought lead back toward philosophy? After all, it was not even a history of philosophy but of the human sciences, of practical moralities, and of political rationalities, and Foucault wrote little of the great philosophers. I think it is in a draft preface to the *The Use of Pleasures* (1986g: 336) that we can find a response. This history of systems of thought 'infers a double reference': it asks of philosophy to explain 'how thought could have a history', and it asks of history to produce an analytic of the historical transformations of thought; it poses to philosophy the problem of the historical relativity of the search for the universal and the absolute, and it poses to history, the effectivity of thought, its consequences for the formation of individual and collective experiences that present themselves as universal. Foucault's problem, then, is one of the unbridgeable gulf between a philosophical practice which works on oneself to change one's being, and an historical domain that discovers the element of thought within the historical forms of social, political, ethical, and discursive practice. Foucault became not so much a philosopher, perhaps, but one who undertakes a philosophical activity as 'an ascesis, an exercise on oneself in the activity of thought' (1985: 9).

We are now at the threshold of a second puzzle, one that truly turns out to be another formulation of this same problem. In a seminal round-table debate with historians, that has guided my own practice of historical sociology (Dean 1991a, 1992b), and to which I find myself returning again and again, Foucault summarises (1981b: 11) his question as: '"What is history, given there is continually being produced within it a separation of true and false?"' The interview is called in English, very precisely, 'Questions of method', and it, more than any of Foucault's massive numbers of communications, has been one I have sought to master. Foucault's question entails four things: how the production of the division between truth and falsity is fundamental to *our* historicity; how this relation operates within those societies that call themselves 'Western' and that claim universal status for a knowledge that is constantly transforming; what historical knowledge can be expected of a history that undermines the truth-falsity division on which it depends; and finally, the general problem of truth.

The latter problem reveals the history of thought as the history of truth. To put it in my own words, the problem of truth is that, if we accept that truth has an historicity, then how can we analyse it? How can we analyse the historicity of truth in the absence of the guarantees of truth? Or, even more directly, how is a history of truth possible, when we realise that truth has a history? Foucault himself sought to analyse 'truth' in relation to the games and rules that structure it, the ways of governing self and others. Yet his posing of this very question was the safeguard that prevented him from offering a bogus solution and from offering an account of the epistemological, political, or moral, grounds from which he worked.

This, quite simply, is Foucault's puzzle. An insoluble one, perhaps, but also one that, if we learn to live with it, leads us to the most productive of enterprises: in the domain of historical knowledge, how we can know without guarantees of truth; in the domain of politics, how we can govern and use power without the guarantee of emancipation and political universalism. In the domain of ethics, how we can live without the assurances of universal moral codes and commandments. This is perhaps why, in that same discussion, he spoke of a new way of founding our practices of power, knowledge, and self, of the will to discover a new way of governing oneself, a 'political *spiritualité*'.

For myself, as a student of a 'sociology' I still seek to come to terms with, these questions have had an extraordinary resonance. After Foucault, no longer must sociological knowledge ground itself in truth. Rather it seeks to induce change in our individual and collective experience by changing our thought about that which is given to us. This is now what I know I meant when, two years ago, I wrote of the idea of a problematising theory in what became the introduction to this volume. Now I know that such a problematisation does not lead to pure chaos, contingency, or irrationality, but new ways of ordering, of 'serialising', of tabulating and cross-referencing, of constructing problems and hypotheses, and of correcting, modifying and even abandoning them in a rigorous manner. I know how it is possible for sociology to become an effective history by means of its 'present-relevance', a term that now displaces Weber's 'value-relevance'.

I now know that, after Foucault, politics no longer has to depend on possessing the right theory, or universal values or foundations. Politics is about confronting values, perspectives, and aims, with one's practice, with the thought that animates that practice. Democracy, I would now say, is an extremely important value within liberal societies, but what is far more important is the confrontation of the notion of democracy with the very texture of the practices of institutions, and of the practices that traverse our daily lives, and our forms of life-conduct. This is a splendid thought for those of the Left who seek to come to terms with a world without a correct line. I have addressed this problem elsewhere (Dean 1991b, 1992a, 1992c).

I now know, after Foucault, that ethics can no longer be confused with the search for foundations, the values that can guide one, the commandments one can follow. There is a history of the self and a history of the techniques of the self that shows that codes, moralities, and values, can only exist in relation to specific techniques and practices that concern the relation of oneself to oneself. The problem is how to form oneself, not in the absence, but in the presence of a plurality of codes, and with a multiplicity of means. Foucault – most assuredly, not a sociologist – offers us a thoroughly sociological sense of self that does not reduce the self to the social. As Deleuze showed, the self is folding of the exterior relation, of the governance of others, back on oneself. The self is neither substance nor interiority. It is the folding back of the Outside to form an Inside, a tissue of foldings that creates an Inside deeper and more remote than any notion of consciousness, identity, or even the unconscious, can capture. After Foucault, it is our responsibility to ourselves to invent new ways of doing this folding, as much as it is our responsibility to invent new ways of knowing and new forms of political participation.

These are the things to which Foucault's thought, his critical and effective histories, can connect us. Hardly sociological, you might say. However, what possible set of purposes could a critical historical sociology of rationality, of power, and of the self, answer to, if it existed without the ones sketched here? How could such an exercise open itself to *our* present, to *my* present, if it could not help us, help me, problematise what we can know, how we govern and are governed, and who we are?

Notes

INTRODUCTION

1 I have here drawn on, but substantially revised, the three forms of theory sketched by Cooper and Burrell (1988).

1 SOCIOLOGY, FOUCAULT, AND THE USES OF HISTORY

1 I am thinking here of the work of Poggi (1978, 1990), Skocpol (1979), Tilly (1975), Giddens (1985), Corrigan and Sayer (1985), and Mann (1986), in the area of the political and historical sociology of the modern state, of the work on the body by Turner (e.g. 1982, 1992), of Wallerstein (1974, 1980) on the modern world system, of the work represented by the papers in Cohen and Scull (1983) within the problematic of social control, and the legion studies on psychiatry, medicine, and sexuality (e.g. Scull 1979, Ingleby 1981, Weeks 1981, Turner 1987a).

2 A very useful brief summary of Bachelard's history of science given in the context of a critical exposition of Foucault's archaeology is provided by Gutting (1989: 14–32). Here I use the term 'epistemological obstacles' to suggest residues of previous and aspects of current thought that block the path of inquiry or unnecessarily limit avenues and arenas of investigation. In this sense, once illuminating accounts of historical transition from traditional to modern societies or notions of industrialisation and urbanisation can become unreflexively used schemas that prevent analysis of definite historical processes.

3 I say this in full knowledge of Foucault's somewhat playful comments, in what is said to be his last interview, that 'I am simply Nietzschean, and I try to see, on a number of points, and to the extent that it is possible, with the aid of Nietzsche's texts – but also with anti-Nietzschean theses (which are nonetheless Nietzschean) what can be done in this or that domain' (1988j: 251). Even here being 'simply Nietzschean' is not really that simple given that Foucault also admitted that his reading of Nietzsche was precipitated and somewhat mediated by his reading of Heidegger (1988i: 250). Nevertheless, none of this game-playing over references really tells us much about how these thinkers were read, for what purposes, to what uses, etc. The bald and unspecified characterisation of Foucault as 'French Nietzscheanism' by born-again humanists such as Ferry and Renaut (1990) is, it should go without saying, highly problematic.

4 It is to the point that Foucault (1991a: 72) cites Georges Canguilhem as the source of the term 'monument'.

5 This intellectual movement is best represented by the work of Robert Castel (1988), Jacques Donzelot (1979, 1984), Nikolas Rose (1984, 1990), Ian Hunter (1988), and the various contributions to Burchell, Gordon and Miller (1991) and

certain of the essays in Miller and Rose (1986). I have sought to make a contribution to this body of literature (Dean 1991a, 1992b).

6 I am well aware of the defence of the philosophy of history from an historical–sociological perspective advanced by John A. Hall (1985: 3–23). I would make only two points in regard to it: first, I am not convinced that Aron, Berlin, and Popper, etc., were entirely mistaken to point out the dangers of the philosophy of history; second, to abandon narratives of progress, reconciliation, emancipation, etc., is not to abandon the quest for 'patterns of history'. Indeed, I would suggest that this abandonment is a condition for such a form of knowledge.

2 PRESENTIST PERSPECTIVES

1 I do not claim to be the first to argue for the pertinence of Foucauldian genealogy to sociological and critical historical studies. I shall mention only two neglected papers deserving further attention here: on 'genealogy as sociology', Huat Chua (1981); and on genealogy and feminism, Ferguson (1991).

2 For a succinct overview of Elias' life, work, and reception, see Mennell's obituary (1990). An interesting, if contestible, reading of the significance of Elias' 'counter-paradigm' for sociology is found in Arnason (1987).

Excursus: Foucault and *Annales*

1 *Folie et Déraison. Histoire de la folie à l'âge classique* (Plon, 1961) is the first edition of the text known in English as *Madness and Civilisation: a History of Insanity in the Age of Reason* (Foucault 1965). The latter is a translation of an abridged version of the former with some additional material. The second full French edition is *Histoire de la folie à l'âge classique* (Gallimard, 1972). The English edition omits over half the text, bibliography, various documents quoted in appendices and over 900 of its notes (Miller 1987: 101). Included in the second edition are two appendices, 'Mon corps, ce papier, ce feu', a reply to Derrida, and 'La folie, l'absence d'oeuvre'. The former has been translated as Foucault (1979d).

3 QUESTIONS OF ENLIGHTENMENT

1 This statement is cited by Lewis White Beck (1963: vii) in his introduction to the collection, Kant (1963). All reference made to Kant's philosophy of history throughout this chapter is based on this extremely valuable collection. This chapter seeks to counterpoise the critical approaches to history of Foucault and Kant. We have here an illustration of that thesis: Kant's disdain for the archival task of archaeology and genealogy.

2 Habermas (1984: 146) also points out that the end is not teleologically given in advance in the Enlightenment philosophies of history.

3 See also Halévy (1927: 220–1). On Malthus and poverty, see my *The Constitution of Poverty* (Dean: 1991a), Chapters 4 and 5.

4 The debate with Habermas is rejoined by Dreyfus and Rabinow (1986: 109–22), and Poster (1989: 70–86). An overview of the Habermas–Foucault 'controversies' is given by Richters (1988). Quite different readings of Foucault on Kant can be found in Gutting (1989: 1–7) and Dolar (1991: 43–56).

5 In this invaluable interview, Foucault (1983b) sites his own critical project in relation to several intellectual trajectories, including those of the French history of the sciences, critical theory, and, revealingly, the twentieth century history of formalism. At several points in the interview Foucault refers to the history of reason, rationality, and knowledge as a mode of critical inquiry. He does not use the phrase, 'critical history of rationality', but does discuss the 'critical inquiry into the history of rationality' (Foucault 1983b: 201).

6 In a piece on Canguilhem (Foucault 1980d) Foucault constructs a similar lineage

which includes the Hegelians, the Frankfurt School, Lukacs, Feuerbach, Nietzsche, and Weber and, interestingly, French positivism from Comte to the twentieth century historians of science, Koyré, Bachelard and Canguilhem himself. We might take note that Habermas is missing in this list.

7 The interview with Raulet (Foucault 1983b) discusses this theme of the critical preoccupation with rationality, science, and knowledge in both German and French thought in the twentieth century at some length. See also Foucault 1980d for an alternative, if similar, discussion. There, Foucault defines the task of Canguilhem to be a 'history of veridical discourses, that is to say, of discourses which rectify themselves, correct themselves and operate upon themselves a work of self-elaboration finalised by the task of "saying the true"' (ibid. 56). This might stand as a close summation of Foucault's own problematic of rationalities.

8 See Hirst and Woolley (1982: Ch. 6). They argue: 'Forms of specification of individuals exist in all societies but they are not necessarily specified as individual subjects, as unique entities coincident with a distinct consciousness and will' (ibid. 118).

9 One, and only one, component of such a task is that by which Foucault (1982: 208) was led retrospectively to characterise the objective of all his work: 'My objective . . . has been to create a history of the different modes by which, in our culture, human beings are made subjects.'

4 WEBER, RATIONALITY, AND THE SUBJECT

1 This point is most clearly made in the analysis of Weber's notion of rationalisation by Hindess (1987: 143) who argues that 'Weber's analysis of rationalisation is problematic not only because it involves a level of structural analysis that is inconsistent with his explicit methodological individualism, but also because it is a form of characterisation based on actors' orientations'.

2 An extended commentary and critique of Weber's neo-Kantian epistemology of the cultural sciences is provided by Paul Hirst (1976: 50–68). The very structure of the free subject founds the possibility of a realm of cultural scientific knowledge. As Hirst has put it, 'in the proposed ontology of the subject is presupposed the whole nature and content of the cultural realm' (ibid. 52–3). One theme of Weber's anthropology not developed here is how the opposition between subject and object underlies his sociology of religion. As Schluchter suggests (1987: 96), the 'systematic standpoint' for Weber's mature sociology of religion 'points to the antimonic structure of human existence with its separation between objective and subjective worlds'. The axes of his typology of world religions refers to the capacity of the subject to engage in a practical form of conduct oriented to the achievement of ends in the external world or a form of conduct which withdraws from practical conduct to pursue absolute values without regard to their consequences. The fundamental opposition between 'world affirming' and 'world rejecting' religions is anchored in such an opposition, as too is the contrast between 'inner worldly' and 'other worldly' attitudes to the world, and ascetic and contemplative or mystical forms of conduct. So too, it would seem, is the opposition between instrumentally rational and value-rational action.

3 The work of Turner (1981) alerts us to the centrality of fate in Weber's historical sociology and sociology of religion.

5 A 'SPECIFIC AND PECULIAR RATIONALISM'? BEYOND THE RATIONALISATION THESIS

1 For recent commentary on Weber, questions of the status and sense of Weber's concept of rationalisation are often posed in relation to the problem of the 'thematic unity' of what might be regarded as a highly fragmented œuvre, a fragmentation

which is compounded for the English language reader by the peculiarities of its presentation in translation. What might be regarded as technical tasks, such as the dating of texts, the discovery of their temporal sequence, and their grouping together, become crucial to the discourse of commentary and of interpretation. There is, however, a familiar resemblance to the recent fashions of a 'return to Marx' and 'return to Freud', especially the dispute over what constitutes the legitimate corpus for interpretation. For example, Tenbruck's reorientation (1980) has been significant for its devaluation of what were previously held to be major texts (*Economy and Society*, Weber 1968, and *The Protestant Ethic and The Spirit of Capitalism*, Weber 1985) and its shift of attention to late, programmatic texts which are considered to contain Weber's mature position if only in cryptic form, principally the 1920 'Author's Introduction' (Weber 1985: 13–31), and the 'Introduction' and 'Intermediate Reflections' of the so-called 'Economic Ethics of World Religions' (Weber 1970: 267–301; 323–59). The 'Intermediate Reflections' (*Zwischenbetrachung*) has, moreover, via the work of Schluchter (e.g. 1979: 61–4), come to occupy a place of central significance in Habermas' reconstruction of the concept of rationalisation (Habermas 1984, 1987b). One might also want to note that recent commentary on issues of rationality and modernity in Weber is, as Roth (1987) has pointed out, based on passages and remarks which together make up no more than a few score pages in a massive *œuvre*. One of the central tenets of Wilhelm Hennis' interpretation (1983, 1987), by contrast, seeks to restore the importance of the whole of Weber's oeuvre, and contends that a comprehensive understanding of one part of it starts to provide an entry into that whole.

2 Habermas, by contrast, argues that Weber broke with the premises of the older philosophy of history and its successors by rejecting evolutionism, naturalism and rationalism (Habermas 1984: 153–5). My argument is that Weber remains within a philosophy of history in so far as history becomes not a space of the dispersion of empirical entities, their temporalities, and their organisation into series, but the locus of a narrative concerning the human actor, its potential and dilemmas. On such grounds, Habermas himself has not shifted out of such domains despite the desire to sublate the philosophy of consciousness.

3 Perhaps one key difficulty with Weber's analysis of rationality is that it seems to be caught between two incompatible principles: one that regards rationality as a feature of the human subject that achieves its expression in a society and one that regards it as a feature of forms of social organisation, and modes of calculation and discourse, as Hindess (1987) has demonstrated particularly clearly. In this regard, it is instructive to compare the historical specification of the conditions of capitalist economic action in the lectures on *General Economic History* (Weber 1927: 276–7) to his general definition of economic action as 'the peaceful use of the actor's control over resources, which is rationally oriented, by deliberate planning, to economic ends' (Weber 1968: 63). While the latter remains at the level of the actor and its attributes, the former locates the conditions of economic rationality at the level of 'objective' modes of calculation and social conditions, e.g. rational capital accounting, freedom of the market, calculable law, formally free labour, and the commercialisation of economic life. The difficulty with this form of characterisation, however, is that all these preconditions of capitalism seem to be simply the expression of the intrinsic anthropological universal of rationality in other domains.

6 ABSENT HISTORY AND ENLIGHTENMENT DIALECTICS

1 The argument of the present chapter is limited to the position that can be discerned in *The Dialectic of Enlightenment* and associated writings of the Frankfurt School at about the same period of the 1940s. I am concerned here to contest Habermas' defence of this text as stopping short of a 'total critique', and his attack on Foucault

in the same terms. For a revealing discussion of this type of contrast see Habermas (1992: 152–5). The present chapter and its argument contain no systematic address upon the intellectual development of the authors of this text before or after its writing. For example, there is no consideration given here to the later writings of Adorno. However, for an extremely useful precis of Horkheimer's work in the context of a discussion of Foucault's contributions on the subject, power, and domination, see Peter Miller's book (1987). I have drawn on it extensively in the following discussion.

7 HABERMAS' MODERNIST TRANSLATIONS

1 For an instructive account, from a different perspective, of Habermas' struggle to free himself from the philosophy of history and to develop a theory of social evolution see Dews (1992: 5–11). I also confess to some puzzlement concerning Habermas' relation to Benjamin who, especially in his 'Theses on the Philosophy of History', so clearly rejects evolutionism (1969: 255–69). Take: 'History is the subject of a structure whose site is not homogeneous, empty time, but time filled by the presence of the now (*Jetzeit*)' (ibid. 263); and the contrast between a 'universal history' with no theoretical armature and the 'constructivist principle', and radical discontinuity, of a materialist historiography (ibid. 264–5). Habermas' appropriation, detailed further in this chapter, appears close to mere lip-service.

2 For informal comments on Heidegger and Nazism, see Habermas (1992: 190–2). Here he presents the thesis that Heidegger's 'history of Being' cannot be derived from the internal development of his philosophy. Instead his later philosophy is derived, according to Habermas, from 'external events', namely his relation to Nazism in the early 1930s. An elaborated version of this thesis is to be found in Habermas (1987a: 155–60). A more cautious and balanced assessment of the relation between Heidegger and Nazism, and of the relations between theory and practice, is given by Hindess (1992). The latter surveys recent debates in France on this issue. On Carl Schmitt, see the various contributions to a special number of the journal, *Telos – Telos* 72, Summer 1987.

3 I am thinking here of the individual and collective work of Michel Callon and Bruno Latour (e.g. Callon 1986; Latour 1986; Callon and Latour 1981). 'Translation' describes the process by which agents and authorities seek to enlist or enrol other agents in their pursuit of goals by interpreting and representing the 'interests' of the latter as identical to or consonant with their own.

4 In this section, I consider the 'ethics of the intellectual' from the perspective of Foucault's genealogy of the human sciences in the 1970s, which is the subject of Habermas' critique. More general issues of politics, ethics, and the intellectual are addressed throughout the later chapters and conclusion of the present work. The work of Paul Patton (1984/5; 1989; 1992) represents one sustained attempt to draw out Foucault's ethical positions. On related issues of Foucault's politics, Gandal (1986).

8 THEMATICS OF STATE AND POWER

1 See chapter 7 on Habermas' criticism of Foucault's conception of power and also Fraser (1989: 32–33), Taylor (1986), and Comay (1986). As Patton (1992) points out, this type of criticism argues around two themes: first, that Foucault's 'descriptive' analyses of power offer no criteria of judgement between oppressive regimes of power and those promoting freedom; and secondly, that there is no alternative ideal based on a conception of human being or human society. The first of these arguments begs the question in two ways: first, it ignores the work that can be done on Foucault to develop a veritable morphology of forms of the will to govern (Miller and Rose 1990; Rose and Miller 1992; Gordon 1980, 1991); and

second, it fails to consider the possibility of drawing distinctions on a non-normative basis between power, power over, and domination, distinctions developed from Foucault's work on governmentality and ethics (e.g. Foucault 1988c; Patton 1989, 1992). The second theme misses the point entirely: as we showed in the last chapter, the radicality of Foucault's position consists in the rejection of universal normative grounds for social criticism. This does not mean that particular 'economies of power' cannot be criticised from various substantive viewpoints, or that Foucault himself always refrains from such criticism. If such viewpoints have no universal grounding it is because they, too, are subject to inspection and contestation.

2 Corrigan (1990: 114) insists on the multiple nature of identity, without which we cannot understand 'the fragility, permeability, difficulty, agony, and yet poetic energy of most human lives which result from attempting to live with and through the contradictory combination of a variety of possible social classifications, possible identities'. Shored of its romantic language and the marxology of the notion of 'contradiction', this appears to indicate the domain of the dispersion of subject-formation characteristic of Foucault's thought, although the analysis of the agency and means of the promotion of forms of subjectification remains wedded to a restrictive sense of the operation of the state.

3 Pasquale Pasquino (1986: 98) makes the point that the 'underside' of civil individuality is already prefigured in Hobbes' remarks in *De Cive* to the effect that 'men only become political subjects *ex disciplina*'. Foucault himself puts this argument for the interdependence of citizenship rights and disciplinary power in more general form: 'The "Enlightenment", which discovered the liberties, also invented the disciplines'(1977a: 222).

4 Although, by the end of the present book, one might wish to say that the province of genealogy is defined in the space marked out by the relations between 'regimes of truth', 'regimes of practices', and 'regimes of the self'.

5 The following passages have relied heavily on Gordon's account of strategy (1980: 250–5).

6 An extremely helpful account of *Discipline and Punish* can be found in Miller (1987: 196–202).

9 GOVERNMENTALITY ...

1 The immediate source of this allusion to the state as the *monstre froid* is Nietzsche's *Thus Spoke Zarathustra* (1969b: 75). The state, he writes, is 'the coldest of all cold monsters . . . [it] lies in all languages of good and evil; and whatever it says, it lies – and whatever it has, it has stolen . . . only there, where the state ceases, does the man who is not superfluous begin. . . .' I owe my awareness of this source to Rose and Miller (1992: 173) whose writings on government represent a substantial development of Foucault's programmatic statements (see also Miller and Rose 1990).

2 The recent literature on police now includes: Radzinowicz (1956: 417–23) which provides a starting point considering Adam Smith and William Blackstone's use of the term; Rosen (1958, 1974) and Foucault (1980e) on the concept of medical police in the history of public health; the pioneering contributions of Knemeyer (1980) on German conceptual history of *'polizei'*, and Pasquino (1978) on French and German usage from the end of the Middle Ages; Foucault (1965) on its relation to the 'Great Confinement'; Hume (1981: 33–34) in relation to eighteenth century conceptions of government; Tribe (1984) with respect to the related issue of 'cameralism'; Oestreich (1982: 155–65) on police and civil prudence in the early-modern state; and Strakosch (1967: 131–7, 183–5) on police and legal codification in eighteenth century Austria. I have tried to summarise this literature in the context of the history of poverty and poor policy (Dean 1991a, 1992b).

3 On different conceptions of oeconomy, its relation to the *oikos*, or household, and to seventeenth century patriarchalism, see Tribe (1978), and my own attempt to link these themes to the understanding of the government of poverty (especially Dean 1991a: 30–34)

4 I must acknowledge the general inspiration for this and the next chapter provided by two exemplary papers presented by Graham Burchell in Sydney in September 1992 entitled 'Practices of the self' and 'Liberal practices of government'.

10 ... AND PRACTICES OF THE SELF

1 Some attempts have been made at working out this problem with questionable degrees of success: Daraki (1986) who, in a rather bizarre fashion, finds something sinister in it, particularly in the theme of the relation between the government of self and others; Bevis et al. (1989) who offer doubts about its placement in the history of sexuality, and who, together with Poster (1986) pose methodological problems and uncertainties. My own interpretation here owes quite a deal to an informal paper presented by Thomas Osborne to the History of the Present Research Network in London in 1992. I can only hope the ideas central to that paper find publication in the near future.

2 I have not explored the latter relation between acts, pleasure, and desire here. For a succinct summary of Foucault's views on how that triad may be used to characterise the Greek, Chinese, Christian, and 'modern' formulae for sexual behaviour, see his overview of work in progress (1986d: 359).

3 The most famous of which comes from the *Archaeology* (Foucault 1972: 17): 'I am no doubt not the only one who writes in order to have no face. Do not ask who I am and do not ask me to remain the same: leave it to our bureaucrats and our police to see that our papers are in order. At least spare us their morality when we write'. I was intrigued by his biographer Eribon's response (1991: xix).

4 See Minson (1980) on Foucault's determinism of power, and Taylor (1986) and Fraser (1989) for versions of the thesis that Foucault has no grounds for justifying resistance inspired by philosophical humanism and critical theory. Patton (1992) offers an interesting response to the latter to the effect that for Foucault the very fact and necessity of resistance requires no justification.

5 The term 'assemblage' is found in Deleuze and Guattari (1981: 49–71). It is a translation of *agencement*, as pointed out by the translator of this piece, Paul Patton (1981: 40). In the present context an assemblage is an ensemble of heterogeneous discursive and nondiscursive practices, and regimes of truth and conduct, which possesses an overall coherence without answering to any determinative principle or underlying logic. Foucault himself used the more obscure and perhaps untranslatable term, *dispositif* – on which, see Deleuze (1992). The English translation of the first volume of the history of sexuality (Foucault 1979b) preferred the awkward term 'apparatus' I seek to avoid here.

6 A short and succinct exemplar of this type of social policy discourse, issued from within the Organisation of Economic Corporation and Development, is Gass (1988).

Bibliography

Abrams, P. (1980) 'History, sociology, historical sociology', *Past and Present* 87: 3–16.
—— (1982) *Historical Sociology*, Shepton Mallet: Open Books.
Adorno, T. W. (1973) *Negative Dialectics*, trans. E.B. Ashton, London: Routledge & Kegan Paul.
Anderson, P. (1974) *Lineages of the Absolutist State*, London: New Left Books.
Armstrong, D. (1983) *Political Anatomy of the Body*, Cambridge: Cambridge University Press.
Arnason, J. (1987) 'Figurational sociology as counter-paradigm', *Theory, Culture, and Society* 4, 2–3: 429–56.
Beck, L. W. (1963) 'Introduction', to I. Kant *On History*, trans. L.W. Beck and E. L. Fackenheim, New York: Bobbs-Merrill.
Bendix, R. (1966) *Max Weber: an Intellectual Portrait*, London: Methuen.
Benjamin, W. (1969) *Illuminations*, ed. H. Arendt, London: Jonathon Cape.
Bevis, P., Cohen, M. and Kendall, G. (1989) 'Archaeologizing genealogy: Michel Foucault and the economy of austerity', *Economy and Society* 18, 3: 323–39.
Bloch, M. (1953) *The Historian's Craft*, trans. P. Putnam, New York: Knopf.
Bogner, A. (1987) 'Elias and the Frankfurt School', *Theory, Culture and Society* 4, 2–3: 248–85.
Braudel, F. (1972/3) *The Mediterranean and the Mediterranean World in the Age of Philip II*, 2 vols, trans. S. Reynolds, New York: Harper & Row.
—— (1975) 'Preface', to T. Stoianovich *French Historical Method*, Ithaca: Cornell University Press.
—— (1980) *On History*, trans. S. Matthews, Chicago: University of Chicago Press.
Brubaker, R. (1984) *The Limits of Rationality: an Essay on the Social and Moral Thought of Max Weber*, London: Allen & Unwin.
Burchell, G., Gordon, C. and Miller, P. (eds) (1991) *The Foucault Effect: Studies in Governmentality*, London: Harvester Wheatsheaf.
Burke, P. (1990) *The French Historical Revolution: the Annales School 1929–1989*, Cambridge: Polity.
Callon, M. (1986) 'Some elements of a sociology of translation', in J. Law (ed.) *Power, Action, Belief*, London: Routledge & Kegan Paul
—— and Latour, B. (1981) 'Unscrewing the Big Leviathan: how actors macro-structure reality and how sociologists help them to do so', in K. Knorr-Cetina and A. Cicourel (eds) *Advances in Social Theory*, London: Routledge & Kegan Paul.
Castel, R. (1988) *The Regulation of Madness: the Origins of Incarceration in France*, trans. W.D. Halls, Cambridge: Polity.
Chartier, R. (1988) *Cultural History: between Practices and Representations*, trans. L.G. Cochrane, Cambridge: Polity.

Cohen, S. and Scull, A. (eds) (1983) *Social Control and the State*, Oxford: Blackwell.

Comay, R. (1986) 'Excavating the repressive hypothesis: aporias of liberation in Foucault', *Telos* 67: 111–19.

Condorcet, M.J.A.N.C. (1955) *Sketch for a Historical Picture of the Progress of the Human Mind*, London.

Cooper, R. and Burrell, G. (1988) 'Modernism, postmodernism and organisational analysis: an introduction', *Organisation Studies* 9, 1: 91–112.

Corrigan, P. (1990) *Social Forms/Human Capacities*, London: Routledge.

—— and Sayer, D. (1985) *The Great Arch: English State Formation as Cultural Revolution*, Oxford: Basil Blackwell.

Cousins, M. and Hussain, A. (1984) *Michel Foucault*, London: Macmillan.

D'Amico, R. (1991) 'The myth of the totally administered society', *Telos* 88: 80–94.

Daraki, M. (1986) 'Foucault's journey to Greece', *Telos* 67: 87–110.

Dean, M. (1986) 'Foucault's obsession with Western modernity', *Thesis Eleven* 14: 44–61.

—— (1991a) *The Constitution of Poverty: toward a Genealogy of Liberal Governance*, London: Routledge.

—— (1991b) 'End of the line', *Australian Left Review* 133: 15–16.

—— (1992a) 'Free thinking', *Australian Left Review* 138: 12–15.

—— (1992b) 'A genealogy of the government of poverty', *Economy and Society* 23, 3: 215–51.

—— (1992c) 'A liberal dose', *Australian Left Review* 145: 16–20.

—— (1992d) 'Pateman's dilemma: women and citizenship', *Theory and Society* 21, 2: 121–30.

Deleuze, G. (1988) *Foucault*, trans. S. Hand, University of Minnesota Press: Minneapolis.

—— (1992) 'What is a *dispositif*?', in *Michel Foucault: Philosopher*, trans. T.J. Armstrong, New York: Harvester Wheatsheaf.

—— and Guattari, F. (1981) 'Rhizome', *I & C* 8: 49–71.

Descombes, V. (1980) *Modern French Philosophy*, trans. L. Scott-Fox and J.M. Harding, Cambridge: Cambridge University Press.

Dews, P. (1987) *Logics of Disintergration: Post-structuralist Thought and the Claims of Critical Theory*, London: Verso.

—— (1992) 'Editor's Introduction', to J. Habermas *Autonomy and Solidarity*, ed. P. Dews, London: Verso.

Dolar, M. (1991) 'The legacy of the enlightenment: Foucault and Lacan', *New Formations* 14: 43–56.

Donnelly, M. (1982) 'Foucault's genealogy of the human sciences', *Economy and Society* 11, 4: 363–380.

Donzelot, J. (1979) *The Policing of Families*, trans. R. Hurley, New York: Pantheon Books.

—— (1984) *L'invention du social*, Paris: Fayard.

Dreyfus, H. and Rabinow, P. (1983) *Michel Foucault: Beyond Structuralism and Hermeneutics*, 2nd edn, Brighton: Harvester.

—— (1986) 'What is maturity? Habermas and Foucault on What is Enlightenment?', in D.C. Hoy (ed.) *Foucault: a Critical Reader*, Oxford: Basil Blackwell.

Eisenstadt, S.N. (1963) *The Political Systems of Empires*, New York: Free Press.

Elias, N. (1978) *The Civilizing Process, vol. one: The History of Manners*, trans. E. Jephcott, New York: Urizen.

—— (1982) *The Civilizing Process, vol. two: State Formation and Civilization*, trans E. Jephcott, Oxford: Blackwell.

—— (1983) *The Court Society*, trans. E. Jephcott, Oxford: Basil Blackwell.

—— (1987a) *Involvement and Detachment*, M. Schrotter ed., trans. E. Jephcott, Oxford: Basil Blackwell.

—— (1987b) 'The retreat of sociologists into the present', *Theory, Culture and Society* 4: 2/3: 223–47.

—— (1991) *The Society of Individuals*, M. Schrotter ed., trans E. Jephcott, Oxford: Basil Blackwell.

Eribon, D. (1991) *Michel Foucault*, trans. B. Wing, Cambridge, Mass.: Harvard University Press.

Falk, P. (1988) 'The past to come', *Economy and Society* 17, 3: 374–94.

Febvre, L. (1973) *A New Kind of History*, trans. K. Folca, London: Routledge & Kegan Paul.

Ferguson, K. E. (1991) 'Interpretation and genealogy in feminism', *Signs* 16, 2: 322–39.

Ferry, L. and Renaut, A. (1990) *French Philosophy of the Sixties: an Essay on Antihumanism*, trans. M.S. Cattani, Amherst: University of Massachusetts Press.

Flynn, T. (1988) ' Foucault as parrhesiast: his last course at the *Collège de France* (1984)', in J. Bernauer and D. Rasmussen (eds), *The Final Foucault*, Cambridge, Mass.: MIT Press.

Foucault, M. (1965) *Madness and Civilisation: a History of Insanity in the Age of Reason*, trans. R. Howard, London: Tavistock.

—— (1970) *The Order of Things: an Archaeology of the Human Sciences*, trans. A.M. Sheridan, London: Tavistock.

—— (1972) *The Archaeology of Knowledge*, trans. A.M. Sheridan Smith, London: Tavistock.

—— (1973) *The Birth of the Clinic*, trans. A.M. Sheridan, London: Tavistock.

—— (1977a) *Discipline and Punish: the Birth of the Prison*, trans. A. Sheridan, London: Allen Lane.

—— (1977b) 'Nietzsche, genealogy, history', in *Language, Counter-memory, Practice*, ed. D.B. Bouchard, Oxford: Basil Blackwell.

—— (1977c) 'A preface to transgression', in *Language, Counter-memory, Practice*, ed. D.B. Bouchard, Oxford: Basil Blackwell.

—— (1979a) 'Governmentality', *I & C* 6: 5–21.

—— (1979b) *The History of Sexuality, vol. 1: an Introduction*, trans. R. Hurley, London: Allen Lane.

—— (1979c) 'The life of infamous men', in M. Morris and P. Patton (eds) *Michel Foucault: Power, Truth, Strategy*, Sydney: Feral.

—— (1979d) 'My body, this paper, this fire', *Oxford Literary Review* 4, 1.

—— (1980a) 'Body/Power', in *Power/Knowledge: Selected Interviews and Other Writings 1972–1977*, ed. C. Gordon, Brighton: Harvester.

—— (1980b) 'The confession of the flesh', in *Power/Knowledge: Selected Interviews and Other Writings 1972–1977*, ed. C. Gordon, Brighton: Harvester.

—— (1980c) 'The Eye of Power', in *Power/Knowledge: Selected Interviews and Other Writings 1972–1977*, ed. C. Gordon, Brighton: Harvester.

—— (1980d) 'Georges Canguilhem, philosopher of error', *I & C* 7: 51–62.

—— (1980e) 'The politics of health in the eighteenth century', in *Power/Knowledge: Selected Interviews and Other Writings 1972–1977*, ed. C. Gordon, Brighton: Harvester.

—— (1980f) 'Power and strategies', in *Power/Knowledge: Selected Interviews and Other Writings 1972–1977*, ed. C. Gordon, Brighton: Harvester.

—— (1980g) 'Questions of geography', in *Power/Knowledge: Selected Interviews and Other Writings 1972–1977*, ed. C. Gordon, Brighton: Harvester.

—— (1980h) 'Truth and power', in *Power/Knowledge: Selected Interviews and Other Writings 1972–1977*, ed. C. Gordon, Brighton: Harvester.

—— (1980i) 'Two lectures', in *Power/Knowledge: Selected Interviews and Other Writings 1972–1977*, ed. C. Gordon, Brighton: Harvester.

—— (1981a) 'The order of discourse', trans. I. McLeod, in R. Young (ed.) *Untying the Text*, London: Routledge and Kegan Paul.

—— (1981b) 'Questions of method', *I & C* 8: 3–14.
—— (1982) 'Afterword: the subject and power', in H. Dreyfus and P. Rabinow *Michel Foucault: beyond Structuralism and Hermeneutics*, 1st edn, Brighton: Harvester, 208–26.
—— (1983a) 'Preface', in G. Deleuze and F. Guattari, *Anti-Oedipus: Capitalism and Schizophrenia*, trans. R. Hurley, M. Seem, and H.R. Lane, Minneapolis: University of Minnesota Press.
—— (1983b) 'Structuralism and poststructuralism: an interview with Michel Foucault' (with G. Raulet), *Telos* 55: 195–211. Republished as 'Critical Theory/Intellectual History' in M. Foucault *Politics, Philosophy, Culture: Interviews and Other Writings 1977–1984*, ed. L.D. Kritzman, New York: Routledge.
—— (1985) *The History of Sexuality, vol. 2: the Use of Pleasure*, trans. R. Hurley, New York: Pantheon.
—— (1986a) *The History of Sexuality, vol. 3: the Care of the Self*, trans. R. Hurley, New York: Pantheon.
—— (1986b) 'Kant on revolution and enlightenment', *Economy and Society* 15, 1: 88–96.
—— (1986c) 'Nietzsche, Freud, Marx' *Critical Texts* 3: 1–5.
—— (1986d) 'On the genealogy of ethics: an overview of the work in progress', in *The Foucault Reader*, ed. P. Rabinow, Harmondsworth: Penguin.
—— (1986e) 'Polemics, politics, problematisations', in *The Foucault Reader*, ed. P. Rabinow, Harmondsworth: Penguin.
—— (1986f) 'Politics and ethics: an interview', in *The Foucault Reader*, ed. P. Rabinow, Harmondsworth: Penguin.
—— (1986g) 'Preface to The History of Sexuality, volume two', in *The Foucault Reader*, ed. P. Rabinow, Harmondsworth: Penguin.
—— (1986h) 'Space, knowledge, power', in *The Foucault Reader*, ed. P. Rabinow, Harmondsworth: Penguin.
—— (1986i) 'What is Enlightenment?', in *The Foucault Reader*, ed. P. Rabinow, Harmondsworth: Penguin.
—— (1988a) 'An aesthetics of existence', in *Politics, Philosophy, Culture: Interviews and Other Writings 1977–1984*, ed. L.D. Kritzman, New York: Routledge.
—— (1988b) 'The battle for chastity', in *Politics, Philosophy, Culture: Interviews and Other Writings 1977–1984*, ed. L.D. Kritzman, New York: Routledge.
—— (1988c) 'The care for the self as a practice of freedom', in J. Bernauer and D. Rasmussen (eds) *The Final Foucault*, Cambridge, Mass.: MIT Press.
—— (1988d) 'The concern for truth', in *Politics, Philosophy, Culture: Interviews and Other Writings 1977–1984*, ed. L.D. Kritzman, New York: Routledge.
—— (1988e) 'The dangerous individual', in *Politics, Philosophy, Culture: Interviews and Other Writings 1977–1984*, ed. L.D. Kritzman, New York: Routledge.
—— (1988f) 'The minimalist self', in *Politics, Philosophy, Culture: Interviews and Other Writings 1977–1984*, ed. L.D. Kritzman, New York: Routledge.
—— (1988g) 'The political technology of individuals', in L.H. Martin, H. Gutman, and P.H. Hutton (eds) *Technologies of the Self: a Seminar with Michel Foucault*, London: Tavistock.
—— (1988h) 'Politics and reason', in *Politics, Philosophy, Culture: Interviews and Other Writings 1977–1984*, ed. L.D. Kritzman, New York: Routledge.
—— (1988i) 'Practising criticism', in *Politics, Philosophy, Culture: Interviews and Other Writings 1977–1984*, ed. L.D. Kritzman, New York: Routledge.
—— (1988j) 'The return of morality', in *Politics, Philosophy, Culture: Interviews and Other Writings 1977–1984*, ed. L.D. Kritzman, New York: Routledge.
—— (1988k) 'Technologies of the self', in L.H. Martin, H. Gutman, and P.H. Hutton (eds) *Technologies of the Self: a Seminar with Michel Foucault*, London: Tavistock.

—— (1988l) 'Truth, power, and self: an interview with Michel Foucault', in L.H. Martin, H. Gutman, and P.H. Hutton (eds) *Technologies of the Self: a Seminar with Michel Foucault*, London: Tavistock.

—— (1989a) *Foucault Live (Interviews, 1966–1984)*, trans. J. Johnston, New York: Semiotext(e).

—— (1989b) *Résumé des cours 1970–1982*, Paris: Julliard.

—— (1991a) 'Politics and the study of discourse', in G. Burchell, C. Gordon and P. Miller (eds) *The Foucault Effect: Studies in Governmentality*, London: Harvester Wheatsheaf.

—— (1991b) *Remarks on Marx: Conversations with Duccio Trombadori*, trans. R.J. Goldstein and J. Cascaito, New York: Semiotext(e).

Fraser, N. (1985) 'Michel Foucault: a "young conservative"?', *Ethics* 96, 1: 165–84.

—— (1989) *Unruly Practices: Power, Discourse and Gender in Contemporary Social Theory*, Minneapolis: University of Minnesota Press.

Gandal, K. (1986) 'Michel Foucault: intellectual work and politics', *Telos* 67: 121–145.

Gass, J. (1988) 'The active society', *OECD Observer* June–July: 4–8.

Giddens, A. (1984) *The Constitution of Society: Outline of a Theory of Structuration*, Cambridge: Polity.

—— (1985) *The Nation-State and Violence*, Cambridge: Polity.

—— (1987) *Social Theory and Modern Sociology*, Cambridge: Polity.

—— (1991) *Modernity and Self-Identity*, Cambridge: Polity.

Goldthorpe, J. (1991) 'The uses of history in sociology: reflections on some recent tendencies', *British Journal of Sociology* 42, 2: 211–230.

Gordon, C. (1980) 'Afterword', in M. Foucault *Power/Knowledge: Selected Interviews and Other Writings 1972–1977*, ed. C. Gordon, Brighton: Harvester.

—— (1987) 'The soul of the citizen: Max Weber and Michel Foucault on rationality and government', in S. Whimster and S. Lash (eds) *Max Weber, Rationality and Modernity*, London: Allen and Unwin.

—— (1991) 'Governmental Rationality: An Introduction', to G. Burchell, C. Gordon, and P. Miller, (eds) *The Foucault Effect: Studies in Governmentality*, London: Harvester Wheatsheaf.

Gouldner, A.W. (1971) *The Coming Crisis of Western Sociology*, London: Heinemann.

Gutting, G. (1989) *Michel Foucault's Archaeology of Scientific Reason*, Cambridge: Cambridge University Press.

Habermas, J. (1984) *The Theory of Communicative Action, vol. 1: Reason and the Rationalization of Society*, trans. T. McCarthy, Boston: Beacon Press.

—— (1985) 'Modernity: an incomplete project', in H. Foster (ed.) *Postmodern Culture*, London: Pluto.

—— (1987a) *The Philosophical Discourse of Modernity: Twelve Lectures*, trans. F. Lawrence, Cambridge: Polity.

—— (1987b) *The Theory of Communicative Action, vol. 2: Lifeworld and System: A Critique of Functionalist Reason*, trans. T. McCarthy, Boston: Beacon Press.

—— (1989) *The New Conservatism: Cultural Criticism and the Historians' Debate*, trans. and ed. S.W. Nicholsen, Cambridge: Polity.

—— (1992) *Autonomy and Solidarity*, 2nd edn, ed. P. Dews, London: Verso.

Hacking, I. (1986) 'Self-improvement', in D.C. Hoy (ed.) *Foucault: a Critical Reader*, Oxford: Basil Blackwell.

Halévy, E. (1927) *The Growth of Philosophic Radicalism*, trans. M. Morris, London: Faber.

Hall, J. A. (1985) *Powers and Liberties: the Causes and Consequences of the Rise of the West*, Oxford: Basil Blackwell.

Hall, S. (1992) 'The West and the Rest: discourse and power', in S. Hall and B. Gieben (eds) *Formations of Modernity*, Cambridge: Polity.

Harvey, D. (1989) *The Condition of Postmodernity*, Oxford: Blackwell.

Hegel, G.W.F. (1956) *The Philosophy of History*, trans. J. Sibree, New York: Dover Publications.

Heidegger, M. (1978) 'Letter on humanism', in *Basic Writings*, ed. D. Krell, London: Routledge & Kegan Paul.

Heller, A. (1990) 'The death of the subject', *Thesis Eleven* 25: 22–38.

Hennis, W. (1983) 'Max Weber's "central question"', *Economy and Society* 12, 2: 135–180.

—— (1987) 'Personality and life orders: Max Weber's theme', in S. Whimster and and S. Lash (eds) *Max Weber, Rationality and Modernity*, London: Allen & Unwin.

—— (1988) *Max Weber: Essays in Reconstruction*, London: Allen and Unwin.

Hindess, B. (1987) 'Rationality and the characterisation of modern society', in S. Whimster and S. Lash (eds) *Max Weber, Rationality and Modernity*, London: Allen & Unwin.

—— (1989) *Political Choice and Social Structure*, Aldershot: Edward Elgar.

—— (1992) 'Heidegger and the Nazis: cautionary tales of the relations between theory and practice', *Thesis Eleven* 31: 115–130.

Hirst, P.Q. (1976) *Social Evolution and Sociological Categories*, London: Allen & Unwin.

Hirst, P. and Woolley, P. (1982) *Social Relation and Human Attributes*, London: Tavistock.

Hohendahl, P.U. (1986) 'Habermas' philosophical discourse of modernity' *Telos* 69: 49–65.

Horkheimer, M. (1974) *Eclipse of Reason*, New York: Continuum.

—— and Adorno, T. (1972) *Dialectic of Enlightenment*, trans. J. Cumming, New York: Continuum.

Huat Chua, B. (1981) 'Genealogy as Sociology: an Introduction to Michel Foucault', *Catalyst* 14: 1–22.

Hume, L.J. (1981) *Bentham and Bureaucracy*, Cambridge: Cambridge University Press.

Hunter, I. (1988) *Culture and Government*, London: Macmillan.

Ingleby, D. (ed.) (1981) *Critical Psychiatry*, Harmondsworth: Penguin.

Ingram, D. (1986) 'Foucault and the Frankfurt School: a discourse on Nietzsche, power and knowledge', *Praxis International* 6, 3: 311–27.

Jay, M. (1973) *The Dialectical Imagination*, London: Heinemann.

—— (1986) 'In the empire of the gaze: Foucault and the denigration of vision in twentieth century French thought', in D.C. Hoy (ed.) *Foucault: a Critical Reader*, Oxford: Basil Blackwell.

Jessop, B. (1990) *State Theory: Putting the Capitalist State in its Place*, Cambridge, Polity.

Kant, I. (1963) *On History*, trans. L.W. Beck, R.E. Anchor and E.L Fackenheim, L. W. Beck ed., Bobbs-Merrill: New York.

Kilminster, R. (1987) 'Introduction to Elias', *Theory, Culture and Society* 4, 2–3: 213–22.

Knemeyer, F-L. (1980) 'Polizei', *Economy and Society* 9, 2: 172–96.

Koselleck, R. (1982) '*Begriffsgeschichte* and social history', *Economy and Society* 11, 4: 409–27.

Lasch, C. (1979) *The Culture of Narcissism*, New York: Norton.

Latour, B. (1986) 'The powers of association', in J. Law (ed.) *Power, Action, Belief*, London: Routledge and Kegan Paul.

Le Roy Ladurie, E. (1974) *The Peasants of Languedoc*, trans. J. Day, Urbana: University of Illinois Press.

—— (1978) *Montaillou: the Promised Land of Error*, trans. B. Bray, New York: George Braziller.

—— (1979) *The Territory of the Historian*, trans. B. and S. Reynolds, Brighton: Harvester.

Löwith, K. (1982) *Max Weber and Karl Marx*, trans. H. Fantel, London: Allen & Unwin.

Major-Poetzl, P. (1983) *Michel Foucault's Archaeology of Western Culture*, Brighton: Harvester.

Mann, M (1986) *The Sources of Social Power*, vol. 1, Cambridge: Cambridge University Press.

—— (1988) *States, War and Capitalism: Studies in Political Sociology* Oxford: Basil Blackwell.

Marshall, T.H. (1983) 'Citizenship and social class', in D. Held, J. Anderson, B. Gieben, S. Hall, L. Harris, P. Lewis, N. Parker and B. Tierok (eds) *States and Societies*, Oxford: Martin Robertson.

Martin, L.H., Gutman, H. and Hutton, P.H. (1988) *Technologies of the Self: a Seminar with Michel Foucault*, London: Tavistock.

Mauss, M. (1979) *Sociology and Psychology*, trans. B. Brewster, London: Routledge & Kegan Paul.

McCarthy, T. (1987) 'Introduction' to J. Habermas *The Philosophical Discourse of Modernity: Twelve Lectures*, trans. F. Lawrence, Cambridge: Polity.

Mennell, S. (1990) 'Norbert Elias, 1897–1990: personal reflections on a remarkable life', *Thesis Eleven* 27: 152–66.

Meuret, D. (1981/2) 'Political economy and the legitimation of the state', *I & C* 9: 29–38.

—— (1988) 'A political genealogy of political economy', *Economy and Society* 17, 2: 225–50.

Miller, P. (1987) *Domination and Power*, London: Routledge & Kegan Paul.

—— and Rose, N. (eds) (1986) *The Power of Psychiatry*, Cambridge: Polity.

—— (1990) 'Governing economic life', *Economy and Society* 19, 1: 1–31.

Minson, J. (1980) 'Strategies for socialists? Foucault's conception of power', *Economy and Society* 9, 1: 1–43.

—— (1985) *Genealogies of Morals: Nietzsche, Foucault, Donzelot and the Eccentricity of Ethics*, London: Macmillan.

Mommsen, W. (1974) *The Age of Bureaucracy: Perspectives on the Political Sociology of Max Weber*, Oxford: Basil Blackwell.

—— (1987) 'Personal conduct and societal change', in S. Whimster and S. Lash (eds) *Max Weber, Rationality and Modernity*, London: Allen & Unwin.

Moore, B. (1966) *The Social Origins of Dictatorship and Democracy: Lord and Peasant in the Making of the Modern World*, Boston: Beacon Press.

Murray, J. (1990), 'Introduction', in P. Veyne *Bread and Circuses: Historical Sociology and Political Pluralism*, London: Allen Lane.

Nietzsche, F. (1969a) *On the Genealogy of Morals*, trans. W. Kaufmann and R.J. Holingdale, New York: Random House.

—— (1969b) *Thus Spoke Zarathustra*, trans. R.J. Holingdale, Harmondsworth: Penguin.

—— (1983) *Untimely Meditations*, trans. R.J. Holingdale, Cambridge: Cambridge University Press.

Oestreich, G. (1982) *Neostoicism and the Early Modern State*, Cambridge: Cambridge University Press.

Pasquino, P. (1978) 'Theatricum politicum: the genealogy of capital – police and the state of prosperity' *Ideology and Consciousness* 4: 41–54.

—— (1986) 'Michel Foucault (1926–84): The will to knowledge', *Economy and Society* 15, 1: 97–109.

Pateman, C. (1988) *The Sexual Contract*, Oxford: Polity Press.

Patton, P. (1981) 'Notes for a glosssary', *I & C* 8: 41–8.
—— (1984/5) 'Michel Foucault: the ethics of an intellectual', *Thesis Eleven* 10/11: 56–70.
—— (1989) 'Taylor and Foucault on power and freedom', *Political Studies* 37, 2: 260–76.
—— (1992) 'Le sujet de pouvoir chez Foucault', *Sociologie et Societes* 24, 1.
Poggi, G. (1978) *The Development of the Modern State*, London: Hutchinson.
—— (1990) *The State: its Nature, Development, and Prospects*, Cambridge: Polity.
Polanyi, K. (1944) *The Great Transformation*, 1957 edn., Boston: Beacon Press.
Poster, M. (1986) 'Foucault and the tyranny of Greece', in D.C. Hoy (ed.) *Foucault: a Critical Reader*, Oxford: Basil Blackwell.
—— (1989) *Critical Theory and Poststructualism*, Ithaca: Cornell University Press.
Poulantzas, N. (1973) *Political Power and Social Classes*, trans. ed. T. O'Hagan, London: New Left Books.
—— (1978) *State, Power, Socialism*, trans. P. Camiller, London: New Left Books.
Radzinowicz, L. (1956) *A History of English Criminal law and its Administration from 1750, vol. 3: The Reform of the Police*, London: Stevens & Sons.
Richters, A. (1988) 'Modernity–postmodernity controversies: Habermas and Foucault', *Theory, Culture and Society* 5: 611–43.
Rorty, R. (1986) 'Foucault and epistemology', in D.C. Hoy (ed.) *Foucault: a Critical Reader*, Oxford: Basil Blackwell.
Rose, N. (1984) *The Psychological Complex: Psychology, Politics and Society in England 1869–1939*, London: Routledge & Kegan Paul.
—— (1990) *Governing the Soul: the Shaping of the Private Self*, London: Routledge.
—— and Miller, P. (1992) 'Political power beyond the state: problematics of government', *British Journal of Sociology* 43, 2: 173- 205.
Rosen, G. (1958) *A History of Public Health*, New York: M.D. Publications.
—— (1974) *From Medical Police to Social Medicine: Essays on the History of Health Care*, New York: Science History Publications.
Roth, G. (1987) 'Rationalisation in Max Weber's developmental history', in S. Whimster and S. Lash (eds) *Max Weber, Rationality and Modernity*, London: Allen & Unwin.
Said, E. (1985) *Orientalism: Western concepts of the Orient*, Harmondsworth: Penguin.
Schluchter, W. (1979) 'The paradox of rationalisation: on the relation of ethics and world', in G. Roth and W. Schulchter *Max Weber's Vision of History: Ethics and Methods*, Berkeley: University of California Press.
—— (1981) *The Rise of Western Rationalism: Max Weber's Developmental History*, Berkeley: University of California Press.
—— (1987) 'Weber's sociology of rationalism and typology of religious rejections of the world', in S. Whimster and S. Lash (eds) *Max Weber, Rationality and Modernity*, London: Allen & Unwin.
Schochet, G.J. (1975) *Patriarchalism and Political Thought*, Oxford: Oxford University Press.
Scull, A. (1979) *Museums of Madness*, London: Allen Lane.
Sennett, R. (1977) *The Fall of Public Man*, New York: Alfred A. Knopf.
Skocpol, T. (1979) *States and Social Revolutions: a Comparative Study of France, Russia and China*, Cambridge: Cambridge University Press.
—— (ed.) (1982) *Vision and Method in Historical Sociology*, Cambridge: Cambridge University Press.
Smart, B. (1982) 'Sociology and the problem of agency', *Theory and Society* 11, 2: 121–41.
—— (1985) *Michel Foucault*, Chichester: Ellis Horwood.
—— (1990) 'On the disorder of things: sociology, postmodernity, and the "end of the social"', *Sociology* 24, 3: 397–416.

Stoianovich, T. (1975) *French Historical Method: the Annales Paradigm*, Ithaca: Cornell University Press.

Strakosch, H.E. (1967) *State Absolutism and the Rule of Law*, Sydney: University of Sydney Press.

Taylor, C. (1986) 'Foucault on freedom and truth', in D.C. Hoy (ed.) *Foucault: a Critical Reader*, Oxford: Basil Blackwell.

Tenbruck, F.H. (1980) 'The problem of the thematic unity in the works of Max Weber', *British Journal of Sociology* 31, 3: 316–51.

Tilly, C. (ed.) (1975) *The Formation of National States in Western Europe*, Princeton: Princeton University Press

—— (1981) *As Sociology Meets History*, New York: Academic Press.

Tribe, K. (1978) *Land, Labour and Economic Discourse*, London: Routledge & Kegan Paul.

— (1984) 'Cameralism and the science of government', *Journal of Modern History* 52, 2: 263–84.

Turner, B. S. (1981) *For Weber: Essays in the Sociology of Fate*, London: Routledge & Kegan Paul.

—— (1982) *The Body and Society: Explorations in Social Theory*, Oxford: Blackwell.

—— (1987a) *Medical Power and Social Knowledge*, London: Sage.

—— (1987b) 'The rationalisation of the body: reflections on modernity and discipline', in S. Whimster and S. Lash (eds) *Max Weber, Rationality and Modernity*, London: Allen & Unwin.

—— (1992) *Regulating Bodies: Essays in Medical Sociology*, London: Routledge.

Veyne, P. (1982) 'The inventory of differences', *Economy and Society* 11, 2: 173–98.

—— (1984) *Writing History: Essay on Epistemology*, trans. M. Moore-Rinvolucri, Middletown, Conn.: Wesleyan University Press.

Wallerstein, I. (1974) *The Modern World-System: Capitalist Agriculture and the Origins of the European Economy in the Sixteenth Century*, New York Academic Press.

—— (1980) *The Modern World-System, vol. two: Mercantilism and the Consolidation of the European World-Economy*, New York: Academic Press.

Weber, M. (1927) *General Economic History*, trans. F.A. Knight, London: Allen & Unwin.

—— (1949) *The Methodology of the Social Sciences*, trans. and eds E.A. Shils and H.A. Finch, New York: Free Press.

—— (1968) *Economy and Society: an Outline of Interpretive Sociology*, 3 vols, ed. G. Roth and C. Wittich, New York: Bedminster Press.

—— (1970) *From Max Weber: Essays in Sociology*, trans. and eds H.H. Gerth and C. Wright Mills, Routledge & Kegan Paul.

—— (1975) 'Marginal utility theory and "the fundamental laws of psychophysics"', trans. L. Schneider, *Social Science Quarterly* 56, 1: 24–36.

—— (1985) *The Protestant Ethic and the Spirit of Capitalism*, trans. T. Parsons, London: Unwin.

Weeks, J. (1981) *Sex, Politics and Society: the Regulation of Sexuality since 1800*, London: Longmans.

Whimster, S. and Lash, S. (eds) (1987) *Max Weber, Rationality and Modernity*, London: Allen & Unwin.

Index